Sir George Trevelyan

Exmouth

Sir George Trevelyan

And the new spiritual awakening

Frances Farrer

Floris Books

First published in 2002 by Floris Books

© 2002 Frances Farrer

Frances Farrer has asserted her right under the
Copyright, Designs and Patents Act 1988
to be identified as the Author of ths Work.

British Library CIP Data available

ISBN 0-86315-377-1

Printed in Great Britain
by Cromwell Press, Trowbridge

Contents

Acknowledgments

So many people helped in the preparation of this brief account of the long and complex life of Sir George Trevelyan (1906–96), so many were generous with their time, their memories and their material, that it seems invidious to mention them individually. I am truly grateful to everyone who helped. As well as stories, photographs and written material, contributions in terms of encouragement and ideas were beyond price.

The great number of people who were keen to contribute is evidence of the regard in which George Trevelyan was held. From anyone who may have been inadvertently missed in this list I hope for the acceptance of an acknowledgement in the largest sense.

Thanks are due first to several members of George Trevelyan's immediate family, including his daughter and literary executor, Catriona Tyson, his sister, Mrs Patricia Jennings, and his nephew, Michael Dower. Many wonderful insights and anecdotes accompanied generous loans of source material and access to photographs. There was also invaluable assistance with checking the manuscript.

Close friends of George who helped include: Mrs Rhoda Cowen, who had known him since childhood and was a fund of good stories; Roger Orgill MBE, George's adopted godson, who voluntarily did some of the research; Anna Benita, whose insights into George Trevelyan's last years were invaluable; and Mary Firth, his colleague for very many years and an early Wrekin trustee.

I would like to thank David Lorimer of Mystics and Scientists, who supervised the project and was wonderfully supportive always; and from the Wrekin Trust, Hertha Larive and Janice Dolley, for their help and encouragement throughout. Palden Jenkins, who set up and runs Sir George's website (see Contacts and Organizations), also made useful suggestions.

Bernard and Ruth Nesfield Cookson were especially helpful, supplying invaluable material about George's time at Attingham, the work of Rudolf Steiner, and the foundation and early years of the Wrekin Trust.

People in the wider New Age movement, including Tom Welch, Peter Dawkins, Geseke Clark and Satish Kumar; and from the

Findhorn community, Elisabeth Tønsberg and Mari Hollander, are gratefully acknowledged. Jean Fischer contributed invaluable material about the Alexander Technique and Walter Carrington contributed memories of F.M. Alexander. George's publisher Alick Bartholomew recalled working with George, and visiting him during his final weeks.

A particular mention is due to Dr Barbara Latto, the widow of Dr Gordon Latto. She was very old and fragile when I met her, and her wish to see the finished book was not granted. She and her husband had a fine partnership in naturopathic medicine. They were of great help to George Trevelyan when arthritis threatened to immobilize him. He was inspired by their work and comforted by their friendship.

Librarians at Gordonstoun School; Trinity College, Cambridge; and in the Oxford library service, deserve thanks for seeking out arcane bits of information and contributing useful thoughts of their own. Thanks are also due to National Trust staff both in London and at Wallington.

Helen Hewlett and Carole McGilvery lent materials; Wendy Hill, Larissa Motiuk and many others offered helpful suggestions; Stan Harding continues to be an inspiration, all of them gave support and encouragement. Thanks to all, and thanks to all who remember George Trevelyan with happiness.

Finally I would like to acknowledge with gratitude the meticulous work of Christopher Moore at Floris Books in preparing the manuscript.

Frances Farrer, Oxford, May 2002

CHAPTER 1

The Trevelyan Family:
Intellectuals, Politicians, Landowners

Our birth is but a sleep and a forgetting:
The soul that rises with us, our life's Star,
Hath had elsewhere its setting,
And cometh from afar.
William Wordsworth

The story of George Lowthian Trevelyan must begin with Wallington, the ancestral home of his family for nearly three hundred years. This great country house was built in 1688 of local Northumbrian dark grey stones, well weathered from their use in forming a medieval tower on the same site. It is substantial, imposing, and self-assured. It is described architecturally as, "square in plan with four ranges 120 feet long around a central courtyard"; and it stands in 13,000 acres of farm and moorland just twenty miles north of Hadrian's Wall.[1] This is craggy, romantic, Walter Scott territory, with a history of clans and battles and Border raids, with long, straight roads, dark mountains, dramatic skies.

Wallington is unusual for a house of its size in that you can see it from the road (albeit from a distance). It is heralded by four forbidding stone griffins' heads which gaze out from the eastern side of the lawn. They were carried as ship's ballast on a return voyage from London to the port of Newcastle-upon-Tyne. The establishment is unequivocally grand, with its acres and estate workers' cottages and Palladian Clock Tower. Its statistics are grand: the original great hall was 44 feet long; on the northern side the estate extends for eight miles. Like most such houses it is stocked with family portraits and antiques; it even has a cabinet of curiosities collected by an idiosyncratic ancestor, Jane, Lady Wilson, of Charlton Park, Greenwich. All this is what George Trevelyan was born to in 1906; it is what he effectively lost in his early twenties, and it was a powerful emotional influence that stayed with him all his life.

The house and estate were acquired by the West Country Trevelyans from the Northumbrian Blackett family through a marriage. The portraits of three centuries' tally of Trevelyans hang in the house; that of the third baronet of the first creation, Sir George Trevelyan of Nettlecombe in Somerset, explains the acquisition. In 1733, this Sir George married Julia Calverley, only daughter of Sir Walter Calverley and Julia Blackett. The Blacketts owned Wallington, and were substantial Northumbrian land-owners with lucrative lead mining, colliery and shipping interests. Sir George died in 1768 before he inherited Wallington, so it went to his eldest son, Sir John Trevelyan. George Lowthian Trevelyan was the fifth baronet of the second (northern) creation, following his father Charles Philip (born in 1870). For several generations, Trevelyan men were called alternately George and Charles. For the sake of clarity George Lowthian Trevelyan, the subject of this book, is called simply George, or later Sir George. Other Georges, such as his uncle the historian George Macaulay Trevelyan, take their second Christian name throughout.

The original, West Country Trevelyans had a romantic legend: they were believed to be descended from Sir Trevillian, one of the Knights of the famous Round Table of King Arthur. Their name and origin is Cornish. The legend is depicted on their coat of arms: a white horse rising from the sea. According to one version of this tale, all the knights were dining on St Michael's Mount when they made a wager that no one could swim ashore to the mainland, and Sir Trevillian was the only one who succeeded. Another version directs the horse back to the Mount in a thrilling escape from the flooded, magical kingdom of Lyonesse. August and serious-minded nineteenth century Trevelyan men attempted for years to authenticate this, seeking evidence and holding frequent family meetings, notably the big Round Table Conference. Even the poet laureate, Alfred Lord Tennyson, became interested in it, and its symbolism was to occupy George throughout his life. This fascination is symptomatic not only of the Victorian era but also of the family's almost genetic sense of chivalry, tradition, and aristocracy. But although the Legend of Lyonesse cannot be substantiated, the family can with certainty trace its ancestry to the Domesday Book (*c.*1086, more than eight hundred years before George Trevelyan), when they were Cornish landowners. A house in the parish of St Veep, near Fowey, was listed in the book and still bears the family name. The shift northwards began in the fifteenth century when a Sir John Trevelyan, twice High Sheriff of Cornwall, married an heiress who brought him estates throughout the south west of England and in Wales. These properties included Nettlecombe, in Somerset, where some members of the family live now.

There is thus a long family history in which responsibility for their land and the people working on it figure significantly, and a feeling of continuity which George Trevelyan felt very strongly. In later years when he developed and refined his thoughts on the relationship between human beings and the planet his early understanding of concepts such as stewardship was central. An aristocratic relationship with *the land* was refocused to an ecological and spiritual relationship with *the earth*, but its origin can be traced to the Trevelyan family tree, with its ancient roots still visible in the West Country.

Trevelyan family loyalties were royalist, so that during the Civil War and the Commonwealth they were under something of a cloud, but their allegiance paid off at the Restoration and the family was rewarded with a baronetcy by King Charles II. Towards the beginning of the reign of Queen Victoria the Northumbrian side of the family began to be liberal, making reforms on their estate and concerning themselves with the wellbeing of the local people. In this they followed a Whig tradition that existed so strongly among some landed families of the time that the term 'squire-radical' was coined to describe it. The second title of baronet was awarded in 1874 to George's grandfather, Charles Edward, first baronet of Wallington, for his work during the Irish famine. By then the Trevelyans were also noted intellectuals and politicians, often advanced in their views, always individual, energetic and controversial. They kept company with artists, academics and scientists. In mid-Victorian times many of them had become aggressively agnostic; they became politically more radical, and George's father developed into a true socialist. This put them at odds with the local gentry but they didn't care a bit: the privileges of aristocracy have always included the licence for eccentricity. Trevelyans could make their friends where they chose, and they chose like minds. These were minds of refinement, cultivation, social concern and high endeavour. There certainly does not seem to have been much in the way of frivolity to be had at a gathering of clever Trevelyans.

Thus aristocracy, land-owning and scholarship formed the core of the family. By the time of George's childhood the owner of Wallington was Sir George Otto, august and ancient former MP for the Border Boroughs in Scotland, Civil Lord of the Admiralty, editor of *Life and Letters of Lord Macaulay*, and author of *Early Life of Charles James Fox*. He considerably restored the family fortunes by his writing, and "a mixture of scholarship and luck," according to his great-grandson Michael Dower. He was independent-minded, quirkily spirited, somewhat daunting. In 1903 he renounced wine for good. Sir George Otto Trevelyan adopted one or two unpopular opinions and made them his own. Against the Jingoism of the times he sympathized with the Boers; extraordinarily for an upper class Edwardian gentleman he supported the suffragettes. He also turned down the offer of a peerage from Lord Asquith. The political magazine *Vanity Fair* described him as being, "in every 'movement'... For ever writing, speaking, questioning, moving, dividing, agitating." As time went by he became increasingly radical, to the point of campaigning for the enfranchisement of the working class.

All the same he was a good deal less radical than his son Charles and their political division appears to have been the cause of lifelong friction. (In their turn, Charles and his son George Lowthian had few opinions — or even sympathies — in common.) If such extraordinary political activity were not daunting enough, grandfather George Otto Trevelyan, the second Classics scholar in his Cambridge year, read Latin and Greek "with an avidity rare even among scholars." He often read the *Iliad* and the *Odyssey* aloud in Greek to his eldest granddaughter Pauline, who apparently lapped them up. When they became old enough the grandchildren were invited to take Sunday luncheon with grandmama and grandpapa at Wallington and some of them found it quite an ordeal: Sir George Otto simply had no conversational gambit for little children, and in the afternoon jigsaw puzzles and readings from the classics formed the entertainment.

Sir George Otto Trevelyan's son Charles married the beautiful and clever Mary Bell (always known in the family as Molly) in 1904. She was the daughter of Sir Hugh Lowthian Bell, Lord Lieutenant of the North Riding, and of his very musical second wife, who (incidentally) was a native French-speaker. The Bells had spent some time on diplomatic business in Germany. They were enormously proud of Molly's half-sister Gertrude, a famous traveller and archaeologist in the Middle East who was reputed to have provided local information for the British government. She dressed exquisitely and spoke many languages; in learning Arabic she had also mastered all its various modulations and could tell precisely which area any Arab came from. Gertrude Bell was remarkable: she went to Iraq, she was a leading light in the task of bringing King Faisal to power, she was a scholar who was called Queen of the Arabs, she collected information that was useful to the great T.E. Lawrence, and the British School of Archaeology in Iraq was founded in her memory. And all this at a time when women did not travel alone!

For her sister Molly, the adventure of life was a different one. She kept the Trevelyan's beautiful stone house in the village of Cambo, a mile from Wallington, and it was a happy and fruitful household. There were six surviving children. Charles and Molly's firstborn was Pauline (1905), George came next in 1906, followed two years later by Katharine (Kitty), Marjorie (1913), then twins Patricia and Hugh (1915), and Geoffrey (1920). Hugh died when he was little more than a year old. Between 1904 and 1928 when Charles inherited, Molly established herself with the 89 Cambo villagers as a socially concerned lady. She started local mothers' groups, worked with the miners' wives and children, initiated educational self-help societies, served on committees.

Charles's brother was the famous George Macaulay Trevelyan, described as a pioneer social historian (*History of England* and *English Social History*), certainly among the greatest historical writers of the era, and from 1927, Regius Professor of History at Trinity College Cambridge. G.M. Trevelyan performed a great service to the study of history, simultaneously popularizing and giving weight to it at a time when many Cambridge academics believed it to be a futile subject. He thus continued the great tradition of popular history set by his father George Otto and his great-uncle, Thomas, Lord Macaulay.

George Lowthian Trevelyan was born into this exceptional family on Bonfire Night under the water sign of Scorpio. Subjects of this astrological sign are described as intellectual, discerning, decisive, often quite witty, occasionally somewhat judgmental. In a book that he co-wrote with Edward Matchett about esoteric astrology, George observed, "Incarnation under this sign is likely to be difficult and painful ... [and it] offers immensely important opportunities for taking 'the longest stride of soul men ever took'."[2] George's rising sign was Leo, and his nephew Michael Dower says he explained inconsistencies or apparent contradictions in his character with reference to this difficult planetary combination. Scorpio is reserved and secretive, Leo open and smiling, this combines the introvert with the actor and public speaker. George

Lowthian Trevelyan was the second child and the first son. He was especially welcome as his birth ensured the succession, but he was subject to the heavy demands of an aristocratic heir.

But for aristocrats as for all other classes, the age into which George Trevelyan was born was the end of a long era. Enormous changes were looming. This was the legendary, last Edwardian summer, the beginning of the end for England's industrial supremacy, imperial power, and rigid class system. Things were beginning to shift, and Charles, though not entirely alone in seeing it, was extraordinary in being able to acknowledge that at last this particular party was signalling it would soon be over. An aristocrat who could do this was a rare soul indeed.

Meanwhile, the family carried on entirely in the manner to which they were accustomed by birth and expectation, dividing their time between London during parliamentary sessions and Northumberland during parliamentary recesses. Charles and Molly's home at number 14 Great College Street was the nearest private house to the House of Commons, just five minutes' walk away. This meant Charles could get up during the first course of his evening meal, walk to the House, vote, and be back in the dining room before the rest of the family had eaten the second course. Until the outbreak of the First World War Charles was a Liberal, and he and Molly gave superb parties for politicians and intellectuals. Half a dozen people would come to dinner, 30 or 40 more would join them afterwards, Kitty records "a roar of talk."[3] Pauline, George and Kitty, the three eldest children, were allowed to stay up for these parties and hear what was happening in the world: the house was a talking shop for people of influence. By contrast, their Northumbrian life in what they called "just a couple of big cottages thrown together" was truly countrified.

Pauline noted that her parents were unusual in eating with their children and spending time with them. "Eating with them" of course meant only the evening meal, the nursery was still the place for their daytime lives, for learning table manners from nanny or governess, and for really being children. The fact that eating with their children was extraordinary offers only one instance of the extent to which comparisons are near-impossible, so unconventional was the family in its own era, so unimaginable is it today. In the country the parties were different again. To sustain the habit of unconventionality, when Charles and Molly were living at Wallington, the servants often joined the company after supper and danced as well. At Wallington the Trevelyans were able to entertain much more grandly and the house became a regular country retreat for half the influential members of the Labour party. Rhoda Cowen (then Harris) recalls: "Wallington was a heavenly place, it had a lovely atmosphere. I used to stay there often as a girl. George's mother was the striking one, she was terrific. Strong. A great personality, and she ran Wallington frightfully well. They had big parties, she put on a very good show."

George's father, Charles Trevelyan, was tall, dark, blue-eyed and good-looking, and described as "tough in mind and spirit." (Indeed the term "spirited" could have been applied as much to his wife and children.) In 1892, after Cambridge, he began his political career as secretary to Lord Houghton, Lord Lieutenant of Ireland; and in 1898 he went round the world with the socialists Sidney and Beatrice Webb. Between 1899 and 1918 he was Liberal Member of Parliament for the constituency of Elland, in Yorkshire. In 1908 he became Parliamentary Secretary of the Board of Education and began to move further to the left, his advocacy of state control losing him many friends. He was vehemently opposed to the First World War and supported a movement called the Union of Democratic Control, described as "the single most important agency of opposition to Government policy during the war."[4] This also brought about some estrangement from his own family. He was especially upset by his brother George Macaulay Trevelyan's mood at the time, and he wrote to Molly, "I am more discouraged by it than anything because it shows the helplessness of intellect before national passion."

For her part, Molly worked with Charles as a political wife, and took part in the Women's Liberal Foundation and the Rural Women's Organization. The family unanimously describe her as "a notable chatelaine" — this skilled speech-maker, domestic administrator, organizer of the family and its social life and that of the house guests. She was also president of the English Folk Dance and Song Society, which had many aristocratic members; and she had a maypole erected annually in Wallington central hall for the spring dancing. Traditional Northumbrian dances included the Morpeth Rant and the Soldiers Joy. George learned Morris dancing because of his mother and was an elegant and enthusiastic dancer of country dances, and indeed practically of all other kinds, all his life. Molly was free-thinking, informal, intuitive, impulsive, a fine hostess and a perfect foil and political partner for her serious husband. It is a matter of record that during their long lives Charles and Molly were invited to four English coronations and attended at least two of them. Their daughter, Mrs Patricia Jennings, still lives at Wallington. She recalls that for one of the coronations, "Mother took her sandwiches in her sponge bag," a very practical arrangement. Sponge bag or not, the large portrait of Sir Charles and Lady Trevelyan in full regalia for the King is properly impressive.

Despite his stated anti-War feeling and a vote of no confidence from his constituency party, Charles continued to serve in the Liberal government of 1911–16. He did not have to go the 1914–18 War because Members of Parliament were exempt from military service. In fact, he would not have gone anyway, as he was so opposed to the War and would have had to be a conscientious objector; fortunately his parliamentary duties saved him the trouble. Charles had his family's serious morality, which included a strong sense of obligation. At the turn of the century when his parents gave up drinking they also gave up jokes, and devoted themselves to agriculture, scholarship, politics and the well-being of their tenants. This purposeful neo-Puritanism was passed on to Charles.

From the first, he was concerned with the welfare of working people. He belonged to a movement to give access to open moorland and mountain spaces to everyone, believing strongly in the importance of healthy freedom of exercise in the countryside. In this at least he was at one with his father. Later he joined the Labour party, believing that the Liberals were not doing enough for the poor, and in particular for their education. Charles represented the Central Division of Newcastle-upon-Tyne for Labour from 1922, to the great discomfort of his parents and most of his family. A family friend commented crossly, "He doesn't alter his life at all!" and he was right: Charles and his family lived very comfortably at Cambo House in the village on the Wallington estate, and when they inherited the title and moved to Wallington there were many who pointed out contradictions between their way of life and their professed beliefs. But while the county grumbled and gossiped the Trevelyans simply steered their own course. They supported the suffragettes, they campaigned for free education for working class children, and in 1914 they opposed the mobilization of troops for the Great War. In 1924 when the first Labour government was elected, Charles was made President of the Board of Education, serving with distinction under Ramsay MacDonald and further boosting the new party's fortunes by steering the fledgling MPs around the House of Commons and explaining how to navigate parliamentary procedure. Later when the Labour government faltered in setting up the welfare system Charles put it largely in place on his own estate and paid for it himself. From 1929 all married men who worked at Wallington received 2s 6d (12.5p) a week extra allowance for each of their children from the confirmation of the pregnancy until the completion of each child's education. Perhaps the county had to eat its words at the evidence of this prototype welfare state. In 1931 he resigned his post as education minister as a formal protest over the government's inactivity in the face of catastrophically rising unemployment.

Cambo village life differed in style from life at Wallington and in London. There were country pursuits, acquaintance with the villagers, and for the children when they reached the age of seven, those formal Sunday luncheons taken with their august and ancient grandpapa at the great house which would one day become their own. Sir George Otto talked to the children exactly as he would to grown-ups, of politics, classics, current affairs, history. No wonder seven-year-old Kitty was apprehensive about her first Sunday visit. She thought Wallington was "like a church... so beautiful that I inwardly bowed before it." Others, however, were less impressed, and one of them recorded that the house was cold, and smelled of artichokes and cauliflowers. By this time Sir George Otto was in his seventies and "hunchbacked with so much thinking and stooping over books." (Back problems, arthritis and deafness run in the family.) Kitty wrote afterwards, in *Fool in Love*, that Grandpapa "gave me chocolate drops out of the drawer and started holding a brilliant conversation about when he was in Gladstone's government. I didn't say anything, and after a time forgot to listen." Luncheon was a proper, formal, Edwardian repast, taken in the vast dining room decorated with Swiss-Italian artistic plasterwork; the family silver and china laid on the long table, ancestral portraits watching every mouthful. Kitty found that, "the butler and footman, who were my natural friends, were suddenly withdrawn, decorous personalities." The grandparental version of Wallington was markedly different from the Wallington of Charles and Molly's era. For one thing, the grandparents had footmen and a butler "and all that sort of thing," an establishment which the younger children found archaic and starchy. Kitty's first luncheon with them contained a particular difficulty. "Mrs Stinchcombe made wonderful pastry, but I was being so polite that I could hardly swallow."

It is unlikely that any such anguish would have attended George Trevelyan's dinners with grandpapa. Trevelyan men were historically minded, with a tradition of participation in the forming of their country's opinions and the making of its decisions, and George enjoyed the talk. He also shared their outdoor interests, as he was an athletic boy, roaming happily around the Wallington estate, up its hills and through its woods. From childhood he was a keen climber and caver, and he became a passionate participant in the Trevelyan Hunt, an annual, three-day man hunt around the Lakeland Fells. This sport had been invented in 1898 by George's uncle G.M. Trevelyan, Geoffrey Winthrop Young and Sidney McDougall, and continues to this day. It involved Trevelyan men and their relatives and friends, with three or more of the fastest runners appointed as hares and given half an hour's start on the rest of the field, who chased them as hounds. Hares start at 8am, hounds at 8.30am, and they are all in play until 5pm. They run in all weathers and latterly women have participated too.

From adolescence George was always a hare, and would find ingenious ways of evading capture, enjoying the chase so much that he would show himself above bracken or from behind rocks to draw the hounds towards him. He was described as, "a brilliant, elusive hare, who took the chase seriously as a matter of life or death and gave all he had to the escape." According to his adopted godson, Roger Orgill, no one could outrun George. They could trap him by manoeuvring him into difficult terrain, but no one ever caught him with superior speed. After the Second World War, it was George who revived the Hunt and became the Master. "George set an example of unremitting determination ... and his knowledge of the terrain and of the wily ways of hares gave him an unrivalled ability to point hounds in the most likely direction ... He set a pattern of defiance on the part of the hares, constantly courting pursuit yet never permitting easy capture." The Hunt has created many family and sporting legends and even its own literature: the quotation comes from its Centenary Yearbook.

But although George was an athlete, and had a fine mind for history and discourse, he was from early on in his life something of a disappointment to his father. In childhood George was not especially confident, which Charles could not find admirable. Furthermore, George's interests were in the realm of the imagination, which was not a place where Charles spent any time. Whether the source of their discord was the traditional dislike of the aristocrat for his heir is not known, but the fact is that they had very little sympathetic communication. There is no doubt that George wished to please his father, but Charles did not take many pains to understand George.

In about 1910 a governess joined the household. Pauline's diary recalls her invention of an outdoor war game of Romans and Picts which employed existing walls on the estate and necessitated the building of further small walls with stones that were lying about. The governess was not the only pedagogue: both of their parents took part in the children's learning and Charles taught most of them to read. Pauline began when she was three. George and Kitty learned together every day before breakfast, sitting on either side of their father on the big flat wooden arms of the chair. Pauline began to learn Latin enthusiastically at the age of seven. Charles and Molly spent a great deal of time with their children. When the family was in London Charles returned home every night in time to bath them, sing to them, and tell them stories in their bedrooms. He often read to the children after supper, usually something historical or biographical. Their mother read Dickens or sang, as a family they all played letter games, card games, battle games, and acted and played charades. (G.M. Trevelyan attributed his fascination with campaigns and warfare, and ultimately with history, to his early passion for playing war games with lead soldiers on the floor at Wallington.) In an era when many middle and upper class parents saw their children only for formal half-hours, and even then not every day, such involvement was extraordinary. Molly was gentle and encouraging, keen on truth-telling and learning poems by heart, good at telling stories, and especially enthusiastic about getting out into the fresh air. Even on wet afternoons she would send the children out to walk, "or you'll be cross by tea-time," and they would splash about, enjoying the rain and wind, enthusiastically jumping into all the puddles. All the children kept their clogs under the settle in the hall of the house at Cambo, so they could quickly run out of doors without the bother of doing up shoe-laces.

However, footwear was not always such an easy matter. When George was eight and Kitty six, a terrible incident occurred. When Molly put Kitty and George to bed she always asked them to put their shoes outside the door to be cleaned, and they often forgot. One night she said, "The next time you forget I shall smack you." At this terrible threat the children were silent; they had never been smacked. By far the worst sanction on their behaviour was the threat of Molly not singing to them at bedtime, which happened if they were caught telling an untruth. But perhaps inevitably, not long after the warning they forgot their shoes again, and their mother made them put their hands out to be smacked. They never forgot their shoes after that. Molly was as keen on physical courage as she was on courage of the moral kind: she expected her children to climb high trees in a high wind, and to balance on a tree trunk to cross a river. Courage was an attribute of George all his life.

The close alliance which was formed early between George and Kitty was strengthened by the arrival in 1915 of twins, which threw them even more into each other's company. It was a precious friendship which lasted all their lives. Kitty wrote, "We achieve a relationship in which the tensions of man and woman are solved, yet the richness and fruitfulness left." According to Rhoda Cowen, "Kitty was much the strongest character in the family. She had fair hair, she was very attractive, and, rather eccentric this, she always wore sandals and no stockings. When she came into a room it was a different place, and there's no doubt she dominated the whole of Wallington. She and George were enormous friends." Other family members describe Kitty as outgoing and ebullient. Certainly she made an impression on all who met her.

The story of the wicker bath chair illustrates the comradeship. Kitty and George were about seven and nine years old when they found an old, wheeled chair in their maternal grandparents' house in Yorkshire. The location of the find was somewhat exotic: the chair was mouldering in the stick house in which were stored logs "as big as a four-year-old child." These logs were thrown entire on to a great fire to heat the parquet-floored games room, and then chained into place so that no sparks would fly out. George and Kitty used to play with the bath chair in the woods, steering it around the trees and directing its course by leaning out of it, rather like sailing a boat. One day they jumped on it for a downhill race, not realizing that they were heading straight for a main road. The chair had no brakes. They careered down the hill, steered sharply to the left, threw their weight over the left wheel, leaped the gutter, sailed down the road (fortunately there was no traffic), then stopped, and the chair began to run backwards. Miraculously, it came to a standstill without injury to the children or to itself. George and Kitty hugged each other and giggled "till the muscles of our tummies ached." This was a typical adventure for them, demonstrating their mutual attraction to danger and their total trust in each other. George in particular always loved exploring. Sometimes he and Kitty would steal out of the house in the early morning before it was light, for the thrill of the strange, cold, greyness, and the pleasure of watching the dawn come up.

At the approach of the First World War the idea of pacifism became a family topic since Charles disapproved of fighting and the children naturally agreed. In 1914 when George was nine and Kitty seven they walked across the bridge over the Tyne in Newcastle, pausing to ask each other, "to save [stop] the War, would you jump over?" — and both cried "*Yes!*" However, the children often found their departures from the majority view confusing. They could not, for example, hate the Kaiser, since their mother at the age of 19 had started off one of his balls in Berlin with his Vortänzer, and George and Kitty could imagine how lovely she must have looked. As a girl, Molly travelled in Europe quite a bit, taking part in a sophisticated, cosmopolitan social life. Her uncle Lascelles was British Ambassador in Berlin at the time of the Berlin ball. (There is an almost Mitfordesque feeling of paradox running through many of the contradictory ideas that seemed to be capable of residing in one Trevelyan head.)

The Trevelyan children could pursue any interest that took their fancy, and pursue it to the maximum. As a family they were uniformly energetic, inquiring, hard-working, and earnest. One more departure from convention was the absence of religion in the household. Though the family followed all and every intellectual avenue Charles was fiercely agnostic, and his perception was the one that prevailed at home. However, when the time came for the eldest children to go to school they were sent to the pacifist Quakers, because he was so strongly against the First World War. Charles could not endorse a kind of education that emphasized the obligation of gentlemen to defend King and Country at a time when he believed it to be ridiculous. George Macaulay Trevelyan also disapproved very strongly of the Great War; with his close friend Geoffrey Winthrop Young he was a conscientious objector and drove ambulances for the Friends' Ambulance Corps. Geoffrey Young, educationist, writer, and accomplished mountaineer, was a hero and role model of George Trevelyan's throughout his life. Young had been greatly influenced by his admiration for the heroic writings of John Buchan, later Lord Tweedsmuir.

According to Pauline Trevelyan, Sidcot School, in North Somerset, gave the children, "a proper attitude towards other people." She wrote, "I think that this is the great characteristic of the Quakers; their evaluation of other people is not connected with either birth or opportunity. I learnt this attitude from my father too; respect for the individual person rather than for their worth in rank or money. I remember that he once said about the Labour Party, 'The leaders are well enough, but the rank and file are pure gold'." Kitty wrote of her schooldays, "I was

happy, and flourished as a flower rooted in good soil, opening to the
sun ... We were trusted and given responsibility" — though she was
often bored by the Quakers' silent meetings for worship, and found her
own relationship with the deity only in private, and out of doors. When
Charles said, "They at any rate won't ram religion down your throat,"
he had forgotten the fact that children learned passages from the Bible
during lesson time and first thing in the morning, and there were discussions on questions such as, "What is a soul?"

In sending his eldest three children to Sidcot to receive a liberal,
inclusive outlook that categorized no one, Charles departed from family tradition: George Otto and his three sons had gone to the more intellectually rigorous Harrow. In Somerset, George Trevelyan developed
his passion for underground exploration, and he helped to found a club
to explore the caves within the Mendip hills. He also did his first woodwork there. A subsequent headmaster wrote of George, "his love of the
countryside of his native Northumbria and Somerset, and his spirit of
questing and exploration, all contributed to his integrated philosophy
of life." The school today makes the same claims as it did then, to be
strong in drama, art and music. While he was a pupil there George
developed his interest in drama. Charades had been a popular family
pastime, poetry was a serious study for the Trevelyan children, and an
appreciation of Shakespeare and the great visionary poets stayed with
George all his life. In the year 2000 a new library and resource centre
was dedicated to George Trevelyan, whose memory is held in high
regard at Sidcot School.

In 1928, Charles and Molly inherited the title and Wallington,
moved into the grand house, and found it to be in very poor repair.
They set to work to replace the roof and instal bathrooms and electric
light, and from Easter 1929 they opened parts of the house to the public during weekend afternoons free of charge. In time, other radical
enterprizes were begun: discussion groups and study weekends were
held at Wallington. Northumberland's first Ramblers' Hostel, which
became its first Youth Hostel, was opened in its stables. Since he did
not approve of living off income from tenants Sir Charles placed the
money from rents into the land or social services. He believed that private ownership of large properties by individual people was no longer
appropriate, and the implications of this began to develop in his mind
into a complicated plan with far-reaching effects on his heir.

In the year when Charles inherited he was President of the Board of
Education, and his government bill to raise the school leaving age to

14 and give grants to parents on low incomes was rejected. As we have seen, his response was to put all the measures in place on his own estate. However much the county and the gentry liked to criticize and gossip, no one could say he was inconsistent in his behaviour towards his employees; Charles put his money where his mouth was to an extraordinary degree. His idiosyncratic behaviour went further even than this: he was so keen on the Soviet system that he lent about £70,000 to the Soviet government. (History assures us that it was repaid.) He and Molly had enthusiastically visited the USSR in 1935. Mrs Jennings still uses a very wonderful Russian doll tea cosy with a voluminous padded skirt which keeps the teapot warm. They brought it back as what she calls, a "tourist trophy."

Molly herself was efficient and hard-working. The traditions of her own Yorkshire family compelled her to rise an hour early every morning for 23 years "to do the tapestry," an impressive, pre-Raphaelite depiction of the legend of Sir Trevillian which now hangs in Lady Trevelyan's Parlour. Sometimes Kitty helped, pulling the needle from underneath as her mother stabbed it through the canvas from above. Molly's local interests included the welfare of the working families, and the local dramatic society, in which she was a leading light.

Every summer the family moved north from Great College Street. In her diary Pauline noted, "not many domestic items were duplicated ... so when we set off to Wallington ... our luggage included things like sewing machines and nursery fireguards — all the things you would have thought we might have two of. This vast quantity of luggage, of detritus, went backwards and forwards between London and Northumberland several times a year and took up an entire guard's van on each occasion." Wallington was supported by a "small" staff of just twelve female indoor servants. With the work of catering, cleaning, tending and valeting the family and their guests was included the task of emptying chamber pots every morning as the house had so few bathrooms. In this it was not deprived: bathrooms were a rarity in country houses in those days.

From the early years of their ownership of Wallington the house was a focus for Labour party socializing. The visitors' book after 1929 shows the signatures of Stafford Cripps, Nye Bevan, Jennie Lee, Hugh Dalton, Michael Foot, Hugh Gaitskell, Barbara Castle, and Clement Attlee, among others. Beatrice Webb and leading Fabians stayed, and some luminaries from the arts world including George Bernard Shaw, Sir Lewis Casson, Dame Sybil Thorndike and

E.M. Forster. The number of guests recorded in 1929 was 101; by 1934 the figure had risen to 160. The house was always full of family and guests; it was a place for serious talk and outdoor pursuits, a continuous country house party which was unusual because it was without frivolity. It is from these boyhood experiences that George Trevelyan began to form the ideas of the country house party as a forum for creativity and intellectual pursuits which were to find such spectacular realization at Attingham Park in Shropshire.

Thus family life as lived at Wallington was rarefied, not in the manner of traditional aristocratic family life, but rarefied all the same. George Trevelyan's nephew Michael Dower sums up the family. "We were brought up to think we were special, the intellectual aristocracy. Huxley, Arnold, Trevelyan, Macaulay — we were all related. I believe George took from the family the manner, rather than the matter. George was the very welcome son, but I think Charles may have wanted him to be an intellectual or a politician, and it was clear he would be creative in a different way." He also remarks that George was temperamentally unsuited to be an historian or landowner, the other occupations at which Trevelyans excelled.

Wallington was a wonderful place to grow up, the children roamed the countryside, climbing, walking, scrambling and running, they read and studied and listened to clever talk, there were family dances and tenants' parties. In the library after dinner they played word games and guessing games and Mah Jong. Their intellectual gifts were stimulated and strengthened by constant exercise, almost not a moment was lost. They all learned poetry by heart. Kitty wrote of learning a poem a day from her governess as the governess was brushing Kitty's hair, and years later Kitty and George could still recite beautifully many epic poems, handing alternate verses back and forth between them. Socially, however, "we were absolute outrés." Friends of their own intellectual level came to stay, or the children went away to stay with their friends in other parts of the country. (An acquaintance recalls her visits with awe: "The Trevelyans were always terrifying, so clever — and there was nothing to drink!") In Cambo they knew everyone; at Angerton they knew the Leatharts, at Belsay the Middletons, at Capheaton the Swinburnes. Otherwise they mixed locally only a little. Another obstacle to socializing was that there were no cars, and although all the children had ponies and the use of a pony and trap, the distances were too large for such slow transport. So they stuck at Wallington until one by one they went away to school. George went to

Sidcot in 1913, when he was seven, the others generally went away after their tenth birthdays. Kitty later recalled her schooldays there,

The question of religion was one with which Charles Trevelyan appears not to have engaged very much, and when one day Miss de Bunsen, an Anglican friend, charged him with neglecting this crucial element in his children's upbringing he apparently drew himself up and said, "I will be God to them." Whether this was meant as a joke is not clear, but it is true that the children were not baptized, did not go to church, and at home they were not taught any scriptural lessons or given an understanding of any deity. Somewhat incongruously, Charles always attended the annual sermon under the Wesley Tree half a mile from Cambo with one or other of the children. After one of these sermons, at Kitty's request, the family began to have a weekly meeting called Sunday Reading. Charles and Molly would read an improving book such as *Conduct Stories* or the life of Buddha, then they would sing from the Labour hymn book, perhaps:

When wilt Thou save the People
O God of Mercy, when?

or sometimes:

England, arise, the long long night is over ...

And always, famously, finishing with the Red Flag:

With heads uncovered, swear we all
To bear it onward til we fall.

Pauline and George enjoyed the Sunday Readings and in particular *The Evolution of the Idea of God* with which they were concluded. This book was popular with Fabians because it demolished world faiths with its material analysis, but Kitty called it, "the cleverness of man picking faith to bits with his nibbling mind." Somehow, despite these Sunday Readings and his Quaker schooling, George always maintained that it was a conversation at Moatlands, the home of the Harris family, that started him on the long spiritual path in his twenties. Indeed, the Harris family always credited themselves with introducing him to the deity. George had gone to stay there with his friend Rhoda in 1928, and she recorded that at the time he was "searching desperately for some true meaning to life, of which he had not a clue."[5] Mr Harris told him, "what matters most is God," and in Rhoda's account, "George began to know that this was true." No doubt he listened with proper attention for he had immaculate manners, but the message appears not to have made much immediate impact. He was then at Cambridge, reading history in the Trevelyan tradition. Like the rest of the family he was also deeply inquisitive, profoundly searching. But his disposition still looked to criticize, to test against evidence, and his curiosity took him in many directions before it returned to this point.

CHAPTER 2

Apprenticeships:
Scholar, Athlete, Craftsman

The Youth, who daily farther from the east
Must travel, still is Nature's Priest,
And by the vision splendid
Is on his way attended.
William Wordsworth

In 1925, George Trevelyan went up to Trinity College, Cambridge, to read history. "All the Trevs read history," says his daughter, Catriona Tyson. It was true at any rate of three generations, almost as long as history had been an academic subject. Trinity is long-established, august, classical: in all respects the proper academy for the Trevelyan family. One of the greatest historians of the day was George Lowthian's uncle, George Macaulay Trevelyan, who after his appointment as Regius Professor in 1927 did a great deal to bring the subject back into favour not only within the academic hierarchy but also with students. As a freshman in 1892, GMT had heard from the then Regius Professor, Sir John Seeley, that history was a science and had nothing to do with literature. G.M. Trevelyan, however, wrote best-selling history books which many considered to be great literature, and which have stood the test of the century. In the inaugural address for his Regius Professorship he said, "the appeal of history to us all is in the last analysis poetic. But the poetry of history does not consist of imagination roaming at large, but of imagination pursuing the fact and fastening upon it." Under his influence the emphasis in historical study began to shift from politics, war and diplomacy to institutional and social change. The phrase, *imagination pursuing the fact and fastening upon it* could describe his nephew George Lowthian Trevelyan at the time: a clever, eager, curious mind, with a poet's imagination, seeking factual information.

The reassessment of the scholarly definition of history had parallels in other subjects. Cambridge, like the rest of the country, was recovering from the effects of the First World War, when the colleges had functioned at much reduced capacity. Fewer than half the pre-war number of men were in residence in 1914 and soldiers were billeted in the colleges and encamped in fields around the town. Rupert Brooke famously chronicled the war in poetry; W.H.R. Rivers, director of the Psychological Laboratory, treated shell shock. Some academics had been involved in war work, many students had gone to fight, and although by 1920 all the normal activities of the University had been resumed it was some years before the academic focus was re-established. Science advanced, as did agriculture. New subjects were being introduced and some of the older ones were coming under close scrutiny. Among the new subjects was engineering (formerly mechanical sciences), among the new approaches to old subjects was the changed view of history itself, largely that of George Macaulay Trevelyan. The outstanding achievements of Rutherford in physics, Keynes in economics, Housman and Leavis in literature, Wittgenstein in philosophy, are similarly indicative of the massive upheaval in existing academic disciplines during the 1920s and 1930s.

Among the undergraduates, some rather precious Cambridge societies were returning to life. They included the Heretics, whose fourth rule required members to reject all appeal to authority in the discussion of religious questions. This led to Bertrand Russell's view that the Ten Commandments should be approached like a Cambridge examination paper, and therefore, "only six need be attempted." The super-exclusive Apostles, by contrast, were utterly secretive. G.M. and R.C. Trevelyan were pre-war members, as were Maynard Keynes, Roger Fry, E.M. Forster, Leonard Woolf, Lytton Strachey and Ludwig Wittgenstein. George's grandfather, George Otto Trevelyan, joined the Apostles in 1859. It is said that when Tom Driberg visited the former Apostle and exiled traitor Guy Burgess in Moscow in the 1950s, Burgess would not reveal any of the Apostles' secrets — although he had been prepared to betray his country. Meetings were held on Saturday evenings, coffee and sardines on toast (known as whales) were provided, papers were read. There was also an annual dinner in the Ivy.

Academically and socially in post-war Cambridge there were attempts at retrenchment as well as movement towards change. The period is marked by increasing political polarization, with rumours of the rise of nationalism in Germany reaching the Cambridge cloisters, and the early stirrings of left-wing Cambridge intellectuals who included the legendary spy trio of Burgess-Maclean-Philby (later augmented by Blunt). In May 1926 some undergraduates went to drive Hull trams and help break the General Strike. (However, it is fair to say that the attraction of driving trams and buses was seen by some of the young men as a stronger motivating factor than principled opposition to "even the most hardened socialism.") By 1936 the mood had shifted so far that many young intellectuals volunteered to fight on behalf of the Republicans with the International Brigade in the Spanish Civil War.

Women came to university in increasing numbers. During the 1920s there was much discussion about the admission of women. They had been admitted to the Tripos examinations in 1881 but not allowed to assume the titles of degrees. Women were there on sufferance; they were still not welcome in the colleges even as wives and many people said they deplored the increasing tendency for the Fellows to marry young. Fellows were not supposed to marry before the age of 30. Oxford had admitted women to full membership of the university by full vote of Convocation before 1920 but Cambridge academics were still busy with votes and reports on the matter, and regularly asserted that the Tripos exams were not suitable for female students. They made confusing and contradictory claims, saying on the one hand that the Tripos examinations were too demanding for women, and on the other that women were, "assiduous note takers unable to manifest the polite indifference of men at lectures." In 1921 when the academics voted in favour of allowing women to join the university, a mob of 300 male students stormed and wrecked Newnham College memorial gates and the decision was not put into practice. Cambridge did not finally came into line with Oxford until 25 years later, when they offered women full university membership.

At the women's colleges many activities were still those of the contemporary girls' boarding school. Hockey and lacrosse were played; students visited in each other's rooms at 9pm for jugs of cocoa. Mistresses of Girton insisted on women students wearing gloves and hats when they were in the town. That they were in a position to make such a ruling hardly makes Girton seem the setting for the early years of adult life. There seems to have been relatively little social mixing between sexes; indeed, Girton College was built some way out of town to prevent it. All this perhaps renders less surprising the reason given for the rule made in 1925 to prevent students (men) from owning motor cars. This was that if they did, they would go and seek low female company in the fenland villages surrounding Cambridge. It was imagined that if students were grounded and the proctors could enforce the midnight curfew, youthful innocence would be preserved. The college functionaries known as proctors patrolled the streets after dark, and the Students' Handbook explained that they were, "taking cognisance in general of any violation of morality or decorum." But despite the clumsy restrictions on social life, these were lively decades. There were rags, societies, sports, and after 1926 the daring, experimental Festival Theatre created by Terence Gray. With some justification Gray described it as, "the most progressive theatre in England."

Cambridge University's boast that its intake was democratic was backed by the large number of special grants and scholarships given to less well off students: up to one third of the intake. To support the claim to egalitarianism, Peter Giles, Master of Emmanuel just after the Great War, said: "It has frequently been complained that the cost of education in the residential universities of Oxford and Cambridge renders access to them possible only for the rich. This was never true, and at all times the bulk of students were drawn from the sons of clergymen, doctors and other professional men whose means were often enough strained to provide their sons with a university education." Thus the Cambridge University definition of inclusive democracy was the sons of impoverished professionals plus the single grammar school boy per county per annum to receive a scholarship. In the year in which George Trevelyan went up to university, two men failed to secure degrees. One was Christopher Isherwood of Corpus Christi, considered the best history scholar of his year; the other was Cecil Beaton, who wrote, "Daddy didn't seem to mind my coming down from Cambridge without a degree, but he's been getting in rather a state since then." The admission of Cecil Beaton had been accomplished at a five-minute interview, though the college was full, because the Master still remembered Beaton *père*. If the pre-war class structure had had its foundations shaken, the building was still largely intact.

And after all, these were the Roaring Twenties, the era of the Bright Young Things, those wonderful, rich, empty-headed P.G. Wodehouse characters who slept all morning and danced all night. Into the lives of men such as Bingo Little and Oofy Prosser nothing much more disagreeable than a beastly relative ever intruded and if such chaps went to the 'Varsity at all, they got in by the five-minute interview and friendship with the pater method, and did not let it affect their lives unduly. "Who was that lad they used to try to make me read at Oxford? Ship-Shop-Schopenhauer. A grouch of the most pronounced description." Such frothy talk is light years from the Trevelyan family although some aspects of the social parallel are close: George Trevelyan was one of many young men with a private income; some of the undergraduates still kept manservants.

George, however, was far from idle. He studied quite hard, and he zealously continued his sporting interests. By the time he got to Cambridge, George was, according to his nephew Michael Dower, "a very capable climber." This enabled him to take part in one of the great Cambridge sports: roof-climbing. Several books have been written about this extraordinary, dangerous, apparently compulsive, possibly even heroic activity. The risks are at least as much to do with the chance of being caught as they are with the heights, ledges, chimney climbs and hand holds. *The Roof-Climber's Guide to Trinity* proposes that Trinity is the aristocrat of college climbing, with a choice of pipe or pinnacle, and a sheer face of solid stone.[1] It explains that the Great Gate is 60ft high and can be tackled from the side. Comments such as "the south side has easier pipes" give strategic clues. Further vital information includes the reminder that the night porter passed through every court every quarter of an hour. George excelled at this jape, as he did at many athletic endeavours. He also climbed with the Cambridge Mountaineering Club, and with his lifelong friend Gurney MacInnes, who was of similar build and fitness. They were great sporting companions. In addition, George fenced for Cambridge University, and was an excellent swimmer.

George was not only athletic, he was also handsome, charming, polished, and — very attractive, this — somewhat shy. However, while he was an undergraduate he became, he said, "dissatisfied with my body," and in 1926 went to consult a new kind of specialist, F.M. Alexander, the originator of the Alexander Technique. F.M. Alexander was very fashionable in London, having arrived from the Southern Hemisphere in 1904 with contacts and introductions among members of the upper class and the acting profession, and established a practice teaching his new perception of posture and breathing. He believed that the Technique benefited the health not only of the body but also of the mind, and regarded the people who consulted him as pupils rather than patients. At their first meeting, George received one of the best shocks of his life. Alexander surveyed him and asked, "Young man, what have you been doing to yourself?"[2] George had gone in search of greater fitness, "finding oneself not as strong as one wished," only to discover that all the exercise he had been doing to strengthen himself was causing more trouble because of the way he used his body while he did it. He was presented with the extraordinary notion that the answer lay in "non-doing." "I had established a habit of use which was pulling the body to pieces," wrote George. "The first lesson was a revelation of wonder and a tremendous flash of vision that this man had found a great truth and the possibility of really establishing the true co-ordination of the human body."

The principle of the Alexander Technique is concerned with deliberate use of the body. The central idea is that of the head leading every movement: thinking of the correct head-neck-back relationship in every activity will ensure that all activity is carried out with the minimum effort. Stresses created by habitual wrong usage are seen to create profound long-term problems. The Alexander pupil must learn to move and breathe differently, effectively to re-learn what until then have become habitual patterns of movement. The discipline of considering every action before deliberately taking it represents a significant change. George recorded, "my curiosity became greater and greater." He began to watch Cambridge runners and he saw that they were using their bodies wrongly. "Obviously the rightly used body must tend to lengthen, not shorten." In time he found that the discipline of considering action in advance applied to every part of his life. If every movement that had been perceived as natural and automatic was found after all to be habitual and damaging, what about every thought pattern? Later still the idea came: might the implication be that his very thoughts were not capable of originality, but were governed by his ability (or otherwise) to use certain tracks that had been taught to him? And might these tracks, like the learned reflexes of his body, be erroneous or even negative? The hugeness of this notion astonished him, and revealed itself fully only over time. George was both excited and nonplussed.

> Somehow one must stop doing those things which pulled one
> out of shape, reduce those tensions and allow the misplaced
> structures to fall back into their normal position and
> conditions. Give them a chance ... Make the change by non-
> doing, not by doing. It seemed sense! If the trouble lay in
> what I was *doing* then the remedy lay in stopping doing that
> thing, not in doing something else.

In weighing up these entrancing ideas George revealed that he was having to turn his world view upside-down. He had learned in his first lesson with F.M. Alexander that he was to be held responsible for making the wrong movements. "*I* was doing them," he wrote, "I myself was positively pulling my body out of shape as I walked and fenced and ran... the more I did, the worse the conditions would become. If in walking I pulled my back right in, what must I be doing in the violent efforts of mountaineering and the rapid adjustments of fencing?" Having accepted this uncomfortable news, another revelation was that his excellent brain did not seem to help him in the attempt to learn new ways of controlling movement. He made repeated reference to it at the beginning of the Alexander training: up to then his brain had been a reliable tool for understanding. "All the education etc. was of no avail when faced by a habit which felt right ... It became clear that the practical test of intelligence was the ability to control against habit and to accept and act on a new idea. This training seemed to offer a way there."

George took up the Alexander Technique with a passion. His family recall that at Wallington during university vacations he would talk unstintingly about it, and his sister, Mrs Patricia Jennings, says that although initially they were quite interested, after a time they almost had to beg him to talk about something else. Oddly, increasing acquaintance with the Alexander Technique made George regret his lack of scientific training. This seems inconsistent with his joy on finding that F.M. Alexander was unqualified. "For here is Alexander, who indubitably changed himself from a badly co-ordinated fellow to a very finely made man and can do so to other people — more or less, and this simply out of his own wits, and not out of training in physiology." George also wrote, "It became clear that the practical use of intelligence was the ability to control against habit and to accept and act on a new idea. This training seemed to offer a way there." He enjoyed F.M. Alexander's discovery of a theory of movement because it was uncluttered by assumptions inherent in a formal training. He admired Alexander's originality of method, based on years of observing his own body and drawing conclusions from its changes and the inadequate responses of medical people to them. Yet for himself, George Trevelyan wished for a proper and formal knowledge of physiology.

Perhaps it was the Alexander lessons and concomitant reassessment that influenced George to change his degree course from history alone to history and economics, adding a year to his undergraduate life. He does not seem to have made much practical use of the study of economics, however. His greatest admirer could not say that he ever had any grasp of humdrum, everyday financial management, simply trusting as aristocrats traditionally had done to the belief that money simply magically turned up. This, and his lack of interest in or aptitude for the task of running the estate, greatly disappointed his father. George's daughter, Catriona Tyson, says, "George would have been hopeless running an estate, he had no idea about money, none at all." George was not an administrator or a manager, either of finance or people. His talents and interests were elsewhere, much more concerned with imagination and inspiration than with the business of getting one's daily bread.

During the 1930s, disappointed with the slow progress of the Labour Party in setting up the early Welfare State, Sir Charles Trevelyan brought socialist principles into the running of Wallington. He saw the anomaly of someone with his principles owning such property. He also saw that his elder son had neither inclination nor talent for estate management, indeed that left in George's hands the property might simply disintegrate. Charles had a strong wish to preserve the house for the future. His way became clear.

For some years he discussed with the National Trust, an organization in which his brother G.M. Trevelyan had a strong influence, the possibility of making them a gift of Wallington. It was the first such gift from a living owner, and there were major difficulties in arranging it. The first was that Sir Charles wished to continue to live in the house until he died, and retain in perpetuity the optional use of a portion of it by a member of the family. Another was that he did not propose to provide any revenue funding with which the Trust could run the house. Because of this the detail took a while to work out, but at last, in 1937, the Deed of Gift was made. In 1941 the Deed of Settlement was signed, an irrevocable agreement that Wallington belonged to Sir Charles until his death. One of his daughters asked him why he did not want the Trust to take over during his lifetime and he replied, "because I am an illogical Englishman," which she thought perfectly apt. Sir Charles did newspaper interviews and went on the wireless to explain his action to the nation, saying how easy it had been to give away Wallington and how he had always had a vision of the public use of the house. Under the headline, SIR CHARLES TREVELYAN'S SURPRISE GIFT DECISION, *The Times* wrote:

Sir Charles is not a showman. The homely Norfolk jacket,
cycling breeches and hose, and heavy hob-nailed shoes are
his favoured dress. Even menial tasks he does not scorn. He
will paint a gate on his estate alongside a labourer. He will
dance a country dance on the lawn at Wallington with
visiting school children.

First, there was this socially inclusive gentleman with strong principles, then, as he himself said:

I have had to think a good deal about the future of the
countryside ... I do not believe in private ownership of land ...
Great houses like this, and the great estates around them, are
part of an order of society which is passing away ... There are
four things I want to ensure:
That the control of the estate and the enjoyment of its surplus
values should no longer be in private hands.
That Wallington, its grounds and its valuable contents, should
be accessible for all time to the people, and should never
pass into selfish or unsympathetic ownership.
That the Wallington Estate should not be broken up.
That the connection of my family with Wallington should not
be severed.

Although this decision cannot have been a complete surprise to
George, the final realization of it was a terrible blow. Can it really be
true that the first he knew of the gift was when he read about it in *The
Times*? Certainly that is the legend. If true, it is symptomatic of his
remote relationship with his father. His friend Rhoda Cowen recalls:
"George and I used to go to the same parties in London. It happened
that George was staying with us at our London house in Phillimore
Gardens when he opened *The Times* at breakfast and saw that
Wallington was given away. It was quite dramatic! It was the first time
anybody had given away such a place. George was dreadfully shocked,
he stood quite still, went white, and was silent. Then he said the odd-
est thing, I shall always remember it: 'My hairbrushes don't belong to
me any more!'" Such a weird response to the loss of a mansion and
13,000 acres can perhaps be attributed to the effects of shock, and compared with the incomprehensible triviality of some of the concerns of
the dying. Had George not believed that the house would really pass

from him? In *The Gold and Silver Threads*, Mrs Cowen says: "It had been discussed but he had no idea of his father's true intentions: Wallington was his inheritance, and much of his upbringing had been geared for him to live there."[3] Years later he said that "as a socialist" Sir Charles had given Wallington away, "but also because I was a bit rum. I was doing things he didn't understand." Mrs Jennings believes that it was George's passionate involvement with the Alexander Technique which was the sticking point for Sir Charles. Whatever the real cause, the loss hit George very hard. Rhoda Cowen says, "He was bemused and terribly insecure. He'd never been brought up to work, you see."

Never been brought up to work. It is an extraordinary idea. Death duties and financially troubled estates notwithstanding, there were still many families in which the necessities were provided from the cradle to the grave, as the makers of the Welfare State later put it. In keeping with Sir Charles's egalitarian principles all the Trevelyan children on arrival at adulthood received the same amount of money from the estate, with no preference for gender or age. This meant that George's income was relatively modest — but it was viable. It allowed him to pursue what interested him. In the idle idiom of the day he could have chosen to be a Bright Young Thing and run about like Buffy Fink-Nottle getting into madcap scrapes with policemen's helmets. Fortunately his mind was too curious and his intellect too advanced for such fluffy nonsense. George Trevelyan pursued his interests sincerely and seriously — but with no thought of making a living from them, or indeed from anything at all. This airy disregard for commercial considerations stayed with him all his life. The notion that money would always turn up somehow was one which freed him from dull, constricted thinking, freed him from the conventional, enabled his mind to go in what directions it chose — and from time to time caused no end of nuisance for those around him.

After Cambridge, what was he to do? He had already determined to take up the training to be an Alexander teacher as soon as it was available, which F.M. Alexander predicted would be in not less than three years' time. So there was this time to fill. There followed a period of experiment, of trying different avenues. Viewing a life story with hindsight it can appear that everything a person did was the correct and logical and obvious move for the time, and that the sum of them adds up to an inevitable outcome, taking every element into consideration. With George the avenues were apparently diverse and yet they led to a conclusion that united them. When he left Cambridge he had in mind to go down the avenue of architecture. He was particularly affected by church architecture.[4] All his life he retained this passion, and he campaigned strenuously and often successfully to save buildings. There are many stories about his minute knowledge of churches and houses. Catriona Tyson recalls, "You could be driving through a village and he would tell you all about the church, or if you told him you were going somewhere he'd say, 'stop at the church and in the fourth misericord along there is a beautiful carved figure'— and it would be somewhere he hadn't been for years. His memory was quite remarkable for detail." He also had a fabulous bravado in the matter of walking to people's country houses or stately homes if he wanted to look at them, with the charm of one who expects to get away with it. "George could always get into people's houses even when they weren't officially open. Old ladies were particularly susceptible, he'd get them round his finger," Mrs Tyson says.

However, this particular magic did not always work quite perfectly. The writer and academic, Bernard Nesfield-Cookson, tells of driving George Trevelyan home from Dorset one Sunday during the 1960s, after the two men had shared the platform at a conference. The day was dark and wet, and both of them were tired. Their route took them through the village of Montacute and George decided that he could not miss the chance of seeing Montacute House. This magnificent Elizabethan house was begun in the 1590s, now belongs to the National Trust, and is usually open to the public. However on that day there were notices all around it saying it was closed. Bernard Nesfield-Cookson was in favour of giving up, enough almost in itself to provoke George to proceed. They pressed on down the long drive, parked the car, wandered around the back of the great house, and peered through the ground floor windows to see if they could find a way in. There were sounds of banging and hammering. Sir George, caver, mountaineer, roof climber, explorer and amateur of private houses, said he would find a way. He had reached a doorway when he and his friend were stopped by the estate manager. "What do you think you're doing here?" he demanded.

Instantly, George was at his most engaging. "Well, we were driving past, you see," he said, "I know something of the house and I've always wanted to look at the wonderful heraldic glass, I do hope you don't mind. As a matter of fact, my father gave his own house in Northumberland to the Trust ... [pause] and by the way, my name is Sir

George Trevelyan." This last shot usually did the trick, but this estate employee was tougher than most. "Then you ought to know better, sir!" he replied straightforwardly, and turned them out. Bernard Nesfield-Cookson remarks, "In the 30 years I knew and worked with George, this was the only occasion I experienced him with his tail between his legs." Tail notwithstanding, George took it in good part. All part of the game, and so on. Many of his friends recall with horror his habit of walking into other people's houses. Ruth Nesfield-Cookson calls him, "a natural trespasser," and the musicologist Mary Firth says, "Going anywhere with George was always a bit of a risk, one lived in a gentle agony about what he might do next."

George Trevelyan's interest in church architecture had started when he was young and it developed into a more general interest in architecture as a discipline and later still as a metaphor. When he left Cambridge this fascination joined with the family link with Germany to create for him a focus on the Bauhaus group. Both the Trevelyan and the Bell families were keen on Germany, and all the Trevelyan children spoke good German. Pauline spent a year at Salem, the school set up by Dr Kurt Hahn, and it is likely that George visited her there. Charles Trevelyan admired much in German culture, especially its affinity with forests, nature and walking. When setting up outdoor youth groups at Wallington he had looked towards German youth movements for inspiration, abandoning them only when the more sinister influences began to appear. At home, the Trevelyan family sang German folk songs from a book Sir Charles had brought back. The English translation was written in pencil over the top of the German lyrics by his mother; George kept the song book for many years. (Kitty also had strong links with the country and in 1935, to the great disquiet of the family, married a German musician, Georg Götsch. "They didn't think much of Götsch," says Mrs Jennings, with massive understatement.) Thus after Cambridge Germany was an obvious destination for George. During his six month stay with various friends he travelled, walked, enthusiastically took up gliding, and made contact with the Freischar youth movement. This particular "free crowd" differed from predecessors of the same name in being genuinely free of religious or political affiliation, and committed to community and a common experience of nature. All the while, George was also investigating possibilities for his next step.

In the late 1920s, Germany was the place where the most exciting new architecture and design were being done. The Bauhaus had been formed in Weimar in 1919 by Walter Gropius; in 1925 it moved to Dessau as the embryonic Nazi movement began to gain ground in Bavaria and render Weimar unsafe. Gropius believed that art could not be taught, but that craft could. He had no faith in the system of Technische Hochschule specialization for architects and believed that training should be in workshops. In some respects this view was traditional: craft industries and the old craft guilds had continued to flourish in Germany throughout the nineteenth century in a way they had not in England.

The Bauhaus adopted avant-garde teaching methods concerned with creativity, the development of craftsmanship, and changing concepts of craftsmanship and its relation to the demands of industrial production. In its fusion of art and design, and in its idealistic view of the lives of craftsmen and the quality of the product, the Bauhaus took much of its inspiration from the Arts and Crafts Movement which had flourished in Great Britain at the end of the previous century. The goal in both cases was idealistic: to promote creative manual work to improve the quality of people's lives. The English had looked to the past for authenticity in design and had attempted to establish a new, Utopian social order through the redemptive role of craftsmanship in an industrializing society. Bauhaus philosophy of design, and design practised in the modernist manner, were to influence architectural thinking for the rest of the century. Furthermore, Gropius had a perception of unity that was to influence not only architectural thinking but a breadth of thinking in many areas. The word holism was not yet coined, but was surely anticipated by some of the perceptions of Walter Gropius, which sound very like the later George.

> The concept of unity underlies Gropius's work in every
> sphere: the essential oneness of things. In establishing the
> Bauhaus, Gropius's primary aim, therefore, was 'that the
> principle of training the individual's natural capacities to
> grasp life as a whole, a single cosmic entity, should form the
> basis of instruction throughout the school.[5]

Turning to craftsmanship

George's mind had been tending towards architecture and he met some members of the Bauhaus Group and talked seriously about it, before a chance remark caused him to change his thinking and move towards

craftsmanship. He said, "I had gone to Germany and come back keen
on architecture, but a friend of mine had said, 'What about crafts?' and
I thought: 'Yes, that is what I am looking for!' I very soon knew that it
was building furniture — that was the nearest craft to architecture."
Back in London George telephoned his father to announce his new
ambition but Sir Charles answered brusquely, "Yes, what do you
want?" a response which apparently upset George dreadfully. George's
daughter Catriona Tyson believes that George was frightened of his
father, and the naturopath Dr Barbara Latto said of the relationship,
"His father wanted him to have an academic career, or a political one.
His father didn't approve of the Alexander Technique, or the furniture,
he didn't want him to do anything manual. George had the constant
disapproval of his father; he was always criticized. Sir Charles was so
much of an aristocrat — he did rather take advantage of that — it came
through in his treatment of George." This view is held by many of
George's friends, and yet in contradiction to it, family members say
that Sir Charles was not much interested in his children's careers and
did not advise or guide them.

Whatever Sir Charles's opinion, in 1929 George went off to one of the
best furniture-making workshops of the time, those of Peter Waals, at
Chalford in Gloucestershire. Waals had been a pupil of the great Ernest
Gimson and had worked as his foreman until Gimson died in 1919.
Gimson himself had been a protégé and friend of William Morris. Both
Waals and Gimson designed in a way that continued the Arts and Crafts
tradition established by Morris in the previous century; moving on, however, from the intensely medieval influence. They set out to produce high
quality pieces of simple, pure design; what William Morris called, "good
citizens' furniture." George took up an apprenticeship as a paying pupil
and set to work, and according to his daughter Catriona, "George was
amazed at how good he was." He wrote:

> There was such endless joy in losing oneself in the making of
> fine things in a workshop where a dozen superlative
> craftsmen were doing the same. I would walk from Burleigh
> over the hill in the dewy morning, take cheese and beer in a
> pub beside the canal, and only chafe that the workshops
> closed at 5.30 and one could not work into the night.[6]

He would not use machines, preferring the activity of "handling and
thumping the great mortise chisels" with his own effort. George's

bench was next to that of the foreman, Ernest Smith, one of Gimson's original craftsmen, and George's first piece was a bed made in walnut to a Gimson design. George slept in it for the rest of his life, and he died in it in 1996. His instructor was Percy Burchett whom George described as, "a tiny man, neat, gentle and polite, but absolutely firm in his demand for perfection in workmanship." The material also excited him. He used walnut and what has been described as "immaculately detailed" English oak. "I had a passion about wood and building in wood. I lived there for nearly two years in a wonderful dreamland: walking in the morning over the Cotswold Hills and dropping down and then taking up my tools again." All the time he was making furniture, George was also practising the Alexander Technique: taking long breaths, using slow movements, resting between actions, observing and modifying the use of his muscles. Although he would not have used the word at that time, his furniture-making was a form of meditation. A link between working with the hands, deliberate movement, and observation of the breath, brought a quality of introspection which was very different from what had been possible for him up to that time. George wrote, "I had had lessons enough from FM to apply the Technique as I sawed and planed and cut dove-tails. I saw, of course, that FM was a very great craftsman in co-ordinating the human body."

Many beautiful pieces of George's manufacture or design still exist and they are always proudly shown by the people who own them. When Richard Tyson, George's son-in-law, asked late in George's life which of all the multitudinous things he had done he was the most proud, George answered, "the furniture." They were works of art as much as of craft. George specialized in perfect inlay and the perfect making of joints. He was full of admiration for the high standard of work in the workshop where he learnt, and of the way in which the skills of Gimson and Waals dove-tailed. He wrote, "Though Gimson was, of course, the inspiration and genius, he used Waals from the outset in close co-operation. The association of these two men was an essential factor in the evolving of the Cotswold tradition." (The phrase "Cotswold tradition" is a George Trevelyan coinage which came into general use to describe these pieces of what Ernest Gimson called, "wonderful furniture of a commonplace kind.") Architecture and craft had become closely entwined among members of the Arts and Crafts movement, notably Philip Webb, whom Gimson admired. George wrote:

It is a puzzle to some that, apart from his exquisite plaster
work and his spindle-back chairs, Ernest Gimson was not a
working craftsman. He was an architect designer — but with
what a difference! Too often when architects design furniture,
their lack of true feeling for material and construction is
revealed to the craftsman's eye ... His genius was such that
he could put himself completely into the understanding and
experience of a craft, so that as far as makes no matter, he
was the craftsman in that skill. He thought as a craftsman,
knowing exactly what he could ask of the men, and he had
their complete confidence through the inevitable 'rightness'
of each design.

The ten or so craftsmen worked in silence in a large shed in the
Cotswold town of Chalford. Each piece took many weeks to complete
and George Trevelyan often gave his finished work away. His daughter says, "He had not a commercial instinct in his head." This was harmonious with the outlook of the members of the Arts and Crafts
Movement. It was often observed that they made no attempt to recon-
cile art and industry but based their philosophy on truth in art through
individuality, the study of nature and the unity of the arts. The work of
manufacturing fine craft pieces, in Chalford as at the Bauhaus, had not
resolved the problem of making itself pay. The furniture made in the
Gimson workshop has proved itself to be worthy of collectors' attention and from time to time exhibitions are held. *Honest and
Unsentimental,* sub-titled "Sir George Trevelyan and the Arts and
Crafts Movement in the Cotswolds," was held in Bath from June to
September 1996, a few months after his death. The title was taken from
an essay for an exhibition of Gimson's work held in Leicester in 1969,
in which George wrote:

The Gimson-Barnsley-Waals tradition drew on a native
genius going back through centuries of handling timber in
the building of ships and houses and the great tithe-barns.
Thus as woodwork this tradition stands unrivalled in its
honesty and unsentimentality, linked with Morris but
untouched and untempted by the exaggerations of Art
Nouveau, the Bauhaus or other continental trends. There has
been nothing like it anywhere, and nothing to touch it.

About Gimson's design George wrote:

> ... in great sideboards or delicate drawing-room pieces,
> cottage chests of drawers or tiny inlaid boxes, there was
> always the same perfection and fitness for purpose, combined
> with astonishingly vivid touches of imagination.

The workshops survived through the 1920s and 1930s because a small number of faithful clients continued to buy the pieces, but in 1938 Peter Waals died and coincidentally there was a workshop fire. Perhaps inevitably, the workshops closed. George continued to design fine furniture all his life, and, before his hands lost their flexibility, occasionally to make more of it himself. But in 1931 the moment arrived for the first Alexander course, and he returned to London to begin.

This study gave George immense pleasure. As with all his other interests, he went into it very deeply. He began working with F.M. Alexander in a group of seven trainees, developing the habit of constant self-observation and the skill of teaching the Technique. Although Alexander had been teaching the Technique to pupils in London for several years it was the first course for training new teachers, so there was a spirit of discovery and even invention about it. According to Walter Carrington, who trained in the group that followed George's, the participants on the first trainee course kept in touch for many years. When it ended several of the new graduates went to teach with Alexander himself, but George set up a practice on his own — and after a couple of years gave it up. "I reached a stage when I simply could not keep it going, and I had to pull out into more understandable fields," he said. Most people attribute this to his lack of business instinct. "He simply hadn't enough pupils," said Walter Carrington, though in fact none of Alexander's first teachers succeeded immediately in setting up independent practices with this new discipline; most of them worked part time in F.M. Alexander's established practice. The insights that George gained from this study and from the lifelong discipline of self-observation, represented huge shifts for him. He wrote:

> The danger is in talking of what the work does... Certain
> changes in use take place, but so slowly that in most of us
> they are hardly visible... The risk is that a man's vigour and
> interest in using himself will pass before he has made the

change... We say our troubles are due to what we are doing.
We are doing our maladjustments. Most are inherited. It is
true but from a practical point of view it isn't. They are so
much part of us.

On the difficulty of setting up a practice in the new Technique he
observed: "The world won't listen to a new thing except from someone
who has shown they can do something in an accepted way." Sixty years
later, giving the F.M. Alexander Memorial Lecture in York in 1992,
George said, "What FM achieved was the marvellous demonstration of
the absolute psycho-physical unity of the human body. It was an outstanding holistic demonstration. We now realize that holism is a very
profound and all-encompassing conception." As with Alexander, so with
the Bauhaus, and the understanding of unity put forward by Gropius.

The Alexander experience was for George a profoundly important
step along the path towards self-realization, the first real step towards
an understanding of the holistic viewpoint that perceives every living
thing as linked and interdependent. Since the Trevelyan children
enjoyed private incomes the financial failure of his teaching was not
disastrous. Because Sir Charles did not believe in primogeniture the
individual incomes were equal and thus not huge, still, they removed
the burdensome necessity of making a living. Walter Carrington
observed that there were many young men around London at that time
with nothing to do and enough money to enjoy their idleness: George
could have been one of them if he had been so disposed. Instead he
took on serious studies: craft furniture making, teaching, a new philosophy of health. When Alexander teaching failed George sought other
employment. He had remarkable energy and if a thing did not turn out
in the way he might have envisaged he took from it what lessons
there were and did something else. About him nothing is written
anywhere, or recalled by anyone who knew him, that indicates
depression or disillusionment. He worked hard, he applied himself,
and he was exhaustingly enthusiastic, no matter whether he was
climbing a mountain, learning a new skill, teaching, chairing a conference, leading a meditation, or running as a hare in the Trevelyan
Man Hunt. Whatever the activity, he did it with all his heart and
mind until it came time to stop, and then he harboured no regrets.
Throughout his life, *What next?* was an eager cry for him. Where is
the next exciting thing to have a go at? All the same, the ideal represented by the Alexander Technique had been hugely important to

him, and his failure to bring it to a wider public must have been disappointing. The idealistic concern was infinitely more important than the financial one, and once again, he had to wonder about a purposeful occupation.

Gordonstoun School

Just when George was looking for something to do after attempting to teach the Alexander Technique, fate dealt him a wonderful opportunity to exercise his physical, intellectual and artistic skills, and to carry on learning at the same time. Of the opportunity of teaching at Gordonstoun School, George said, "I was rescued by a great friend, Kurt Hahn, the head of the public school, Gordonstoun, who recognized that I was a great teacher going hopelessly wrong, introverted by being cut off so completely, trying to do this thing that nobody understood. Therefore I had to chuck out the thing that I had given my life to and I found myself at thirty, without a training, without a profession, without a qualification in the world's point of view at all. At that stage, in the middle of my life, I had to re-start, and Gordonstoun was the obvious link. Kurt Hahn picked me up and threw me into very, very full activity — mountaineering, being in charge of crafts, teaching history and literature." (*Kindred Spirit*) This was a rescue not so much from crisis as confusion, and lack of direction. The Alexander Technique had seemed the answer but had proved, at least for George, to be an impractical profession.

George Trevelyan almost certainly met Dr Hahn in the company of the mountaineer, poet and educational philosopher Geoffrey Winthrop Young, a close friend both of Sir Charles and of George Macaulay Trevelyan. Kurt Hahn was a former diplomat who in 1920 had founded a boys' school called Salem, in Bavaria. It was broadly after the pattern of British public schools of the Victorian era, but with a novel emphasis on outdoor pursuits, self-monitoring and community service. A contemporary says Salem, "produced the more liberal sort of German." It was housed in a wing of Schloss Salem, one of the homes of Prince Max of Baden, with whom Hahn shared a belief in the importance of awakening in the young a sense of duty as citizens. Dr Hahn was clever, charismatic, idealistic and determined, and ran his school along somewhat unconventional lines, simultaneously continuing some of his original political work for Prince Max. He believed this political link helped to keep his pupils in touch with current affairs.

Among his strong principles besides public service were health, decent
social behaviour and a certain amount of solitude every day. Two concepts were present from the beginning: "Help your neighbour," and
"Give service for peace."

Many of his key ideas were taken from the 1897 New Curriculum
of Dr Cecil Reddie, the innovative first headmaster of Abbotsholme
School, in Derbyshire. Kurt Hahn had met an Abbotsholme hiking
party while walking in the Harz mountains, and had been much
impressed by the young Abbotsholme masters and pupils. Dr Reddie
had brought climbing and canoeing into the curriculum. He also
believed that as his pupils were likely to be in positions of influence in
later life, their formative experience should be rounded, and accordingly he ensured that they visited northern factories, mills and mines,
staying as guests of working families.

Dr Hahn's opposition to Nazism grew with the rise of the Nazis
until at last, in response to the Potempa murders in autumn 1932, he
wrote a circular to all Salem Old Boys demanding the condemnation
of the Nazi murderers. He did this in the knowledge that the letter
would fall into Nazi hands, and his action was described by Dr Eric
Meissner, himself later of Gordonstoun, as, "the bravest deed in cold
blood I have ever witnessed."[7] The Potempa murder story was told by
Meissner: "A few months before Hitler became Chancellor, five S.A.
(*Sozialitische Arbeiterpartei*) men were imprisoned and tried. They
had trampled a Communist to death in front of his mother. Hitler sent
them a telegram of appreciation and praise. He called them his com-
rades. He was right, they were." As early as 1923, Prince Max of
Baden had written, "The spirit of civil war is sweeping the whole
country ... the younger generation, victims of deception, have come
to believe that you can be a murderer in Germany without being dis-
credited." Hahn was imprisoned and was considered to be in great
danger; not only had he spoken against the Nazis, he was also Jewish.
However in 1933, after the intervention of the British Prime Minister,
Ramsay Macdonald, he was released under surveillance. It is generally accepted that Hahn's release was also aided by Lord Tweedsmuir
(John Buchan) whose adventure stories had inspired the
Trevelyan/Winthrop Young Lakeland Hunt. Within weeks, Dr Hahn
was smuggled out of Germany in a marvellous escape from a tennis
match which had been arranged on the Swiss border for the purpose.
During a break in play, Hahn, still in his tennis whites, was whisked
away to England. George's uncle, George Macaulay Trevelyan,

helped in this, as did the Prince of Baden-Wuerttemberg, another friend of Sir Charles.

Next, G.M. Trevelyan with Geoffrey Winthrop Young and the Prince helped Hahn to found a new school along similar lines to Salem. This was Gordonstoun, eight miles from Elgin and three from Lossiemouth, on the north coast of Scotland. Gordonstoun began in May, 1934 with two English boys transferred from Salem by Geoffrey Winthrop-Young (who was working at Salem at the time) and eleven local pupils. Later, Winthrop Young made another transfer from Germany: that of Prince Philip of Greece, then at preparatory school. In the following year there were 52 pupils including 17 Germans; of the remainder about half were English and half Scots. John Bartholomew was a pupil at that time and recalls that most of the arguments among the pupils were between English and Scots: the presence of the Germans caused no strife. By September 1937, the school roll had risen to 121, and by 1940 to 135. The fees varied with the incomes of the parents and to begin with not all the teachers were paid. This somewhat experimental enterprise found a great many distinguished friends. The first list of Governors to be made available in 1937 includes the names of the Archbishop of York, the headmaster of Eton, the vice-chancellor of Aberdeen University, the master of Downing College, Cambridge, the director-general of the BBC, G.M. Trevelyan, Regius Professor of Modern History at Cambridge University, and Geoffrey Winthrop Young, Reader in Comparative Education at London University.[8]

The idea of the school was to focus on the development of the individual within the context of the group, with emphasis on both the ideal and practicality of service. Thus far in expressed intention it did not depart very much from the contemporary British public schools, but a different emphasis was placed on building character. At Salem there had been dedicated teachers for what they called character training, and this arrangement was retained at Gordonstoun. Boys kept their own progress record charts which were not subject to inspection. They understood that if they cheated over how many times they had taken the early morning run, or done their daily exercises, or even fulfilled their own punishments, they were only cheating themselves. This emphasis on individual responsibility for individual progress extended to the way in which academic work was done. Gordonstoun boys also took on local duties such as keeping watch on the headland for boats, in the absence of a lighthouse. The importance of this task is so obvious that the boys, who worked in pairs, never slept on duty. George

Trevelyan and a few of the pupils built the first coastal lookout station in 1936; it continued in use by the boys until the school was evacuated to Wales in 1940, and throughout the War by local watchers, and was not replaced until 1948. Senior boys worked in the local fire service, and still do. Thus the responsibility of each pupil for himself as an individual, and for his actions within his community, were seen to be linked.

The Gordonstoun perception of these and many other community service efforts is the participation of all for the general good; an essential aspect of it is the mixing of all people, without snobbery over ability or financial status. Dr Hahn's convictions about international understanding had been among the factors that put him at odds with the German hierarchy. The objectives of Gordonstoun, then as now, were self mastery achieved through adventure and experiment which tests mind and body; and compassion learned through the opportunity and ability to help others in distress. Hahn's biographer says, "in the ideas themselves there is no great originality... The originality lies in the man, in his combination of qualities, and in the experience of life and politics that he brought to the work." Cecil Reddie should perhaps have some of the credit for the ideas, but original or not, to this day the views of Kurt Hahn are often quoted.

It happened that in 1936, Hahn was looking for like-minded teachers who were physically fit and academically able. Here was young George Trevelyan, the nephew of his benefactor, a craftsman with a Cambridge degree in history, an understanding of teaching, and an athletic prowess which some of his more fervent admirers have said was practically at Olympic level — and he was looking for a job. The situation was quickly resolved. George found the project exciting. He loved challenges, he loved innovation, and it is hard to imagine that the romance of Hahn's escape from Nazi Germany left his poetic imagination unmoved. The location of the school represented another draw: rugged, mountainous terrain, perfect for a climber and caver brought up in the Border country. There is some question over whether or not there was a salary for George. The school started with little money and few pupils and many of the early members of staff received only their board and lodging, so perhaps for George Trevelyan the job could have been regarded as one more apprenticeship.

The remote location of Gordonstoun was not allowed to lead to insularity within the school community. According to Adam Arnold-Brown, an early Gordonstoun teacher, Dr Hahn consistently set out, "to bring to our notice world affairs in order to mitigate the inward-facing tendency of all isolated communities ... One boy would read the news, another would comment upon it. Then Kurt Hahn would elaborate, fill in, expand, explain and attempt a glance at the future. Our interpreter of world affairs was well qualified to tell us something of what was going on."[9] Sometimes Hahn translated for small groups of boys and teachers as Adolf Hitler was speaking on the wireless. "Here were two men with utterly opposed convictions. Both men were of strong character, but one desired to impose his will upon mankind, the other to strengthen the individual will and the power for good."

The school sits surprisingly well in the context of innovative, unconventional public schools of the 1920s and 1930s. These include Dartington, with a liberal arts focus that included professional performance; Millfield, which has an exceptional variety of sports facilities and subject options and provides for 50% of pupils to be subsidized by the other 50%; maybe even Summerhill, a controversial residential school focusing on free, individual choice. This was a period of reconsideration of schooling, as of so many other areas of life. Post-war Britain was still engrossed in reassessing its certainties. Hahn was concerned that the worlds of action and thought were "no longer to be divided into hostile camps." He wished to build up, "the imagination of the boy of action and the will-power of the dreamer." This idealism also found expression in attempting to span social division by ensuring that many pupils from poorer homes were enabled to attend Gordonstoun. Between 20% and 25% of the parents voluntarily paid more than they needed so that others could pay less. The wealthier ones themselves determined how much extra they would pay — and yet the system worked. There was and is a commitment to bringing a number of pupils in from abroad, in order to foster the spirit of internationalism that the Nazis had been so concerned to destroy. Geoffrey Winthrop Young called it, "more than a school: a movement."

George took to Gordonstoun a clutch of skills that could almost have been tailor-made for the place. His combination of high quality craftsmanship and athleticism with scholarship was of huge importance to Kurt Hahn. The term *holism* was not in use at the time, but in his concern with the *whole boy*, whose strength of character and balanced outlook were as important as his scholarly ability, Hahn in some way anticipated it. The concept was the one with which George Trevelyan was to engage for the rest of his life. In Nazi Germany Dr Hahn had seen how the highest aspiration can be grotesquely distorted.

What was needed was to bring the notion of the whole boy back into the liberal arena. The intention at the school was always to push one-self to constantly improve. Pushing oneself was something George did as a matter of course. He never gave way to tiredness, just as in later life he never gave way to pain.

At first many local people were suspicious of the new school, and they had to be courted. George threw himself into it with characteris-tic zeal. Indeed, of all George's qualifications for Gordonstoun, his enthusiasm may have been the most important. You can hear him cry-ing, *Wonderful!* — the emphasis strongly on the first syllable, which was pronounced *wan* in the aristocratic way. Whether keeping lookout on the clifftop, teaching history, or making the huge Austrian oak table for the library with five of the boys, he was whole-heartedly involved. This table deserves a moment of its own. It is still in use in the library, and much admired. Gordonstoun old boy John Bartholomew, brother of George's publisher Alick Bartholomew, describes it as, "a monastic, refectory-style table: solid, yet graceful. It couldn't have simpler lines. A fine piece." He calls it a monumental work, believes it to be at least 12ft long and says it is massively thick. It bears the inscription, "George Trevelyan 1936," and the initials DN, PCK, RDL, MR and TB-F.

George's infectious energy was always a tremendous bonus for those around him; an impromptu lesson illustrates it. At short notice he had to take over a history class because the usual master was ill. He was told that the class was doing the French Revolution, and that was more or less all of his brief. He walked into the classroom and asked the boys, "What are you studying?" They answered, "The French Revolution." George asked, *"Why?"* The boys replied that they were to be examined on it. "I don't mean that," said George, "I mean, *why a French Revolution?* Why was there a Revolution in France in 1789?" — and then he talked electrifyingly for the entire period. Totally unpre-pared, he gave the boys a vivid impression of the events of the Revolution and with it an excitement about historical study that trans-formed their view of the subject. Apparently the lesson was not espe-cially related to their examination material but it gave them not only a new appetite for history but also an invaluable insight into the use of imagination in academic endeavour. George's own enthusiasm was transmitted no matter what he was teaching. It conveyed all the fun of the investigation and the triumph of the ultimate discovery.

During the Gordonstoun years, his confidence in his own ability grew. Everything he had done until his acquaintance with the Alexander Technique had been along lines which could have been prescribed by his family. His job at Gordonstoun had more or less been put in his way by his uncle George Macaulay Trevelyan. Nevertheless George was not valued by Sir Charles, he was not quite the desired eldest son, and he had always lacked confidence. This may have been attributable to the dazzling achievements of the rest of his family, especially those of his father, grandfather and uncle. For the first half of his life George had not such a great opinion of himself and although his confidence grew over time, during the Gordonstoun period he was still somewhat the uncertain young man. John Bartholomew says that he seemed reserved, but that he was possibly shy, somewhat inward-looking. "I remember him reading to us, English Literature. He didn't have much of an impact." However, he also remembers that, "the boys had tremendous respect for him." The consensus at Gordonstoun was that he was at any rate "interesting," if still somewhat shy. For himself, the full realization of his abilities was relatively slow in coming. Gradually he began to understand how well he could teach all sorts of things, and what a marvellous effect he could have on the state of mind and the motivation of his auditors. Even more gradually, he began to value it.

It was inevitable in 1939 that Gordonstoun School would experience difficulties. With Britain once again at war with Germany, suspicion of the German headmaster and members of staff coupled with rumours about what went on at the school began to build locally into an attitude of outright hostility. It was rumoured that Hahn was a spy, even that the school was a military base. The school's proximity to a small airfield which might become an enemy target was probably the deciding factor on the list of factors which led to the move to Wales during May and June 1940. Somehow, in Wales no one was suspicious of either the school or Kurt Hahn, and despite difficult physical conditions the school population was able to thrive. George went to their initial evacuation home at Aberdovey, then to the one at Berthddu. The boys constructed sand pits for athletic high and long jumps, and for their community contribution they cut and fetched firewood for local people. The school records noted that during War Weapons Week: "Mr Trevelyan produced two plays, *The Fifth of November* and *Prairie Rose*, with the third form." Furthermore, "He caused a sensation with his rendering of The Hungarian Hair Artist." The same magazine recalled that, "Mr Trevelyan and three or four boys have spent their spare time during the whole two terms making puppets, and at the end of term they produced *Twelfth Night* as well as an enthralling battle between a Knight in armour and Hugi, Merlin's pet dragon. They did several shows for the benefit of the local people." Mr Trevelyan the adventurous sportsman is remembered on Llyn Cae, "taking the more energetic of us on up to the summit," where within a few minutes, "Mr Trevelyan's party came into the mist and from then on we had to steer by map and compass."

In Scotland the school had regarded seamanship as its main sporting activity but the evacuation to Wales placed difficulties on continuing it. They established a seamanship centre where the boys could spend weekends, 33 miles away at Aberdovey. This led to a very significant independent offshoot: Outward Bound. The first Sea School was founded in Aberdovey in October, 1941, to provide moral as well as physical training to urban and rural young people in an intense period of adventure over periods of about four weeks. It was to be a democratizing experience. Early brochures offered, "character training through adventure and testing experience." Hahn believed that young people were made dependent for too many of their formative years and needed to test and prove themselves. He thought their situation, artificially kept in the dependent position of learners well into their young adulthood, was contradictory. Hence the emphasis on outdoors, physical effort, group responsibility. Outward Bound made another important point: no boy or girl fails through lack of physical strength or aptitude; the experience is what counts. Within 25 years there were 19 Outward Bound Schools: six in Britain, the others in the USA, Australia, New Zealand, the Netherlands, Germany Africa and Malaya.

This development was entirely sympathetic to George Trevelyan, for whom adventure was crucially important. Throughout his childhood in Cambo and Somerset he had taken great joy in constantly pushing himself physically further, and as he grew up the tales of his participation in the Trevelyan Man Hunt, exploring in the Mendip caves and climbing the roofs of Cambridge testify to the continuation of this. His godson Roger Orgill said that even after disability struck him later in his life, "There was always one more climb for George." Such energy was harmonious with the aspirations of Gordonstoun and its offshoot organizations. In 1943 when George named a schooner *Garibaldi* for the Outward Bound School he said, "If ever youth loses the thirst for adventure, any civilization, however enlightened, and any state, however well-ordered, must wither and dry up." After Outward

Bound came Atlantic College, another legacy of the innovative energy of Kurt Hahn and his staff.

From the beginning of the Second World War Gordonstoun School employed female teachers; this became necessary as the younger men were called up. Among them was Helen Lindsay-Smith, a formidable woman in her late thirties who had been taken on the staff to teach the younger boys of prep school age. She had been born in India, the daughter of an Indian army officer, and like many of her contemporaries sent back to boarding school in England, in her case the Royal School in Bath. When the First World War came, Helen had to spend it in England, staying with maiden aunts (mostly in Ireland) during the school holidays and thus not seeing her parents for 10 years. These wartime schooldays were her teenage years, and in the normal run of things it was expected that she would return to India when she finished her schooling, to locate and marry a suitable army officer. However, Helen refused to do it, preferring to stay in England and find work as a preparatory school teacher. It was a radical move for a young woman of her class at the time. Perhaps the fact that she was, "half-Scots, half-Irish, and very dramatic," according to her daughter, Catriona Tyson, had something to do with it. Apparently she was also tall and rather beautiful, and always superbly turned out. The assumption that marriage was the only career for women was pervasive: immediately their schooldays were over the all-consuming occupation of young girls was generally that of finding an eligible husband. For Helen to choose not to marry if doing so meant accepting a young man chosen by her family was not only odd, it was almost outlandish. For her to choose to make her own living was also very unusual. Helen Lindsay-Smith was determined, clever and independent. She taught in prep schools during term times and became a governess to children home from school during the school holidays.

Helen was five years older than George, and like him, something of an eccentric within her family. But while Helen had openly rebelled against her fate, George had not. He and she began to go about together. They walked on the hills and on the rough, romantic north Scottish coastline, and in time Helen was invited to stay at Wallington during the summer holidays. She was not a notable success with the Trevelyan family (themselves not the easiest company); nevertheless in 1940, she and George were somewhat precipitately married. From the outset it was a troubled relationship. There was friction over opinions and over the fact that George made almost no concession to the married state, carrying on doing his own things and following his own interests like a bachelor. After their marriage both of them stayed only a few more terms on the teaching staff of Gordonstoun School, for it had become time for George to serve his country.

The Trevelyan attitude to the Second World War was the opposite of its attitude to the First; they were in no doubt that Hitler and Fascism were wholly bad and must not be allowed to take over Europe. Therefore George joined up. He was 33 years old at the beginning, which made him too old for active service, so he volunteered to train riflemen and was attached to the Rifle Brigade of the Home Guard between 1941 and 1946. He had all the experience of training for outdoor life from his time at Gordonstoun, and from his roof-climbing, fencing, walking, mountaineering exploits. He had experience of teaching boys and young men, and enthusing and motivating them, from Gordonstoun and from working on the beginnings of the Outward Bound movement. More or less, he continued doing what he had been doing for some years, but with active service the object instead of community service.

In 1942 (coincidentally the year of the near-revolutionary Beveridge Report on social insurance) George went to the lecture that revolutionized his life. This was the famous lecture on Rudolf Steiner, which he had attended apparently by chance: his spiritually oriented sister Kitty persuaded him to drop in on a weekend conference being held on Rudolf Steiner's agricultural teachings at Heathcote House near Aberdeen. George was interested in organic husbandry, and wanted to know more about bio-dynamic agriculture. During the gathering, Dr Walter Johannes Stein spoke on the subject: What did Dr Steiner mean by Anthroposophy? There George heard for the first time a set of ideas that made complete sense, that appeared to answer all his deep questions, that seemed to square the circle of harmonizing the rational mind with the imagination, that seemed to encapsulate all of his own thinking, feeling and aspiration. The lecture affected George by simultaneously crystallizing and altering everything for him. It seemed to explain all that was puzzling, and listening to it he was so taken over that he famously cried *Yes!* to every point that was being made. It was indeed George's personal Road to Damascus (see further in Chapter 3). Here he took on the great visions of reincarnation and Gaia theory, the notions of spirit as first cause and the complete interrelatedness of all cell structures. It is hard to imagine that these ideas were new to him, and it is certain that his thoughts and aspirations must have been shifting for many years for him to have been able to respond to them so totally.

At the end of the War George was expected to go back to Gordonstoun, where his job had been held open for him, but before that could happen he was ill. Physical illness can create mental states with visionary and philosophical potential, and always the opportunity to take stock of one's condition and progress. George said, "At each of the turning points in my life I have had an illness, and at the end of the War it was jaundice. It was a very cleansing experience." When he recovered he set off to go back to the school, but something very strange happened, something which was always afterwards referred to by him almost with disconnected wonder, as though it were happening to someone else. He got out of the train at Elgin and set off to walk the eight miles to Gordonstoun, but as he walked he found his steps getting slower and slower, and eventually he found he could not go on. It was a turning point which he often recalled in later years. At the 1992 Alexander Memorial Lecture he said, "I remember the sandy road with a leaning Scots Pine tree and I just came to a stop as if an India-rubber rope was holding me from the back or an angel was standing in the way. I knew that adult education was my line. And without a thought, I just turned on my heel, turned my back on schoolmastering, and walked into adult education." (*Direction* magazine). In fact, he turned around with nothing specific to go to and no plan in mind.

As luck would have it another marvellous opportunity was waiting for George, one that, like Gordonstoun before it and Attingham after it, seemed almost tailor-made for him. The army was making provision for some of the soldiers who were about to be demobbed to spend a month getting additional education to help them back into civilian life. The definition of education was geared to the idealistic, post-war Labour Party view of regenerating the nation, and was a broad one. It could mean studying the arts, law, civics, or joinery and carpentry. There was even a Post Office course, for soldiers who had worked in the Post Office and needed to do some revision before they returned there. Such a liberal and liberalizing idea was entirely to George's taste; much better than instructing people on firing rifles or even than going back to Gordonstoun to teach teenagers. One of the places where this interim education was provided was at Newbattle Abbey, just outside Edinburgh. It bore the title of Army Formation College. George was taken on in his army rank as Captain to lecture in English and history, with a responsibility to a broad interpretation of the arts. His interest in drama soon brought him into contact with Dr George Firth, who headed the Fine Arts section, and they formed a friendship. Dr Firth and Mary (not yet his wife) were musicians.

George Trevelyan was eager to learn about music, of which he had little knowledge. He had a boundless curiosity about practically all arts and philosophical subjects, about crafts and the making of things, and, since his first contact with the Alexander Technique, about the human body. About science he was almost wholly uncurious, the big exception being astronomy, in which he became quite expert. When he wanted to pursue something he would always find good teachers, a facility which transferred marvellously to Attingham College. Something would begin to occupy his questioning mind and he would either seek out an expert or one would seem miraculously to present themselves to him. Later this was put down not to luck or coincidence but to the law of manifestation, a concept much talked about in the Findhorn Community and in New Age circles in general.

So George started at Newbattle, perhaps a little tentatively at first, soon coming into this own. Teaching adults in one way or another was becoming his life's work, and everything he had done to date contributed to the success of it. He was in his element. Another big change took place at this time: he and Helen adopted a baby called Catriona. Both of them wanted children but Helen was getting old for child-bearing, so the ten-day old girl who had been born in Aberdeen became their family. Catriona had a delightful temperament, curious, imaginative and sparky, and was a welcome addition to the household.

Back at Newbattle the staff were getting to know each other. Mary Firth recalls, "I first met George Trevelyan when he was dressed as a Rifle Brigade captain with a beret stuck on his head. I could see he had a lively mind, although I think I was assuming his intelligence because he was a Trevelyan and the family was well known, of course. He was curious and energetic; he wanted to know what we were planning and whether it would be interesting. After he joined the college I remember having great arguments with him about his drama because he would alter scripts to make a point and I didn't think you should. We had quite a spat over his interpretation of *Julius Caesar* because he cut it. I said he altered the meaning, he said, 'that's just what I meant to do!'" This was a friendship that enjoyed intellectual skirmishes, and that grew over a long time into deep affection. George spent two happy years at Newbattle Abbey. He lived with Helen and Catriona in a flat near the Edinburgh Botanical Gardens and stayed at the Abbey on choir nights (though his absences from home were not much appreciated). His interest in liberal arts developed, and he was able learn and teach at the same time, a combination which he always relished. "He wanted to know many things," Mary Firth says. "He was building up an enormous reservoir of knowledge, all the time." At the beginning of the 21st century it is next to impossible to imagine the appreciation with which all this learning was received. The current mode of regarding education as a commodity that must always produce a saleable skill has damaged the spirit of joy in simply exercising the mind. This perception can surely be only transient. At the time that George and the Firths were teaching not only soldiers but also civilians would avidly pursue whatever interested them, and give their scant free time to it. The habit of linking free time with consumerism was still some way off.

Luckily for the Firths, George also continued to maintain his interest in furniture design. After the War there was little manufactured furniture. This made setting up home, as George and Mary Firth were trying to do, next to impossible. They asked the joinery department what to do about it and someone said, "Let's ask George Trevelyan!" George said he believed he could lay his hands on, "a few sticks of Gloucestershire oak." These sticks were actually fine timber which had been left in the Waals workshop after it closed. George located the wood, designed some pieces, and contacted the Waals craftsman Owen Scruby who had continued working after the closure. In time, tables, chairs and cupboards of exquisite craftsmanship found their way to Scotland for the musical household that was just beginning. Many of the pieces are still in use and, like so many of George Trevelyan's design works, are much cherished by their owners. If the Firth household benefited in many ways from George's friendship, the next George Lowthian Trevelyan undertaking was to benefit greatly from the friendship of the Firths, because as we shall see in Chapter 4, after Newbattle came Attingham. But first a moment for taking stock.

CHAPTER 3

Midpoint

Forty, halfway through a life, is an obvious moment for taking stock and often the time when people are about to do their best work. It was then that George Trevelyan began, somewhat tentatively at first, to express the complex ideas that were to make him famous. When a few decades later the movement which became known as the New Age of spiritual understanding and enlightenment started to gather momentum, George was its standard bearer and its greatest exponent. His own inner development had been achieved through years of training, reassessment and inspiration, and he was ready to use it to the benefit of all. Came the hour, came the man.

The cliché that inspiration comes to those who are ready to receive it, or indeed that to have a vision on the Road to Damascus you must first be on that road, is certainly true of George. His friend Rhoda Cowen (née Harris) thought he was seeking spiritual answers from his late teens and possibly before. The freedom to think the unthinkable was part of his inheritance from Charles Trevelyan, whose enthusiasm for wild ideas found by far its greatest exponent in George. Further gifts from his background, among them agnosticism and a Quaker schooling, brought a liberal attitude to religion. There was nothing rigid or narrow about George's search, so when in 1942 he first encountered the radical and esoteric thoughts of the Austrian philosopher Rudolf Steiner, his mind was free to receive them.

Upper class radicalism did not generally concern itself with deep thinking or esotericism. In George's immediate family, Charles Trevelyan was a political revolutionary and George Macaulay Trevelyan a radical intellectual; they were both materialists to whom George's ideas seemed insubstantial and inconsequential. Even within his own definite parameters, however, Charles was an extremely contradictory man. He was a supporter of the working class who approved of the Russian Revolution and lent money to the USSR, yet when his son and heir George Lowthian Trevelyan decided to become a craftsman, he was horrified. It was manual work! His daughter Pauline recorded that Charles would happily paint a gate with his estate workmen, and said he told her, "the rank and file are pure gold" — but for his eldest son to study the Alexander Technique was utterly beyond the pale. To Charles, the practice of the Technique counted as manual work (and coincidentally he thought the Technique itself was a crazy fad). For most of his life George was afraid of his father; for his part, Charles was excessively critical of George. The relationship upset George terribly and was at least part of the cause of his youthful diffidence. It made the treading of his own path both courageous and essential.

As in most difficult relationships, there were as many similarities as differences between the protagonists. Both men were purposeful, determined and conscientious, and they both held contradictory attitudes; in particular, the concepts of social equality, family and rank were in conflict within George just as much as they were within his father. People remark that George was always aware of who he was and whence he came, and that although he mixed easily and happily with all sorts and conditions of people, there could be an edge to him if someone omitted the "Sir." When the idea of adopting a brother for his daughter Catriona was proposed it was forcefully rejected by George because of the potential for dispute over the title. There could be no question of an adopted boy from who knew where attempting to claim a Trevelyan baronetcy. George's attitude in such matters was probably indistinguishable from Charles's.

But the concept of aristocracy is infinitely more complex than simple, material concerns with property and title and orders of precedence might suggest. It encompasses quasi-mystical beliefs concerning the significance of links with the land; indeed, some aristocratic families see their continuing existence as essential to the soul of the nation. These notions gained force in Victorian times, when the rise of the newly rich industrial middle class drove the landed upper classes back to an emphasis on blood lines and continuity. A fascination with heraldry and medieval chivalry arose at the same time. This esoteric perception is itself a kind of suspension of reality, creating a bond or brotherhood like some secret society. Such esotericism held great appeal for George, who believed in the importance both of stewardship and legend. Hence the tale of the Trevelyan link with the court of King Arthur was greatly to his taste. In Victorian times, august Trevelyan men assembled at a Round Table conference to try to find links within the family coat of arms with Sir Trevillian, a Knight of the legendary Holy Grail. If they had succeeded they could have claimed as part of their history the myth of Sir Trevillian's ride out of the sea at St

Michael's Mount, in Cornwall. In his New Age incarnation George afforded great significance to this tale and to St Michael's Mount itself; but for a conference of materialistic politicians and high-minded scholars to make such a serious effort to verify it seems magnificently paradoxical.

George was brought up to understand responsibility for the land and for the people who worked it, and responsibility for the people who sustained the Wallington household and estate in all ways. Charles Trevelyan's idealistic paternalism led eventually to the creation of an independent, miniature welfare state. (In fact, Charles's aristocratic concept of responsibility was far more harmonious with a paternalistic welfare state than it was with competitive industrial capitalism.) Notions of belonging to the land are also strong in Germany, the country with which the Trevelyan family had its closest relationship. Landscape is of crucial importance in Teutonic folklore. Medieval themes of darkness and danger, forests, the fear of forests, animals, castles, mountains, and magic, are pivotal within it. A twelfth century perception of the natural environment formed a backdrop for George's athletic exploits up mountains as well as underground. From childhood, he explored his internal world through exploring the countryside, and contemplative solitude was essential to his peace of mind.

Wandering around the Wallington estate as a boy, investigating, climbing, exploring, George framed his observations within the imaginative setting of poetry. His mother taught all her children to learn poems by heart and George loved to play with the ideas they offered. His poetic understanding is at the root of his frequent recommendation to "seize an idea for its own beauty," and in his agnostic youth he relished the impressionistic potential of poetry, the chance to sketch his own meaning, paint his own colours. He loved words, sound and rhythm, he loved abstract ideas. All his life he would launch himself unexpectedly into a line, a verse, or even a whole poem, often in the middle of an otherwise ordinary moment, and "even at breakfast!" his friends recall, marvelling. Such romanticism played well with the late-twentieth century movement away from mundane materialism. George often quoted nature poets such as William Wordsworth:

Our birth is but a sleep and a forgetting:
The soul that rises with us' our life's Star,
Hath had elsewhere its setting,
And cometh from afar.

And:

> The Youth, who daily farther from the east
> Must travel, still is Nature's Priest,
> And by the vision splendid
> Is on his way attended.

And later:

> All are but parts of one stupendous whole
> Whose body nature is, and God the soul.
> *Alexander Pope*

Over time this led to:

> Never the spirit was born; the spirit shall cease to be never,
> Never was time it was not; end and beginning are dreams.
> *Bhagavad Gita*

George's poetic imagination employed in the service of abstract thought was among the strongest of his tools for gaining access to inner wisdom and a pure relationship with himself, but during the first part of his life this intuitive activity played second fiddle to his rational training. After the discovery of Steiner's thought, the emphasis reversed, and the understanding of the two sides of his brain began to synthesize. George would quote Shelley: "Poetry is the breath and finer spirit of all knowledge; it is the impassioned expression on the face of science."

Exploring the internal and external landscape were lifelong activities, and the years that George Trevelyan spent at Sidcot, the liberal, Quaker boarding school in Somerset, provided wonderful scope for them. As a pupil there he began seriously to pursue his interest in caving. It is easy to make the connection between caving and the unconscious mind, that which is dark and hidden, dangerous to negotiate, subject perhaps to sudden rushes of light. Caving in the Mendips was something he returned to later in life when his body was tortured by the dreadful Trevelyan arthritis. There were also exceptionally good facilities for drama, George's forte. With his love of words and his extraordinary memory for verse went a great gift for oratory. In addition George loved to assume characters, and is remembered for the enthusiasm with which he threw himself into them. (Somehow, in the light of acquaintance with the Trevelyan family, it is not surprising to know that his sister Kitty was coached for the leading part in the Sidcot production of St Joan by no less a mentor than Sybil Thorndike.)

The Society of Friends, known as Quakers, had been chosen as mentors for the eldest three Trevelyan children because of Charles Trevelyan's opposition to the Great War. The Quakers were a Christian Protestant sect founded in the seventeenth century and dedicated to non-violence and social reform, two objectives which were sympathetic to Charles. Quaker meetings replace conventional religious services and emphasise meditation and the freedom of all participants to contribute their thoughts. Sidcot School was academically less demanding than Harrow, the traditional academy for Trevelyan men, and in many ways had more human qualities. It was egalitarian, encouraging children to be kind, inclusive and democratic, to hear all points of view.

Elements of aristocracy, poetry, a liberal and unconventional Christian schooling, physical excellence, an affinity with nature, paternal rejection, sensitivity, an enquiring mind, and a degree from Cambridge university in the family subject of history (with the improbable addition of economics), travelled with the young George to Germany. He went on a quest to broaden his horizons and seek a *métier*. On the way he found the avant-garde designers who made up the Bauhaus, people with a new understanding of the organic nature of buildings, an emphasis on natural shapes, an apparently revolutionary take on architecture. Back home, however, his interest shifted. As cited earlier, George wrote, "A friend of mine said, 'What about crafts?' and I thought: 'Yes, that is what I am looking for!' I very soon knew that it was building furniture — that was the nearest craft to architecture." The concept of structure, construction, of the organic development of furniture as of buildings, formed another key element of George's understanding and later teaching. He later linked with structures of churches and buildings with the natural concepts within Goethe's theory concerning *the being within form.*

George's return to take up a furniture-making apprenticeship in the Cotswolds inevitably brought more opprobrium from his father. It is tempting to use the word 'contrary' about Charles Trevelyan. It often appears as though nothing that George could have done could have pleased him, just because it was George who was doing it. For George himself, however, the period in the Waals workshop was a time of great learning. He had learned enough of the disciplines of the Alexander

Technique to practise them at the bench, and to use his time of apprenticeship as a two-year meditation. The revelations that had come from
his lessons with the great F.M. Alexander were essential to the re-
thinking of his life. George was already much excited by the notion
that he was a creature of habit, with habits of thinking that might be
quite as wrong or inappropriate as his habitual thinking was proving to
be. Indeed, he began to perceive that his very emotions might be habitual. His contemporary, Louise Morgan, recorded her thoughts on the
teaching of F.M. Alexander. "You have to keep an open mind if you are
his pupil," she wrote, and remarked on, "Beginning to *see* light on *feeling*. It appears that what *feels right* may be very *wrong*. All the things
which feel *right* for me to do are *wrong*. So I must not do the wrong
thing — that is, the thing that to me feels *right*."[1]

These ideas were entirely sympathetic to George, who delighted in
the notion that all the assumptions of his scholarship, background and
culture, needed re-examining. While making furniture he contemplated
all he had been taught. In the workshop there was comradeship, concentration, hard work, perfectionism, craftsmanship — and perhaps
above all, silence. George liked to exercise his mind as much as his
body and the habit of constant re-examination of assumption was put
firmly in place in the Waals workshop. Neither the demands of this
exercise nor the skills necessary to meet them ever left him. When he
began to speak in public he recommended the exercise of mental re-
examination to everyone, often concluding, "Don't just believe what I
say, try it out for a day or two and see how you like it. If it's no good,
let it go! I have a clear technique for exploring such ideas. You need-
n't prove it like a scientist. Take the idea. Try it out. Live with it.
Because ideas are living beings they draw conviction towards them!"
(The concept of ideas as living beings came to him later, through
Rudolf Steiner.)

The workshop also gave George the experience of working and living within a group, and he gained a feeling of power from the shared
endeavour. The craftsmen working silently together created an atmosphere which he believed enhanced the quality of each individual man's
work. George encountered this again at Gordonstoun, where he was an
unconventional schoolmaster in an unconventional setting. The school
was working on an altered emphasis on pupils' levels of personal
responsibility. Dr Kurt Hahn transformed the traditional boarding
school structure because he believed that children were kept artificially
dependent for too long, and he set out to re-balance the relationship

between the generations. The discipline of self-monitoring exemplifies this. If punishments were given for wrong behaviour, the boys themselves were entrusted to do them, and no one would check that they had. They were thus made responsible for their own truthfulness, for their relationship with their consciences. This emphasis on personal responsibility for individual development was unusual for the time, although later in the century words such as self-realization, empowerment, and self-esteem could have been applied to the intention of this system.

By these long steps and through various apprenticeships George Trevelyan reached his mid-thirties, when his thinking was transformed in a single evening — indeed, in a single hour when he had his huge mystical experience. It happened at a lecture on Rudolf Steiner and anthroposophy given by Dr Walter Johannes Stein. Stein had known the Austrian philosopher/scientist Steiner personally for many years, and was a dedicated exponent of his ideas. George had gone to the talk with his spiritually oriented sister Kitty, only because he had an interest in organic agriculture. Those who say there is no such thing as chance will shrug off this explanation, but it is the one he gave ever afterwards. He recorded that he cried aloud, *Yes, Yes, Yes*, to some very big ideas. The pre-existence of human beings. *Yes, obviously*. Earth as a training ground for souls. *Yes, indeed*. Reincarnation through many lives. *Obviously yes*. The universe as mind and living thought, earth as a living creature. *Yes, Yes!* He wrote, "I felt that Dr Stein was talking directly to me and my whole being innerly shouted out to him in affirmation and total acceptance of all the great concepts. I abandoned my agnosticism completely in that lecture, which was a turning point in my life." Here were huge conceptual shifts, the biggest being the central one, did we invent God, or did God invent us? The answer to this question had suddenly reversed for George, and from that time onwards he acknowledged that the universal mind was all-powerful, and he understood humans to be an idea within the mind of God. This was the foundation on which Steiner's discipline, known as Spiritual Science, was built, and it was in almost total opposition to George's upbringing and intellectual training. He wrote, "My whole soul inwardly shouted affirmation." It was with his soul that he accepted these ideas, not his brain. In one bound went from the material interpretation to the spiritual one, from exoteric to esoteric. He wrote, "For that whole hour no negative response rose in me. The agnosticism of thirty-six years faded like morning mist." And again, "The lecture by

Dr Walter Johannes Stein in 1942 lifted me clear of agnosticism and released the spiritual vision.."[2]

The ideas presented in the talk (on: What did Dr Steiner mean by Anthroposophy?) were the ones he spent the rest of his life studying and re-examining. This framework of thought with which he felt immediately in total accord put into entirely different perspective everything he had felt to be important until that point. For the next four years he studied anthroposophy under Dr Ernst Lehrs and there has been some speculation that he might have chosen to go and train as a Steiner teacher, and make practical use of the new discovery. If this had been his thought several things operated against it. One was that Helen was not of like mind with him on it (or on many of his subsequent spiritual endeavours). Another was that he needed to make a living, for his allowance from the Trevelyan family was not enough to support his family. Steiner schools then as now operated on a shoe-string. Whatever the reason, that was not the course he took, but his involvement with Steiner remained with him all his life.

Anthroposophy was the word Steiner used to describe the new science that he proposed. It is made from two Greek words, *anthropos* (man) and *sophia* (wisdom/ knowledge). It means the knowledge or understanding of man, and its first recorded use was in 1742. Steiner used it to encompass his perception of the material world and the animal kingdom, a perception in the light of soul and spirit, and not only in the material, scientific analysis. At its basis was the notion that in addition to the physical body, humans and animals have three non-material bodies. Steiner called them the etheric, the astral, and the ego. The first term referred to the mysterious life force; the second to the consciousness and feeling shared by humans and animals; the third to the thinking part of human beings. This scientific philosophy synthesized and harmonized the workings of George Trevelyan's rational and poetic mind and satisfied it completely.

Much later, in *Operation Redemption*, George described Steiner as "a great scientist who also from his youth possessed complete clairvoyance, so that the reality of the spiritual worlds was obvious to him... he saw that this faculty must be transmuted into thinking that was consonant with scientific method... the human mind must be able so to lift its thinking that it could blend in consciousness with the world process. Then true investigation of higher knowledge by immediate experience would be possible ... This would be worthy of the evolved intellect of our age."[3]

The ideas in their fullness concern the nature of man and the universe, placing spirit at the centre of creation. Steiner said, "We are forced to recognize the existence of objects over and above those we experience in sense perception. Such objects are Ideas. In taking possession of the Idea, thinking merges itself into the World Mind. What was working without now works within. Man has become one with the World Being at its highest potency. Such a becoming realized of the Idea is the true communion of man.."[4] The universe as mind and living thought became a theme for George, who would explain that concept was the first cause, that all life forms and the planet Earth itself had been conceived in the divine mind, that the material world was simply idea made manifest. The perception that while matter changed but did not die, spirit neither changed nor died, led to a belief in reincarnation. George studied many of Steiner's lectures on the subject of repeated lives on earth, and life after death. The garden compost heap gives the simplest demonstration of the proposition that matter changes but spirit does not. "Dead" plants, classified as waste matter, readily re-form into nutritious material from which new plants are grown. In the same way, discarded animal bodies decompose into useful material. Matter only alters, and does not die.

Plant metamorphosis became another fascination for George after the Stein lecture. Part of the theory holds that the spirit or *idea* of a plant reinstates itself from the conceptual plan, something envisioned by Wolfgang von Goethe and expounded by Steiner. George fully accepted the concept of "the being within form," a "science of the invisible." Much later, he wrote, "The inner being in each of us is immortal. It cannot be touched by 'death' which will break down the discarded sheath of the body. This recognition of the spiritual entity in man has immense implications. We are a creature of body, soul and *spirit* — and the spiritual being within us, the true 'I,' is imperishable. It always was and always will be."[5]

This concept of reincarnation includes the idea of earth as a training ground for souls, one which few people brought up with conventional Christian teaching can find acceptable. Rudolf Steiner had rediscovered the Cosmic Christ, a concept known to esoteric Christians who see Jesus as the human vehicle for the Cosmic Being of Christ. George found this entirely acceptable, and with it the accompanying conception of Buddha as the one who "prepared the way 600 years before the event at Golgotha, by showing the path to enlightenment." George wrote, "the Buddha is now working in close association with Christ for

the redemption of mankind through illumination of understanding."[6]
George joyfully embraced the idea of an eternal spiritual entity in
human beings, "the spiritual being within us, the true 'I', is imperishable. It always was and always will be." Reviewing his own life he
began to see everything that had happened as pre-ordained, a useful
construct for one who had taken so many disappointments. Eventually
he came to believe that he was working out the combined negative
karma of the Trevelyan family (though it is hard to imagine that in the
800 years of its existence the family had not accumulated a far worse
karmic debt than even George was capable of settling on his own).

On the night of the Stein lecture, however, the full realization of
these ideas for George Trevelyan was some considerable way off. The
thoughts presented there became the material with which he spent the
rest of his life, and indeed could have spent many more lifetimes still.
It put him at odds, or perhaps at even greater odds, with Helen. It put
him further out on a limb from the Trevelyan family. Almost at once
Steiner became his vocation, his purpose, his study, and his being. He
never deviated from it, and as far as one can tell, never doubted it.
From the point of the lecture to the day he died, George was a crusader
for the unseen worlds, for the idea that the inner world was infinitely
greater than the outer, and for the crucial importance of engaging with
spiritual effort. All this took place at the midpoint of his life, drawing
on all that had happened up to that time.

Many people say that the spiritual movement in Great Britain was kept
alive during the twentieth century by Sir George Trevelyan's untiring
promotion of it. Even if this is too large a claim, it is true that without
him much less progress both in quantity and in quality would have
been possible. Although his insights were not unique, his interpretation
of the most exciting and radical thinking, and the scale of his influence
on the way in which spiritual endeavour developed in this country and
in parts of mainland Europe and America certainly was. The term New
Age can be variously interpreted and is very loosely used, but perhaps
the proposition that a change in thinking is essential if the human race
is to draw back from the brink of destroying the very planet that we live
on will suffice. It gave rise to all kinds of new ideas, some thrillingly
radical, some silly, which in essence were and are spiritual. The New
Age movement acknowledges that spirit is at the heart of all life. It
acknowledges the growing need in humankind for a spiritual dimension to life, a profound need which is often not answered by the estab-

lished religions. For George Trevelyan, this need and the consequent search was more than profound, it was all-engrossing. *Magic Casements* is his own and truly wonderful anthology of poems for spiritual seekers, containing many of his favourite poetic encapsulations of esoteric concepts. The crucial importance of engaging with them is shown in one of George Trevelyan's favourites, *A Sleep of Prisoners,* by Christopher Fry, and he loved to quote from it:

> The human heart can go the lengths of God.
> Dark and cold we may be, but this
> Is no winter now. The frozen misery
> Of centuries breaks, cracks, begins to move;
> The thunder is the thunder of the floes,
> The thaw, the flood, the upstart Spring.
> Thank God our Time is now when wrong
> Comes up to face us everywhere,
> Never to leave us till we take
> The longest stride of soul men ever took.
> Affairs are now soul size.
> The enterprise
> Is exploration into God.
> What are you waiting for? It takes
> So many thousand years to wake
> But will you wake for pity's sake?

CHAPTER 4

Attingham: Teaching and Learning

We have dreamed dreams beyond our comprehending,
Visions too beautiful to be untrue.
Sidney Royse Lysaght

The arrival of George, Helen and Catriona Trevelyan at Attingham Park, in Shropshire, was the beginning of 23 extraordinary years. George's work in this period was regarded by many members of his family as the most significant of his life, and to the lifetime achievement question, "What was his contribution?" they reply at once, "Attingham, and the furniture!"

The story began in 1947, after the famous turning back on the road to Gordonstoun and the useful transition period teaching soldiers at Newbattle Abbey. Helen Trevelyan saw an advertisement in the paper for a proposed adult college in Shropshire. It was the idea of Martin Wilson, the county secretary for education, and was to be financed by the county with help from the independent Carnegie Trust. However, George thought he was not properly qualified for the job and he did not apply. Dr George Firth chanced to meet a Carnegie Trust member in a train. Dr Firth asked whether George Trevelyan had applied, was told he had not, and replied, "Leave it to me." Subsequently George applied without any hope of being interviewed but was given the date and travelled south to join the interviewees. On the same train was another Newbattle teacher who had done similar work before the War; both he and George fully expected him to get the job. George went before the board — and was astonished as during the day, one by one, all the other applicants were dismissed, leaving only him. He wrote, "I went for the interview and recall meeting 24 or 25 other people who all seemed to be more qualified than myself in academic fields. However, I was offered the wardenship of this new residential centre and it was the answer to my dream." Members of the interviewing panel said he seemed to have been made for the job, and history proved them right.

George returned to Edinburgh hugely elated if somewhat apprehensive. (It is thought that the other Newbattle candidate took a different train.) He explained the whole wonderful prospect to George Firth. They talked about putting Attingham Park back in order, planning a programme, attracting students, and they determined that it would probably take a year. "October, a year after this moment. A note in our diaries!" cried both the Georges.

The adult education college set up within Attingham Park by Shropshire County Council was extraordinary in helping to transform the quality of many people's lives at a troubled moment in the nation's history. Its foundation was the continuation of an idea from before the Second World War. Several short-term residential colleges had been established during the 1930s, to help train the workforce in the period of terrible unemployment; and during the war years discussion about adult education of various kinds had continued. The Vice Chancellor of Oxford University, Sir Richard Livingstone, was a keen exponent of residential educational opportunities. In 1941 he wrote: "All over the country great houses will be vacant, calling for occupation, purchasable for a song. Why should not each local education authority start its own House of Education?"

When the war was over there was a general acknowledgement that the nation needed replenishing. For the second time in a century all the energy of all the people had been focused on fighting the enemy or defending against attack. Afterwards the exhaustion was not simply due to coping with food shortages and wrecked cities; it was also a weariness of spirit. The phrase was *loss of morale*. The camaraderie generated by fighting a common enemy had gone and the victorious British people found that much that had sustained their pre-war lives lay in ruins. It was seen that there was a need not only for physical sustenance but also for nourishment of the intellect and emotions, of the mind and spirit. The foundation of the Welfare State brought new practical ideas to fruition in everyday life; and new hope, new thoughts, new artistic enterprises were equally needed for England to rekindle its energy. As in 1918, a massive reassessment was under way.

George Trevelyan's vision of country houses as cultural education centres differed from his father's in the detail but was similar in principle; indeed it is quite possible to regard his work at Attingham as the development of something begun at Wallington. Sir Charles Trevelyan's idea was to make accessible the great houses of England for people to experience living and learning within the historical and cultural environment that had played so central a part in the nation's development. Therefore he opened his own home as a meeting place for politicians and rebels, and the place where the Youth Hostel movement was given its greatest encouragement.

Both Sir Charles and George were acquainted with the Folk High Schools for adults which had been set up in Sweden and Denmark. These were the realization of an idea of Bishop Grundig in the 1840s, set up to provide what he called "enlivenment" on short courses in which the positive energy of participation was emphasised. The Danish Folk High Schools provided much of the inspiration for Attingham. George saw the application of the principle in England using country houses as adult colleges offering short residential courses on a great variety of subjects. He talked frequently about enlarging the imagination. For him the subject matter, while important, was less significant than the expansion of the mind and vision.

Attingham was the second adult college to be established in Great Britain. In time there were about 25, all affiliated to the National Institute of Adult Education (NIAE). As one of the first wardens of such an establishment George joined the Institute, and he became a respected representative at its gatherings, giving great encouragement to colleagues who were looking for ideas. It is fair to say that no other adult education college had such a varied, imaginative programme as Attingham, or perhaps such an elevated ambition. (In the matter of finance, however, George was less than expert. Indeed after Attingham's first year with George in command of everything, control of the budget was retrieved by the county authority.) The course content, added to the influence of the place, was intended to light sparks that would permanently alter participants' lives, even if they did not go away with a fully fledged new skill. At the practical weekend courses George was often heard vigorously encouraging students, "If a thing is worth doing at all, it's worth doing *badly!*" From a skilled craftsman this might have been thought mischievous, but the point was a serious one. In a weekend, no one was likely to achieve mastery of a craft any more than they were likely to gain a deep knowledge of a new subject — but it might be possible to inspire them, and energize them. Indeed, it generally was. This was equally true of the literary courses, the countryside courses, the drama courses, the many other kinds of exploration that intrigued George Trevelyan enough for him to seek out teachers for it. As an Attingham student you would usually work quite hard and learn as much as it is possible to learn in a short time. That was one

aspect of it. What may have been the more important element was that
the excitement of enquiry and the spirit of endeavour would have been
sparked in you as much as it was in the Gordonstoun schoolboys who
were suddenly called upon by Mr Trevelyan to answer *why* they were
learning about the French Revolution.

The first publicity information about the Shropshire Adult College
came out in April 1948 on a single sheet of paper. It said the college
would accommodate thirty students in residence (more attending
daily) on courses lasting from a weekend to a fortnight. It promised
that the atmosphere would be friendly and informal, with lectures, discussions and common activities during the evenings. It announced a
wide range of cultural possibilities, with current affairs, social problems, history, literature, music and drama, also crafts, gardening and
bee-keeping. It mentioned that the accommodation would sometimes
be available for use as a conference centre. "The aim of Attingham is
to stimulate many and varied interests" it said, assuring the public that:
"no one need be deterred by the feeling that he or she is not a scholar."
After a couple of years the leaflet had grown in size but was still very
welcoming, telling its readers: "The aim is to present subjects in a way
which anyone can understand and enjoy. Previous knowledge is not
necessary and the atmosphere is easy and informal. All enquiries and
applications should be addressed to: The Warden, Attingham Park,
near Shrewsbury. Telephone Upton Magna 255."

The charge for a full weekend including residence and tuition was
25/- (£1.25). Single lectures were charged at 1/- (5p). The leaflet
pointed out that the portion of the cost of Attingham falling on the rates
(council tax) was, "rather less than one halfpenny in the pound." Here
are some of the possibilities offered by the programme:

> The Story of Farming. Prehistoric Agriculture to modern
> breeds of live-stock.
> Growing up in a Difficult World. Children needing special care.
> Increase of juvenile delinquency.
> Judging of Preserves.
> Geology for Everyman.
> Country Housewives Course. Your Home in Spring-Time.
> Kitchen and garden, new life in clothes and soft furnishings,
> making your home attractive.
> Literature and Life. Nineteenth and twentieth centurywriters
> and social reform.

Adventure on Holiday. Canoeing, climbing, cave exploring, gliding, sailing and camping.

Appreciating English Art.

Adventure of Man in Society.

Great Drama II. Ibsen and Peer Gynt, Shropshire Drama Group.

Music for Young People. The Art of Listening. Dr George Firth, director for Scotland of the Arts Council for Great Britain. Mary Firth (pianist). An Opportunity for those under 35.

This last item, The Art of Listening, was a favourite subject, often repeated. In George Trevelyan's view listening was as active as speaking, both were important skills, neither was to be undertaken casually. A facet of this which he often put forward was the idea of the *living word*. He determined that the teachers were to speak from the heart, direct to the hearts of pupils, without notes. Later the notion of the *living idea* was added. These were concepts George had taken from the works of the Austrian philosopher and educationist, Rudolf Steiner. *Living ideas* meant two synthesised things: one that ideas had life of their own; two that living with them in one's mind predicated living differently. The suggestion was that people might think differently, and see if thinking differently would affect their lives. His intention always was towards a more positive, optimistic attitude. The broad Attingham programme started as an exciting experiment in reinvigorating the creative and imaginative spirit and very slowly began to include a few directly spiritually focused topics. Its progress was entirely a manifestation of George Trevelyan's own life journey. A unique grouping of people and ideas was drawn towards him as to a powerful magnetic force. *Controversial* is an appropriate description: many people outside the walls of Attingham found it somewhat disquieting, despite the testimony of the many within who found it inspiring. Locally there was opposition even to the liberal arts curriculum, even, amazingly, to the practical skills courses such as gardening and bee-keeping. Some said public money was being put to frivolous use at a time of rebuilding the nation. Letters were written to the local newspapers, fulminating because post-war Britain had still not enough housing for its returning heroes, never mind courses on Shakespeare. Such criticisms were probably inevitable and can partly be met by the proposition that man cannot live by bread alone. At the time they were answered by the College's consistent popularity with students, its tiny budget, and by the efforts of George himself acting as a missionary for it, knocking on doors, speaking in libraries and public halls, giving interviews to newspapers. Even so, it is perhaps in the nature of things that some within the College felt he did not do enough of this essential promotion.

Attingham Park, near Shrewsbury, is a fine Georgian mansion built in 1785 and set in 5,000 acres of parkland through which flows the river Tern. The house and estate has many of the characteristic features of such places: its mile walk, lined with trees and rhododendrons, follows the river and circles back to the house; the dining room had a Pompeian red ceiling executed by Italian craftsmen. This became the main lecture room and could seat 170 students. (At the end of their time there, they managed to get 200 into this room.) The residential accommodation could sleep thirty at the beginning and expanded greatly as the fabric of the house was revived. As it was among the first of the residential adult education colleges there was no particular precedent for the curriculum. All of the colleges were breaking new ground, but none of the others attempted anything like such an enterprising or ambitious curricular scope. (During the 1970s public finance began to be withdrawn from such institutions and many of them closed.) A substantial part of the house was leased for the college from the National Trust at a nominal rent.

Its former owner, Lord Berwick, had bequeathed Attingham to the Trust, and his widow lived in apartments on three floors on its east side. She had a housekeeper and other occasional help, and could often be seen walking in the grounds with her little dog, or showing visitors around the part of the house that was open to the public. Catriona Tyson (then Trevelyan) says, "Lady Berwick lived in one wing in an extraordinary time-warp, with funny old maids on the staff, that sort of thing. There were state rooms, it was another era entirely." Catriona visited the private wing from time to time and says that Lady Berwick, "was always very nice to me." She was a gracious and dignified presence, she always attended quartet concerts and occasionally lectures, and from time to time she invited George and Helen and members of the college's administrative staff to her rooms for a glass of sherry. Lady Berwick was always interested in the work of the college and in her role as president of the Shropshire Women's Institute she actively promoted it.

The Trevelyan family had part of the house for their own use which more or less amounted to a wing. Catriona Tyson says, "We lived in the smaller part of Attingham: the orangery. My mother called it the flat,

which I think was a bit silly really because it had eleven bedrooms."
However the eleven-bedroomed apartment on three storeys was often
used for entertaining visiting speakers and there was some justification
for Helen's description: officially the Warden's part of any such establishment is known as a flat. Roger Orgill recalls that the Trevelyan
apartment had partition walls, and, though extensive, was somewhat
informally constructed. He is the son of Mrs Gwen Orgill, the college's
first Domestic Bursar, and he and his sister Judith also lived at
Attingham. Roger was fourteen years old when he first met the man
whom all the staff called GLT, and he recalls feeling somewhat over-
whelmed by the unfamiliar experience of an adult showing an interest
in his life. His school holidays from the age of fourteen onwards were
spent exploring the estate (often in conflict with the gamekeeper), the
Shropshire hills, and the old sandstone quarries where George introduced him to caving and to roped climbing.

Roger Orgill says George called climbing and caving, "the great
sports"; and that he also took a great interest in Roger's canoeing and
boat building efforts on the river Tern. "My ventures included the
restoration of a dinghy which I taught myself to sail," says Roger
Orgill. "George allowed me to learn through experience. He would
never intervene, he simply provided words of advice, for example how
my woodworking might improve if more time were given to preparing and sharpening the tools." Thenceforward, "holidays at Attingham
were looked forward to with great anticipation." The two of them
would often arrange competitions for running or climbing, which
George always won. "He was very competitive at times," says Roger
Orgill. George's other great outdoor passion was caving and underground exploration and he took the teenaged Roger Orgill on an
excursion to a new cave system in South Wales. This was Ogof-
Ffynon Ddu, one of the largest systems in Britain. The outdoor world
was vital to young Roger and in adult life he became George's successor in appreciation and use of landscape, taking on many of his
important adventure activities, including Outward Bound. During his
childhood Roger Orgill was free to attend any of the courses that took
his fancy, as were all the Trevelyans and all members of the household. In addition, "all meals were communal affairs shared with students, staff and visitors" and the exotic nature of the visitors could
provide extraordinary pieces of luck. "I remember finding a spare
breakfast-time seat next to someone who I soon discovered was
Yehudi Menuhin," Roger Orgill says.

To some observers it seemed as if, at the age of 41, George Trevelyan had regained a sort of Wallington. There is certainly something piquant in discovering the disestablished aristocrat once more set up in a country mansion where he can so stylishly entertain his guests. For the fraction of a moment it may be possible to exchange Attingham in the mind's eye for the great house in Northumberland, "bursting with guests and Lady Trevelyan gathering us all together after luncheon, on the steps from the beautiful saloon to the terrace, to ask us to choose what to do that afternoon — swimming in the lake, climbing the rocks at Rothbury, or all round the house and stables without touching the ground, or walking over the moors."[1] George was, of course, fascinated by the local history. The name St Eata's Ham had become Atcham, then Attingham. Atcham Church, opposite the gates, is dedicated to St Eata, and is an ancient foundation containing stones taken from the nearby Roman town of Viroconium. Visitors found the area around the great cedars and the mile walk particularly peaceful and George sometimes speculated that some of the saints of olden times might have wandered in the area and contributed to its atmosphere.

The Shropshire Adult College was supported financially by the county in which it was situated, by Birmingham University Extra Mural Department, by some other local authorities, and by the Carnegie Trust. Because Attingham was a pioneer among the country house colleges there was no plan and George was allowed to choose the subjects and the lecturers, always remaining conscious of receiving public money and of the necessity of attracting students. That is, it still had to make ends meet. George himself received a very scanty salary. Astonishingly, it was still possible in the post-war period to employ very capable people in professional capacities and not pay them a living wage. Indeed, in some situations it was almost a condition of employment to have another source of income; apparently there were enough people around of high qualification and some private money to make this possible. With his tremendous enthusiasm for a great span of interests George set joyfully about this task. He believed that at last he had found his life's purpose, and that all his experiences, particularly in the crafts movement, had led him to this point. His aim, in the words of William Blake, was, "to open the mind of man ... inwards," and he always said that if a subject was worth thinking about he would consider running a course on it. He spoke of a short escape not *out of* but *into* reality, and of "encouragement to exploration" (*exploration* was a favourite word). He wanted the lecturers to offer students a real excitement in their subjects in a short time.

There were two types of course: those open to the public (most weekends and the summer holidays) and those given by organizations for their members. About 3,000 people stayed at Attingham every year and an equal number came to concerts and single events. George joined the open courses whenever possible and often gave the introductory talk. In *Exploration into God*, he wrote: "I knew that I could enthuse people on any subject I wanted to know about. Thus in the post-war period I broke into theme after theme and subject after subject. I saw that it was a question of finding the Integrating Ideas, which would relate the subject to a wider context... then the visiting professor or expert could take us to a deeper understanding. This was in line with holistic thinking."[2]

Michael Ford attended a course there in 1951, as a teenager from the sixth form of Moreton Hall, near Oswestry. He recalls, "George Trevelyan could take an enormous interest in anything. Every course that he was involved with became a personal interest. He went into it almost literally body and soul, his appearance even seemed to change subtly with the course. I went on a weekend course entitled The Stand Against Communism which I think was the first connection of my school with Attingham. Afterwards we did other things with them — astronomy, outdoor theatrical productions and a *Twelfth Night* course." There were many local links, and not only with schools.

Initially the money to support the college was limited by the caution of the grant-giving bodies, so George went from door to door locally, and on speaking tours throughout the county, publicizing it and gaining support. The building needed a great deal of work to prepare it for use and some local people helped; the earliest Workers' Educational Association students decorated and cleaned the interior. Catriona Tyson, recalls that the place was something of a barn when they arrived there, having been first neglected and then used to billet soldiers during the War. It was cheerless, cold, and empty. Roger Orgill says, "I frequently painted walls, and I remember once working late at night with George, both of us balancing on a hand rail to reach the opposite wall over a stairwell. Suddenly George let out a yell: he'd painted over his hand! He said, 'I know now why human hand prints are mixed with animals in prehistoric cave paintings!'" Improvements continued throughout George Trevelyan's time there, and continued to employ the efforts of the students. George often told the story of members of one of the early Creative Leisure courses making the first bedspreads for the residential students, to the design of his friend, the potter David Ballantyne. They simply screen-printed old white cotton sheets — very effectively, apparently. Living conditions for the first few years were simple but the course fees were very reasonable, the tutors were of extraordinarily high quality, and in any case, immediately after the War, no one expected luxury.

In 1948 and for several years afterwards there was still food rationing and students brought their coupons along with them to their study weekends, not to help out, but of necessity. Fortunately Gwen Orgill was marvellous at doing deals with local suppliers. There were attempts to continue the War Garden idea of growing the necessary vegetables, an example of the *living idea*, as the organic garden was also seen as an ideal. An ancient Attingham gardener named Carter, remembered with awe for wearing his stiff Edwardian collar even when gardening and for always maintaining a waxed moustache, got the garden into a state so healthy that it was even a paying enterprise. Apparently he was not keen on the organic ideal but acquiesced in it because George asked him to, and then made a spectacular success of it. Several other old Attingham retainers were taken on to the college's domestic staff, people who had been in service all their adult lives. Roger Orgill says they very much enjoyed the new regime. Local people recalled that during the 1920s and 1930s, news of the imminent arrival of a member of the Berwick family, being driven from Shrewsbury station in one of the Attingham cars, would somehow be magically transmitted along the route so that any villagers or farm workers who happened to be about could stand to attention, caps in hands, ready to touch the forelock as the car passed by. This sort of feudalism is even more startling when set in the context of the date: it was scarcely a couple of decades before the adult education college was set up to provide intellectual sustenance for all.

Using George's connections, Mrs Orgill went to Denmark to look for domestic helpers among people in the Folk High School movement who wished to learn English. The international staff members mixed well and were flexible about their duties; at the beginning there was far too much to do for anyone's tasks to be narrowly defined. Roger Orgill explains, "My mother was the Domestic Bursar, which broadly speaking meant that she was responsible for the hotel side of the enterprise. But if there was a crisis in the secretarial department she would do that too, working half the night. It just worked like that."

Courses were given on almost any subject which could widen the vision, and for which suitable teachers could be found. From early in the College's life they were often fully booked in advance. An early residential course was offered for the English Folk Dance and Song Society, a lifelong passion which George Trevelyan inherited from his mother. It was held in August 1948 and attracted 40 students. For a similar course in 1950 George had to organize outdoor seating for 650 people to watch the dancers: an indication of swift growth. The place also had its own attraction. It seems to have been a power house, an energy vortex which people never forgot, an experience which was memorable almost regardless of what was being studied. The intention of reviving the national imagination was being thrillingly realized. There were also vocational courses. The breadth of provision of high quality study for the sheer enjoyment of it is almost breathtaking. There was literature, history, architecture, archaeology, music (for players and non-players), drama, crafts, painting, heraldry, geology, and nature studies (during nature studies courses George took great delight in waking the household at 3.30am to hear the dawn chorus). In autumn and spring, one mid-week period in four was set aside for evening events. There were concerts given by musicians of the calibre of the Amadeus quartet, there were special single lectures, and many amateur dramatic productions. The list of people who taught there reads like a roll-call of contemporary people of ideas: Benjamin Britten, Sir Nikolaus Pevsner, Patrick Moore, Sir John Hunt, Sir Edmund Hillary, Edward Barnsley, John Nash, Professor Anthony Blunt. Adding the Trevelyan charm to the attraction of Attingham, it seemed enough for George to pick up the phone for powerful people to go there and teach for a weekend for quite a moderate fee, and for the student enrolment to be oversubscribed.

The less well-known lecturers were generally experts drawn from universities, and mid-week there were courses for specialized organizations, local authorities, education departments, industrial concerns, university departments, and for groups of working people such as furniture salesmen. In 1951 the Twelfth Night Festival included lecturers from the Arts Council and the University of Wales and recitals given by members of the Glyndebourne Opera company. (Twelfth Night was always celebrated at Attingham, and Roger Orgill recalls accompanying George, "leading a candle-lit procession from the kitchen to the dining rooms, carrying on high great platters of food, to the accompaniment of the Boar's Head Carol.") Among the many course titles

were: Humus on the Farm; Celtic Christianity in the British Isles;
Costume, Music and Poetry through the Centuries; Orchestral Playing;
and Wochenende in Deutscher Sprache. The lecture series on soil ero-
sion and forestry given during the early 1950s were remarkably pre-
scient. They were offered at least in part because George's great friend
Lady Eve Balfour was president of the Soil Association; and they were
offered at a time when the Association and its concerns were popularly
regarded as the preserve of cranks. Richard St Barbe Baker, founder of
the Men of the Trees and another contemporary ecological expert
(though the term *ecological* was not in use at the time) spoke of the
importance of forestry for soil and water conservation. However, a representative of the Ministry of Agriculture, Food and Fisheries, standing
in the traditional, gentleman's pontificating posture with his back to
the fire, said firmly, "Trevelyan, I tell you now, there is no future in
organic farming!"

One of the early students was Dick Alcock, who became a youth
leader on adventure courses, taking young people canoeing, cycle tour-
ing and camping. He came from a strong Church of England background and was interested in the work at Attingham because it seemed
to him to have a moral base. "I was greatly impressed by Sir George,"
he says. "In particular his breadth of vision and knowledge. I especially remember his vision for things we all didn't think much about at
the time, such as resources. He was a great philosopher for our growing dependence on material things; he took the lead for getting people
to think about things we all take for granted, like food." At the time,
the notion of finite resources was almost outlandish. In a country
recovering from the privations of war and rationing, the suggestion that
material goods might be voluntarily limited was fairly startling.

In summer the courses became much more general: Bees and Plants,
for example, and The Story of Steam. Some courses included travel to
houses, castle and churches, following some more of George's own
great passions: architecture, history, storytelling. There was also a
good quantity of Shakespeare; The Archaeology of Roman Britain;
Appreciating English Art; and, Growing Children, their needs and our
difficulties. Dr Geoffrey Beard describes it all as "a bold experiment"
and says few colleges could have had such a wide range of programmes. It was intended to appeal to a great many interests at a great
many levels. One of the slogans was, *Where Tom, Dick and Harry (of
any age) may learn enjoyably.*

Summer sporting courses might include a fair amount of walking, hill-walking, climbing: exertion of the kind George Trevelyan so much enjoyed. He was very competitive in physical skills and in the evenings sometimes engaged in challenges with students. Such games were in a tradition of pre-war climbing meets, such as the famous Cambridge University Easter gatherings led by Geoffrey Winthrop Young, which explored the rock faces of Snowdonia. George was seldom happier than when he was out of doors. "There was always one more climb for George," says Roger Orgill, who, however, believes that, "his ability on the Trevelyan Lakeland Man Hunt to charge downhill, seemingly out of control, certainly contributed much to his later infirmities." (George fairly early in life began to show indications of having inherited the Trevelyan propensity to arthritis, which manifested severely in his middle years. Few members of the Trevelyan family, in which the disease is inherent, can have suffered as badly from it as he did.)

The natural environment was perceived by both George and Roger as an invaluable setting for making contact with the inner self; and Roger remembers the two of them lying flat on the roof over the great portico at Attingham, identifying stars and constellations, and speculating on the nature of the universe. He talks of the relationship between the inner and outer landscape, a profound one for both of them. "Outdoor people think about inner things," he says. Later in his life, when he himself was leading youth groups in mountain adventure, Roger Orgill often observed that, nights spent in the mountains with tents and sleeping bags were "natural opportunities for discussions exploring philosophical and esoteric topics." From fairly early in his time at Attingham it became the habit for George to rise at four in the morning for an hour or so of meditation, a practice which he continued throughout his life. He often received intuitive knowledge at these sessions and he always acted upon it. In New Age terminology this is known as *guidance*, George preferred the word intuition. Under whatever name, he held it to be vital to the conduct of his life in the material world that he consult his inner self daily, and abide by its rulings.

For students as well as teachers the college at Attingham established a wonderful reputation very early in its career; for himself, George loved all of it. Because of his social background his own friends who heard about it and were enthusiastic often came from London; there was almost a following, such as F.M. Alexander had enjoyed when he first arrived in England. George's friend Rhoda Cowen (formerly Harris) said, "They were marvellous people that went there. A lot of my friends who I met in London said, 'aren't you coming to

Attingham, it's wonderful!' but I didn't want to go. He started a new form of encounter, socially and spiritually. He was a very good host. They had fascinating talks from some very odd speakers: most people were willing to speak there. An extraordinary atmosphere, most exciting. In the 1960s my daughter heard about it from friends, she just got into her car and drove — but of course it was always full up, so there was nowhere for her to sleep! She slept in a bath!"

From the great number of inspiring courses, one outlived Attingham's existence as an adult college. In 1952, with his friend Helen Lowenthal, who had been associated with the Victoria and Albert Museum, George founded the Attingham Summer School on the Historic Houses of England. It was primarily for American art and architectural historians and conservationists and was very professional, drawing professors as students and famous academics as lecturers. Among the teachers were Sir John Summerson of Sir John Soane's Museum, Sir Nikolaus Pevsner, the authority on national architecture, and Alec Clifton-Taylor, specialist in the history of building materials. The first ten days were spent at Attingham, then there were four days looking at great houses of Derbyshire and a week in a different part of Great Britain. George enjoyed sharing Britain's artistic past with visitors and he loved the vigour and enthusiasm of the American students — who for their part adored this charming, vigorous English aristocrat. He even enjoyed the logistical planning of the expeditions into the rest of the country: on one occasion, a convoy of ten vehicles left for Derbyshire. The final dinner of the course was reminiscent of scenes from an earlier Attingham. George could play the country house host and simultaneously make fun of it: he often played a gramophone recording of Noel Coward singing The Stately Homes of England, a piece of stylish nonsense that satirized decayed elegance.

The courses in the Creative Leisure stream, and those for crafts, were especially memorable. When George said exuberantly, "if a thing is worth doing, it's worth doing *badly*!" he meant that the experience of creating is more important than the standard of the finished article. His old mentor Edward Barnsley spoke at some of the craft courses and Attingham was used during the 1960s for meetings held by the august Society of Designer-Craftsmen on subjects such as The Place of Crafts in Our Time and The Training of Craftsmen. Painting, woodwork, sculpture, fabric printing and calligraphy were among the offered crafts and some of the activities were housed in huge tents. This was the only time in the year that children were accepted, and a wonderful informality pervaded the house, with George visible every-where, supporting and encouraging.

Jeff Lowe was one of the early tutors. He wrote: "We went away exhausted, enthusiastic and ready to take steps forward. A fundamental change of energy always takes place. George brought the energy, lecturers took it on, and students took it from them." There was something profound about the engagement in a common task that always made the product of the courses greater than the sum of the parts. Evening activities on the more practical courses often included bonfires and songs; George specially enjoyed, "When will they ever learn?" He also loved to take expeditions into the Shropshire Hills and on one occasion he and Lowe made a night expedition to plant bogus archaeological relics at the Roman site at Wroxeter. Apparently they foxed the archaeologists.

Creative Leisure courses generated one particularly important project: George was mad keen on heraldry and its symbolism. Heraldic shields made during courses were used to decorate the College. Jasper and Molly Kettlewell, makers of stained glass and mosaics, were tutors. With George they conceived the idea of creating a mosaic combining the arms of the Berwick family with those of Shropshire County Council and the Trevelyan family. This remains at Attingham. It led to the making of twelve mosaics representing the signs of the Zodiac for the round entrance, and to the making of the final mosaic of the Unicorn, which was presented to George on his retirement. He kept it with him until his death and it is now in the Findhorn community. The importance to the psyche of engaging with others in a common task is one that the Attingham situation provided for very well, and it was often remarked of the endeavours on short courses that the whole was greater than the sum of the parts. The elements within it were not just the group of people, the quality of teachers, the end-product, but the intangible, immeasurable product of harmony, community, and joint and several effort. Perhaps the zodiac mosaics exemplify this especially.

Music was also important to George. The first open course was on understanding and enjoying the great composers, and was given by George and Mary Firth. (Dr Firth was one of the earliest supporters of the Edinburgh Festival.) It was the first of a great series of music courses inspired by the work of the great musician and scholar, Sir Donald Tovey. Professor Tovey published the highly regarded Tovey edition of Beethoven Sonatas, as well as the Tovey edition of 48 Bach Preludes and Fugues. He wrote a cello concerto which was played by

Pablo Casals, and coincidentally also worked with George's uncle Robert, who wrote the libretto for Tovey's opera. The strong influence of Sir Donald Tovey is indicative of the calibre of the teachers who came to Attingham. Others in the music series included the Easter Orchestral course conducted by Bill Jenkins. It was another subject area with a life of its own: people came back year after year. Loyalty to an annual visit often gave students the impression that their course was the only one that took place there and they used the phrase *the Attingham course* in relation to their particular series, as though there were no other.

Music settled down as a regular feature, appearing on the programme three times a year. Mary Firth used to come and give weekends focusing on a single work. She would set off early on Friday morning from her home in Edinburgh, with the long train journey in which to crystallize her planning. "I used to go over everything I was going to do in great detail, because from the moment of arrival there was no time to look at notes. I used to arrive at about five o'clock and some of the students would already be there, and of course the moment you are in contact with the students there is no more privacy. During Friday evening I met all the students. After supper George used to do the introduction to the courses in the hall, and then everyone was keyed up because he made it so exciting. When George had spoken I gave a general picture of the work we were going to study. Analysis began the next day.

"Some people came back for every course, they called themselves 'Mary's family'. This held a potential drawback that new people could feel as if they didn't belong — although usually by the time of the Saturday morning coffee break, everyone was talking to everyone else. I was always in the dining room for Saturday breakfast as it gave me another chance to meet the students. I lectured between 9.30am and 1pm, with a break.

"Saturday afternoon was free, although George sometimes organized outdoor things to do. I needed the time because I gave a concert in the evening and had to rehearse for it. There was another lecture between 5 and 6.30pm, then a meal, then I had a rest, then the concert was at 8pm. On Sunday at 9am I lectured again, and then we listened to the whole work. It was nine hours over the weekend of lectures plus a performance. With a programme like that you might think I would have been tired, but actually it always felt as though time had stopped.

"My relaxation came when the students had gone. One of them said to me that at the beginning of one of the courses she had been anxious that the critical approach to the piece seemed like dissecting a butterfly and pinning it to a board — but that at the end, like magic, the butterfly had all gone back together again, and flown." Geoffrey Toms, who was Deputy Warden from 1968, saw these courses as among the best. "The analysis came first," he says, "but there was an awareness of the beauty too. It was lovely balance and you came out richer by knowing what Beethoven or whichever composer you had been studying was about." A parallel to the musical saturation was found on some literary courses. A weekend might revolve around a visit to Stratford-upon-Avon to see a play, with a minute study of its elements as the work of the group.

George Trevelyan's deep love of poetry and his phenomenal ability to recite from memory is well documented. He saw the value of poetry in expressing great truths succinctly, and in cultivating the imagination. His delivery was slow, dramatic and beautiful; he used the Alexander Technique and took a long breath between each line. This fulfilled two purposes: it helped him to anticipate the meaning of the following line, and it enabled his audience to absorb fully the meaning of the line just spoken. Thus he painted pictures, image by image, word by word, and even people who heard him only once remember how inspiring he was. His mother had ensured that the Trevelyan family grew up as poetry lovers; George and Kitty could enthral an audience for a whole evening as they capped each other with poem after poem, ranging from Border Ballads to Shakespeare, from ancient to modern. George had an equal talent for acting and is among the few people of whom it could genuinely be said that he might well have become a great actor had he chosen to take it up. The Twelfth Night ceremonies are indicative of George's delight in taking on and portraying a character: he loved it, perhaps even a little too much. He was always very aware of an audience and his effect upon it.

In planning his early programmes, George was assisted by the Deputy Warden, John Pilgrim, a residential tutor funded by Birmingham University Extra-Mural Department, and by three Shropshire County Council tutors. George usually accepted the suggestions of the advisory tutors and he had a particular respect for John Pilgrim. The tutors had lecturing duties and did much to widen the scope of the college, finding speakers, promoting the college, and setting up county bodies for special interest groups. Among them were the historian Donald Moore, who was instrumental in setting up the National Museum of Wales, and Bill Rix, a local historian with an interest in the lives of what might be called "ordinary" people. Bill Rix coined the term "industrial archaeologist," discovered the importance of Ironbridge (site of the Iron Bridge built in 1779 and one of the first and most striking products of the Industrial Revolution in Britain), and with George fought hard and successfully to save it. Geoffrey Toms was George's deputy during the final years at the college and took on more of the work as George's arthritis took hold. He is remembered for having made a great success of running some of the final summer schools for American art and architectural historians, and at the same time, Ruth Bell took on more of the administration. The original administrative team included Mrs Gwen Orgill, "Mrs O," domestic bursar for the first 10 years of the life of the college and essential to its creation. However the organization was so novel and adventurous that demarcations were imprecise. Suggestions for course content might come from administrators, teachers might be found mending fences, and the college handyman, Peter Palfreman, became a valued meditation partner of George's. George Trevelyan was easily as democratic as his father.

All this hard work and excitement took up most of George's time, and he also applied himself to local conservation questions. Catriona Tyson says, "George was very good on the civic trust stuff for Shrewsbury — they saved Ironbridge, for example, and other buildings. He was one of the earliest people for conservation, he was at the forefront of many movements that people regard as mainstream now." She acknowledges his infinite variety. "Such an in-depth skill for so many things, that's what was extraordinary about him." Apart from his local civic work George also went about selling Attingham to groups, giving talks and lectures about the place and its facilities. Though he was not highly visible in the family, for Catriona at least this was not so dreadful, since when he did appear he thought up wonderful adventures. She says, "George was not there for ages and ages and then he'd have an afternoon off. Presumably he'd think — 'Oh goodness! My daughter!' — and then he'd invent something absolutely marvellous for us to do together. Once, he took me pony-trekking all round south Shropshire, sleeping in barns, making picnics, it was magical. Another time he made Treasure Island for me. He buried some treasure on a little island in the river and we had to find it. He would take me to churches because he was mad about architecture and he could make it wonderfully interesting. And he knew so much poetry! But with him, it was either complete attention or switched off."

Helen Trevelyan took relatively little part in the college activities.

She and George led rather independent lives, a style of marriage which now might be considered modern but at the time was more unusual. George's absence from hearth and home may be explained by the scale of the project he had taken on and his huge enthusiasm for it, but his preoccupation was certainly not helpful to their relationship. As for George's esoteric side, she simply did not share it, her feet being planted firmly on the ground. Of his numerous interests in this area, she said succinctly, "It's like having 101 insurance policies and hoping one of them will come up."

However, one weekend in 1953 Helen attended a course called You All Can Paint, took up a paintbrush, and painted energetically every day of her life thereafter. She had quite suddenly found her vocation. Other students were using water colours, she used poster paints. George's nephew Michael Dower is one of many who cherish Helen's pictures and show them to visitors. Many people including George saw her work as gifted and encouraged her in it; and she was still painting watercolours of flowers in her nineties.

That year contained another landmark: Everest had been climbed. George learned through a mutual friend that the expedition leader, Brigadier John Hunt, had returned home to Llanfair Waterdine, on the south Shropshire border not far from Attingham. An arrangement was made for Brigadier Hunt to visit Attingham and give an informal talk and Roger Orgill went to collect him by car. He recalls that the journey to Attingham was spent trying to convince John Hunt that the talk did not constitute a public lecture, since the Everest team had promised that none should be given until all the members of it had a full collection of slides. George Trevelyan rewarded Roger Orgill's part in this adventure with a pair of climbing boots.

The College provided an extraordinary number of courses for special interest groups. They included courses for professional people, now generally known as in-service training courses; practical information for members of voluntary bodies and associations; local visits — indeed, it seems fair to say that the college would provide for anyone who wanted to pursue anything at all, as long as the subject was interesting enough to attract a full-size group, and was legal. Some were closed courses, booked by outside organizations who used the premises as a conference house and contracted to pay for services. Occasionally George was invited to lecture on these programmes. Among the wonderful offerings in these large categories during the early days of Attingham, the early 1950s, were these:

Taste and Design in Furnishing for representatives of the Retail
  Furniture Trade
Coal Board Conference (for colliery managers)
Physical Education in the Primary School, a local education
  authority course for Shropshire teachers
Modern Thought in Adult Education. Weekend for members of
  Wolverhampton Local Education Authority and Voluntary
  Bodies
Visit of Berkshire Archaeological Society

Spiritual beginnings

George Trevelyan believed that adult education should bring meaning
to people's lives and could give a lead for the development of the self.
Over many years this came to imply for him a spiritual development.
This might perhaps be defined as any effort or perception that led to a
greater understanding of the inner self and the relationship with a
higher being, whether or not such effort was rooted in formal religion.
In the early years he touched on subjects such as What Can We
Believe? (often with area tutor Margaret Rose) and pursued related
questions on literature and drama courses. Astronomy, music, craft —
indeed practically all the activities — were undertaken with the further
exploration of the interior self as a goal. Sometimes a new form of psychology, or a perception of living in a way that directed the emphasis
away from the material, interested George. He would talk to the people with expertise in it, and to those around him, and set up a course.
Such courses caused concern among some local people. There was
even disquiet about innocent Attingham events such as the Twelfth
Night Bonfire, and occasionally people wrote to the local paper about
such goings-on. According to Ruth Nesfield-Cookson (then Bell), who
worked as George's secretary during the latter half of his Attingham
period, these letters often came from people who had not set foot in the
place. A comparison might be made with the suspicions aroused when
the college was founded in 1947 and people objected that public
money was being squandered on frivolous things. The local authority
dealt with their anxiety about the esoteric courses by simply not attending them: if they did not know the precise content they could continue
to turn the blind eye.

  These tentative beginnings led to the series that became increasingly
important to George Trevelyan. He himself, ever since his encounter

with Dr Stein, followed very much a Christian path, but he always insisted that what he presented was a view that acknowledges the value of all the great religions. His own exceptional skill as a teacher, a presenter of ideas, a person who inspired and energized others, became more and more highly developed. He had no grand idea of playing any part in changing general attitudes and consciousness although as time went by he became aware that the courses on such subjects offered a picture of his own spiritual progress. More is accomplished by example, after all, than by didacticism. But although the presence of such material in the Attingham programme bothered the authorities the dedicated courses were a tiny proportion of the whole; one per term was about the sum of it. From a typical summer programme chosen at random it can be seen that from about thirty courses, three were on directly esoteric subjects. The ratio of 10:1 was more or less maintained throughout George's tenure as Warden. However, spiritual considerations had an ever greater influence on the work in other subject areas.

During the 1950s, George Trevelyan put lecturers from the General Anthroposophical Society at Dornach, Switzerland into the programme. The course was poorly attended and people found the Germanic speakers hard to understand. George therefore decided that he would have to make anthroposophical teaching his own, and present it with other spiritual teachers. He began to draw in speakers such as Pir Vilayat Khan, Father Andrew Glazewski, Bruce MacManaway, Bernard Nesfield-Cookson and Reshad Feild; all of them leaders in their particular areas. Pir Vilayat Khan is both a Sufi and an expert in Essene teaching. (Two mystical disciplines: Sufism is the esoteric part of Islam, the Essenes are said to have taught Jesus Christ.) Andrew Glazewski was a Catholic priest who spoke to all faiths. Bruce MacManaway was one of the earliest exponents of intuitive healing. Reshad Feild is also a Sufi. The interweaving of ideas is such that a sequence that began in 1961 with the poet Kathleen Raine speaking on The Arts as Symbol of the Spirit, and George's own course on Hopkins' "Wreck of the Deutschland," could be seen as part of this subject area. The greatest significance of poems to George Trevelyan was that they expressed the abstract, intuitive side of the brain and contained great truths that could not be encapsulated within the formulae of the scientific mind. "The Wreck of the Deutschland" was one that meant a great deal to him. On one of the courses when he interpreted it for the students, he found himself stuttering at the point where

Hopkins stutters as he relives the nuns' experience of the Christ. In the same, esoteric, subject stream came the consideration of world ecology. This was not a term in general use at the time, yet as early as 1964, with Lady Eve Balfour and several others, George ran a course entitled Life Threatened.

Subjects which were not being dealt with elsewhere began to have a platform in Shropshire. In June of the same year they gave Death and Becoming. This had profound significance within the household, and in planning the course, George said to his secretary, "Do not ever let me be so brave again!" This may have been the first open course on the subject and he believed he had overstepped the mark and would get a bad reaction. In the event it attracted record numbers: 170 attended, and Attingham's 65 beds had to be supplemented by hotel accommodation. George shared the lecturing with Bernard Nesfield-Cookson. Afterwards, Wellesley Tudor-Pole asked George to create the Lamplighter Movement as a successor to the Silent Minute of prayer for peace prior to the nine o'clock news during the Second World War. (A German army officer said of the power of the Silent Minute that the English had some secret weapon that the Germans had no means of countering.) Major courses on these topics always drew a similar number of applicants. Ruth Nesfield-Cookson says that after this first one, "It was a fight to get on George's [esoteric] courses. It was a big turning point, but we still kept the programme balanced very carefully." Nowadays it is hard to imagine how little was available on such subjects at the time. The themes of Death and Becoming were reprised again and again, and formed the bedrock of the association called the Wrekin Trust. Many believe that George Trevelyan may have been instrumental in setting in motion changes in thinking about spiritual matters in the half century after the Second World War. He was forever testing the new ideas that came his way, and he did his testing in precisely the manner he proposed to students, the *living idea*. He was sure that changes in perception were necessary, changes in the perception of — for example — death. He said that if he did nothing other in his life than bring this about he would have made a success.

On 24 January, 1958, Sir Charles Trevelyan died, and George Lowthian Trevelyan inherited the title and with it the mantle of physical and symbolic family continuity. Among the qualities that George inherited from his father was optimism. Sir Charles's biographer wrote of his last years: "Visitors would not find an old, disappointed politician pining for days gone by ... Surrounded by a host of children and grandchildren, Trevelyan remained young at heart."[3] It was to be a significant year for George. Later in 1958, George's close friend and colleague, Gwen Orgill, left Attingham. She died in 1959. Mrs Orgill had been the Domestic Bursar during its establishing years, she had been George's confidante and ally, and had helped to shape the work of the college. These were two great losses very close together for George, who suffered greatly because of them. He spent a long time in deep sorrow, carrying on his work but communicating outside it very little. He withdrew, meditated, and wrote: "I knew without any shadow of doubt that the spark of divinity in us cannot possibly die... this can bring an absolute certainty and subjective proof of the eternal spirit in each of us." George spent less and less time at home, which made Helen feel very lonely. She acknowledged a wonderful term of inspiring courses and said that she and George were talking together more, but all the same felt isolated.

From this time George continued to weave his inner experience into his courses, and when in 1966 Molly Trevelyan died at Wallington on a Friday night, George told his students about it on Saturday morning and asked them to join in a few moments' silence for her. They went ahead with the course, which was successful, and George left for Northumberland on Sunday evening. He left Shropshire exhausted from the weekend and far from well, but returned a few days later elated after a funeral in which all the Cambo villagers had been involved. In the following year the household suffered another bereavement when Helen's 14-year-old great-nephew David Goodwin was drowned in the river Tern. He had shot the weir and been dragged down into the boil by the undertow. The boy had lived with George and Helen for three years, in order to go to school locally. Again a student group was able to sympathize with the family's loss and admire the strength with which George responded to it. On that occasion Helen joined in George's Sunday morning service, reading a Whitsuntide poem she had written herself. Oddly enough, David had opened a conversation about spiritual ideas with George only a few days before he died. The focus on these occasions led in time to further Death and Becoming talks and investigations undertaken by the Wrekin Trust, and to the related research of the Mystics and Scientists group. But that was some way in the future.

The lecturing partnership of George with Bernard Nesfield-Cookson led to some fine work, including a weekend entitled

Architecture and Man. George thought that architecture and the rhythms of architecture, when seen with deep intensity, could move beyond solid form. (The idea of moving beyond solid form came into several courses. It derives from writings of Rudolf Steiner and the poet Goethe.) His working and social relationship with Nesfield-Cookson grew. They shared a love of the work of Steiner, Shakespeare, Goethe, Blake, and the Romantic Poets. Bernard Nesfield-Cookson ran courses on Goethe and on Projective Geometry. The combination of the inspiration of the one with the scholarly knowledge of the other created a fine balance; and in George's later years Bernard Nesfield-Cookson often deputized for him. The Psychosynthesis course in 1964 also had long-term effects. The founder of Psychosynthesis was the medical doctor, Roberto Assagioli, who moved from Freud to a psychology that included the soul, the imagination and the will. Dr Cirinei, who had worked with Freud, was the speaker. The course was the first on the subject to be held in this country. The Psychosynthesis in Education organization was founded in George's study afterwards — the first such association in the UK.

The decade in which all this was going on was the fabled Sixties, the one people often define by saying if you can remember it you weren't there. Starting with sex and drugs and rock'n'roll, taking in the Pill, the Beatles, marijuana and the fashion for going to India to meditate, political unrest, posters of Che Guevara, the incessant use of the word Revolution, demonstrations, Parisian paving-slab hurling, Vietnam, Hockney, Pop Art, Stoppard, Twiggy, the mini skirt, it is easy to compile a sixties list. However lightweight some of the items on it might be, they add up to a massive disenchantment with what came to be called the Establishment, and with the assumptions of previous decades. The Sixties are frequently blamed for all the subsequent ills of the century. It is equally possible to see them as the continuation of a deep unrest from preceding decades, one stage in a century of upheaval. In the frivolous 1920s George Trevelyan had taken life seriously and gone in for the Alexander Technique and craftsmanship in the Arts and Crafts tradition. In the trippy 1960s he found himself at the helm of a place of serious endeavour and experiment. He was on the other side of the Looking Glass in other ways too: his growing understanding of the positive aspects of all life was in contradistinction with the popular expectation of crime, war and disaster, and the compensating idiocies of hedonism and over-consumption. The fact that materialism appeared to have reached its apotheosis was a big factor in the disenchantment and led to the search during the 1960s for meaning in places east of Europe, and during the 1970s in the mythologies of heroic, idealistic eras.

Group living was as bizarre a concept as ecology in the later 1950s and early 1960s. The beginning of the experiment in the practicalities of both was taking place at Findhorn, on the north east coast of Scotland. Peter Caddy, founder with his wife Eileen and their friend Dorothy Maclean of the now world-famous Findhorn community, arrived in George Trevelyan's life by turning up for a weekend on The Significance of the Group in the New Age. Peter and Eileen were living in a caravan on what had been a rubbish tip, and attempting an approach to living that harmonized with the natural environment rather than conquering it. The approach overturned the materialistic emphasis, taking its inspiration from prayer and the acceptance of intuitive instruction (known in the community as *guidance*). Peter and Eileen always acted in accordance with Eileen's guidance and when Peter was offered an invitation to the weekend course at Attingham by someone who was unable to go, he decided at once that it was intended that he take her place. He did not know that this was a hazardous move. Attendance at the more esoteric courses was by invitation only, and Peter Caddy had not been invited. However on the way south he phoned to check that he could attend, and was given permission. When he got in the queue to pay his fees, Ruth Bell told him she expected him to have so much to contribute that he could have a free place. She said this without knowing him, and without knowing that he had not a penny in his pocket. Acting upon intuition was a factor at Attingham too (George Trevelyan never liked the term "guidance"),although to nothing like the extent that it was in the Findhorn community.

The course was exploring the role of groups. The Findhorn group was still very small, nevertheless Peter was the only person there with first-hand experience of living and working in this way. What were the other students to make of this ex-RAF Officer who marched round the Attingham corridors with a battered suitcase containing leaflets entitled God Spoke to Me? They soon heard about the principles of the Findhorn community, for Peter Caddy spoke during the weekend about its way of working according to intuition, about its faith in everything working out "in right timing," and its confidence that the material means for their projects would always turn up. The meeting had lasting effects. Though he was initially cautious, George felt that these might be important ideas. For Peter Caddy, it was the first step to making publicly known what his little group was doing. For George, the link with the Findhorn Foundation became one of the closest of his life. Ruth Bell said that she would not have dared to leave Attingham to work for the Wrekin Trust if she had not first seen Findhorn. Thus the courage and energy for the progress of all concerned seemed to be generated on this early weekend. It all seemed, in the New Age terminology, to have been meant.

The weekend course on The Darkness and the Light, given in 1966, was the first of an annual series on Light, Love and Power. These are the three salient words in the Great Invocation given by the Alice Bailey, the theosophist who founded the Arcane School in 1923, with the object of fusing the work of Buddha and Christ. For two days George built up to the notion that Christ is already here, and that people have only to change their consciousness to be aware of the Christ presence. The atmosphere is described as electric. At the end of the second afternoon George played a recording of Handel's Hallelujah Chorus, moved back to stand behind his chair; and the audience of 170 spontaneously rose to its feet. Such courses always closed with ritual, during which many people used the time for generating thoughts of Light and Peace. George could create a powerful atmosphere that enabled the audience to be more alert and aware. Finally, by tradition, Blake's "Jerusalem" was sung:

> I will not cease from mental fight
> Nor shall my sword sleep in my hand
> 'Til we have built Jerusalem
> In England's green and pleasant land.

The Sunday Services which George offered were always geared to the people attending them. Using writings from thinkers and poets, and closing with music, George gave some widening of the vista, some elevated moments or realizations to take home. Another feature of the esoteric courses was that a few close friends and colleagues were often invited to stay on for Sunday night. Close relationships were formed and developed, thoughts for future courses conceived, and companionship enjoyed over supper. The poet Johann Wolfgang von Goethe had been a big influence on George Trevelyan, and his *wahlverwandschaffen* notion of the creation of one's family from the rest of the world, and not necessarily from the one's blood relations, was one with which the social life of Attingham was in harmony.

Some Attingham traditions were ceremonial rather than strictly educational. They included that of the students circling the house in procession bearing lighted candles, ending with sacred hymns and songs, poetry and meditation. The last part took place in the round entrance, a central point on the lower ground floor which George came to view almost as a chapel. For The Darkness and the Light evening he concluded with a reading by George of T.S. Eliot's "Chorus of the Rock." Like everything in the college such occasions came from George's sense of combined drama, dignity and fun. However not all the traditions were so serious: at New Year courses a kissing bough was hung in the bell room and George made good use of it, attempting to get every woman in the house under it before midnight. He also established a tradition for him to use a kitchen broom to get all the bells in the bell room ringing simultaneously at New Year.

George Trevelyan's great quality as a host was one of the many attributes that made him such a success with Attingham. His background and disposition fitted him superbly as the hospitable master of the house, concerned with the comfort and amusement of all his guests. Roger Orgill recalls the amazement on the faces of new students, walking from the bus stop up the long drive with their suitcases and overnight bags, at being greeted on the steps of the house by members of the household staff, and, once inside, by this charming aristocrat so obviously in his own setting. The actor in George Trevelyan also enjoyed putting on a more or less constant play. Another description might be orchestral conductor. He liked to be in charge, he liked to give the beat, he liked to have all sections of the household orchestra following his baton. Roger Orgill says that Attingham "became a spiritual home to many" and, perhaps surprisingly, "it was a long time before George saw that was happening."

Throughout George's tenure at Attingham the balance between esoteric and general courses was fairly constant. The practical and the academic pursuits were mixed together, with teachers and other professionals coming in for teaching and training, and local interest groups holding their own courses. However, the esoteric studies came to assume greater significance as George Trevelyan's thinking developed along spiritual lines. They are receiving more attention here because they were the foundation of the last 25 years of his life, but this attention is not quite representative of their presence within the Attingham calendar, of which they were about 10%. Over time, other courses took on a more spiritual orientation: courses on

Dickens, perhaps, might consider the perceived deeper meanings. But work within the definition of the word spirituality remained in the minority.

In 1967, the post of Deputy Warden became available and Bernard Nesfield-Cookson applied for it. George and he were keen that he should be appointed. Bernard had a broader academic background than the other applicants, whom the governors dismissed before deliberating on him. However, they decided not to offer him the post but to look for someone whose interests were less similar to George's. This left George without a deputy, and he was far from well: he was suffering from a recurrence of the arthritis that plagued the second half of his life. It was one of few occasions when George showed disappointment: he was convinced that he and Bernard Nesfield-Cookson could have worked well together. However, when Geoffrey Toms was appointed to the post of Deputy Warden and Bernard took over as principal of Hawkwood College in the Cotswolds the solution was a good one for everyone concerned. When George retired from Attingham, Hawkwood inherited some of the esoteric courses, and George became a trustee at Hawkwood and lectured there many times.

Geoffrey Toms saw his Attingham appointment as providing a balance. "I felt we should do courses on topics like Multiculturalism, War and Peace, World Poverty. For a time our different approaches might have caused difficulties, then George became very ill and I more or less took over for about a year. When he came back we simply followed our own lines and worked separately." The difference was one of outlook and approach. "I would be saying that everything an adult college is doing should be based on traditional intellectual lines," says Geoffrey Toms. "For example, astronomy is more important in my view than astrology. Botany, looking at flowers in the field, is more important than something like, say, the image of flowers." There were others who shared this view, however loyal they felt to the undisputed imaginative and energetic powers of George Trevelyan.

Early in 1968, George gave a course designed to help people discover their own ability for public speaking. He felt passionately about this. When he was a young man, Sir Charles had taken him out into the hills around Wallington and challenged him to speak as if to a vast audience, presumably in anticipation of a parliamentary or public career that would demand oratory. As a public speaker, George was exceptional. "A gorgeous speaker, on any occasion," is the consensus view. His linguistic command and his knowledge of poetry were extraordinary. Members of his family recall with wonder how he would "quote twenty lines of Milton straight off, completely *à propos!*" He spoke with the perfect clarity and diction of an accomplished actor. This was attributable in part to his father, in part to the Alexander Technique, and in part to an appreciation of the richness and flexibility of the English language that was shared by all members of his family. Lady Molly had conveyed quantities of poetry into the minds of her children; George's uncle, the historian George Macaulay Trevelyan, revelled in the story of the language of his birth. GMT wrote that the Norman Conquest was the making the English language because it effectively exiled Anglo-Saxon to the status of peasants' jargon. The clergy talked Latin and the gentry talked French, so for the three hundred years when our native language was a dialect it lost its clumsy inflections and elaborate genders and acquired the grace, suppleness and adaptability which are its chief merits. At the same time, it was augmented by French words and ideas. Thus improved, our native tongue re-entered polite and learned society as the English of Chaucer's *Tales* and Wycliffe's Bible, to be enriched into the English of Shakespeare and Milton. George Macaulay Trevelyan said there was, "no more romantic episode in the history of man than this underground growth... of the despised island patois destined... to be spoken all around the globe, and to produce a literature with which only ancient Hellas is comparable." It is hard to imagine George Lowthian Trevelyan departing from this opulent view. He was a great lover of the English language all his life.

At Easter 1968, George visited the little community at Findhorn, and returned full of admiration for the way in which they were growing trees, vegetables, fruits and flowers on inhospitable sand dunes, using very little compost. They were living on their vast, healthy crops while neighbours who tried to copy them achieved nothing. It was the beginning of a long association for George, who became a trustee and a regular speaker for the Findhorn Foundation. He was enchanted by the way they were living the ideal, by the integrity with which they undertook all their tasks. According to Eileen Caddy they were under instruction from God. She would meditate every night, finding the darkness and the silence conducive to receiving guidance. Then she would convey the messages to the community, who would go about their business accordingly. The encounter between Trevelyan and the Caddys was mutually beneficial. Holism was being practically researched at Findhorn and George found it fascinating.

Up to this point the esoteric courses had attracted little interest from younger people, but during the one called The Allegorical Journey, over New Year and Epiphany, 1969, a dramatic group of young people, including two of Lord Harlech's daughters, swept into George's life. Theatrically dressed, the young men wearing capes and earrings, they were entirely outside the experience of George and the students. These visitors were amazed that older generations were thinking about spiritual ideas unconnected with orthodox religion; George was amazed that so many young people, some from wealthy, aristocratic homes, others penniless, were seeking a spiritually oriented life. George could not alter the course that was under way but told the young people that if they could gather a group he would put one on especially for them. At first they said they never planned ahead but then they promised to fill the house for a mid-week course. It was a memorable event for everyone, especially George. He shared the lecturing with Andrew Glazewski, Kitty Trevelyan and a former student named Ludi How, and offered a programme with plenty of opportunity for comeback from the young. George talked informally about Life Seen as an Allegorical Journey, Shakespeare, The Symbolism of Heraldry, The Quest for the Grail, and The Meaning of the Odyssey. He tried to show that the past was not to be jettisoned, but that its strength and aspiration were to be lifted forward. George himself made quite a picture, lecturing to seventy colourfully dressed young people in brilliant sunshine at the edge of the wood. Andrew Glazewski talked about Science and the Approach to the Supreme and when at the end Ruth Bell unveiled him as a Roman Catholic canon, the young people were utterly amazed. More critical observers remember it differently. "This group of wealthy hippies, they even had hippy nannies for the children! They were separate from the big hard world. They were reclining along the mile walk, making flower chains. It really caused a schism among the staff."

George was physically quite poorly and had lately been diagnosed with rheumatoid arthritis, but he neither spoke about it nor gave way to it. He meditated, and ultimately went on a naturopathic regime. Some say he believed he was paying the karmic debt of the Trevelyan family through his suffering, that the age of the family and the inevitable number of its misdemeanours could be equated with the extent of his pain. For her part, Helen was hugely frustrated by his attitude to his illness and to any mention of conventional medical help. She did her best to look after him at such times and did not feel he co-operated. However, the arrival in George's life of the spiritually-seeking young people was in itself therapeutic. George adored them. Essentially they knew they wanted a different world from the one they had inherited, but thought they were changing things simply by shocking older generations travelling the country in horse-drawn caravans with their children and dogs. They knew what they were objecting to but not where they were going. George and Andrew and their colleagues tried to give a vision of the significance of the past and ideas that could take people forward. They were able to balance teaching with fun, so that new ideas were palatable. George had been diagnosed with a dreadful affliction only two months earlier and appeared quite an old man, nevertheless the young people adored and admired him. They found they agreed with what he and his colleagues were saying, and a mutual tolerance and understanding flowed among the party. The young people stopped being defensive when they saw that they were accepted.

Kitty Trevelyan was also a tremendous success with the young. She had joined enthusiastically in the life of Attingham from its beginning, and travelled up from the south of England for many if not most of the specialist courses. Her connection with her brother George, begun so early in life, had remained close throughout their parallel development along similar paths. For people brought up without the need to live in the materialistic world the objections of the so-called counter-culture of the sixties and seventies could be seen as sympathetic. Materialism was coming under the spotlight of the young because their parents' generation seemed to be exclusively concerned with the mechanisms of getting and spending. Contemporary plays and novels and even occasionally the ephemeral world of pop music made strong objections to the arid influence of consumerism. The attempts being made at Attingham to consider and question the current nostrums were part of this discussion.

Since George was committed to presenting many different spiritual paths to the public, he met many ideas and enthusiastically made them his own, retaining those he felt fitted in with his anthroposophical background. He had received training in the Maharishi's type of meditation, and it helped him to find stillness for his battle with the hereditary Trevelyan arthritis. It helped him to be detached, and ready to accept that if he was not to be healed, he must take it as Christ's will that he accept the pain as part of his life's journey. He rejected conventional treatment and more or less ignored the pain, appearing for the most part to pretend it wasn't happening, though it increased exponentially. He said, "it is just amusing to think this pain matters." When during his last couple of years at Attingham he had to be away for periods of treatment, he called it, "nothing but an enforced withdrawal for a time of opportunity for spiritual development, and therefore to be welcomed."

An important element in the treatment of George Trevelyan's arthritis was his contact with Dr Gordon Latto, a well-known naturopath. George often stayed with Gordon and his wife Barbara, who was also a doctor, at their home near Reading. He had been introduced to them by Rolf Gardiner through Lady Eve Balfour of the Soil Association. Rolf Gardiner was a leading practical ecologist; Lady Eve Balfour was a pioneer in organic farming when everyone else was keen on using chemical fertilizers and pesticide sprays. George's health regime consisted of nutritional changes, water treatment, saunas and exercises, and gradually, with enormous determination and working through his pain, he achieved a little more movement. He who had been such an athlete and had taken such joy from physical endeavour, never complained of pain or the loss of vigour. Dr Barbara Latto said he had, "utter and complete determination." There was a 2ft high 'hill' in the Latto garden that he made himself walk up every day, and he always did it although it caused him great agony. Some contemporaries attributed his resumption of walking 30% to Latto, 10–20% to spiritual healing, and 50% to determination. Soon he could only walk downstairs backwards, had difficulty rising from a chair or using his fingers to open a door, and his legs were in callipers. He described it as "a mild inconvenience."He cleverly worked out a way to give fully of himself with his usual energy when in public, but allow time to withdraw and take total rest when necessary. Rhoda Cowen said that the Lattos helped George not only with food, but also by teaching him the importance of moving correctly whatever the pain, of taking control of his own body. This linked up with his knowledge of the Alexander Technique. She believes it is doubtful whether without these therapeutic efforts he would have been able to fulfil the programme he set himself after his retirement from Attingham. Between the Lattos and George's will power the disease was brought under control, and when he maintained his diet, he could move just enough. George said, "I had wasted some time before that because I refused to let any doctor get at me, so I had never had any cortisone injections or what-not. If I had not dithered about looking amateurishly for help, even the permanent damage to my bones could have been avoided. Yet in four to five years, with the help of Gordon Latto, we had my blood absolutely normal ... Five years later I had to have a prostate operation, which Gordon's brother did. He took my blood and tested it before the operation, and to my astonishment he found it was totally normal on every count. This meant I had entered a new stage of my life." (*Kindred Spirit*)

In the summer of 1969, the major esoteric course was The Buddha and the Christ, something of a new direction in that it brought together two anthroposophical speakers, the Rev. Adam Bittleston, a Christian Community priest; Dr Thomas Weihs, a leading figure in the anthroposophical Camphill movement; as well as Chao Khun, a Buddhist. The idea was that the Buddha symbolizes the eternal stillness of contemplation and peace; the Christ symbolizes the dynamic force that permeates all life in the universe. A balanced consideration of these two concepts was intended. However, at the time George's arthritis was reaching its peak and, after giving his own lectures, he withdrew for most of the time.

Over New Year and in the late summer it was possible to run courses for longer than the usual 48 hours, which gave scope for exciting additions to the programme. Drama, crafts and expeditions into the hills were included, and George was in his element. He saw that all education, including spiritual education, was more than information; it is also activity, and sharing group activities. The drama in the esoteric summer schools was recorded by Ruth Bell as being particularly memorable. It was usually directed by Marabel Gardiner. She was the wife of Rolf, mother of the conductor Sir John Eliot Gardiner, and an old friend of George's. She had the wonderful facility of getting even the most staid of the mature ladies to take part. Another aspect of the summer schools was George's great love of architecture and of, "getting buildings moving" by taking the eye along the lines of them. St Chad's Church in Shrewsbury was a favourite for this exercise. One such course was Inner Eye, Outer Eye in the summer of 1969. Letters of appreciation flowed in to George after such courses.

In September when the College closed for a summer break, George went to the Bath Clinic to see if the orthodox medical profession could help him overcome his polyarthritis. He wrote that this time of withdrawal was giving him the chance to experience, "infinite stillness, bliss consciousness. My room is like a sanctuary full of angels and full of light and peace. This is exquisitely monastic, or rather hermit-like. In these nights my rediscovery is that God is Joy... how temporary are any worries." George regarded his illnesses as tools for spiritual advancement. The altered consciousness brought about by pain can indeed be a means to insights which could probably not be obtained in any other way. Periods like this one, and the spiritual turmoil they encompassed, gave George a great deal that was essential in his future work. Meditation was becoming crucially important to him. He was having to live his own phrase: *take courage*. He believed that people should never allow others to project negative ideas on to them, that problems such as lack of world harmony, pollution, and so on, should be overcome with courage, not seen as negative and insoluble. Just before Christmas the chairman of the Attingham governors told him they assumed he would retire in two years' time, at the age of 65. Even this did not dismay him. He had enough faith that his work was continuing to tell them that his secretary Ruth Bell would be retiring with him. It seems possible that his illness and the increasing divergence between his New Age passions and the wishes of the local county council members provided enough reason to make retirement the best solution.

At New Year, 1970, another course was run for young people which formed a link between George, representing the Arthurian stream of ancient wisdom, and the Sufis, representing a wisdom tradition from the east. On New Year's Eve the group dined as King Arthur and his Queen and Court. George and Helen dressed according to their royal status. (Many of his friends are happy to recall how much George loved theatrical costume: "never happier than when he had the dressing-up box open," is one version.) George relished these symbolic occasions and loved the acting, but he did not became entangled in the acted status of regality. He was clear that it was a meaningful pageant, a symbol only. Throughout his life he retained a consciousness of his aristocratic family, his roots, and the importance of continuity to the understanding of human development. no one who met him ever forgot who he was — or felt intimidated by it. Catriona Tyson says: "He was not at all a snob, but he was aware of his family always. If you can imagine those two things co-existing, in him they really did." There were the usual New Year festivities, including the kissing bough, and the group gathered around a great log fire while George and Kitty recited poetry. At the end of the evening, a procession of candle bearers circled the house to greet King Arthur on the colonnade, a trumpet heralded the New Year from the roof, and then they broke into Hark the Herald Angels Sing.

Early in the year, twelve fine mosaics of the signs of the Zodiac were mounted. They were designed by Jasper and Molly Kettlewell, measured about 5ft by 3ft, and were made by a team in the Oxford Room in the corner of the courtyard. Students had raised money for them and the mosaics were presented to George as a decoration for the round entrance. The Kettlewells planned to cover the floor and ceiling, and George rather grandly began to talk of the Rotunda as "the Ravenna of the north." He hoped the mosaics might be a gift from the college to the National Trust, but five years later public finance was withdrawn from much adult education and the college had to close. George did not think the mosaics would be properly seen any longer so he arranged for them to go in to the Telford Technical College. Many people who were concerned with Attingham as an adult education college hope one day the mosaics will find their way back to the place for which they were made.

Time passed, the moment of George's retirement from Attingham came closer, and the rumour that he would be leaving in little over a year got around. The conception of the Wrekin Trust came in March. George became aware of the gossip and decided to say something at the beginning of his final lecture. He began, "rumour reaches me that rumour reaches you!" and assured the audience, "This work will continue." He was committed, though he had not started to think about the practicalities of it.

The following month, George went to London for the first of several Sufi Congresses at which he shared the platform with Pir Vilayat Khan, who said that their meeting, representing western and eastern thinking, had been significant. George spoke of the need to find a new world religion that could unite all religious and spiritual groups. The only criterion should be a belief in a spiritual world view which would leave everybody free to follow their own path, but united in acknowledging the spiritual aspect of man and the universe. It was the first time he had put forward this idea, which was to engage him for many years. He talked of the Maharishi's meditation, the Silent Minute, and Lamplighter Movements. George had said that the uniting of people "for humanity" could only take place through the interfusion of the planes of being, past and present, traditional and new, and he spoke of men and women fulfilling their role as co-creators with the Divine. At this time he seemed to have a new drive. For about sixteen months he had been obeying doctors' orders; now he was claiming that his arthritis was much better even though his knees and feet must still have been very painful.

Interest in the esoteric work was increasing, especially among

young people, and applications for the June course on The Expansion
of Consciousness were so numerous that they had to decide whether to
double the maximum capacity numbers and hold the lectures in a marquee, or run the course twice. George decided to repeat the course.
There were about 400 applications and no more than 340 could be
accepted, many of those having to stay in local hotels and guest
houses. The two courses were to have slightly different lecturing pan-
els. In his retirement year George felt he could be braver about who he
invited to speak. For both courses he invited Paul Beard of the College
of Psychic Studies in London, Rosamond Lehmann, and Lady Cynthia
Sandys, a close friend for many years. They were joined initially by
Ronald Beasley of White Eagle Lodge (a psychic and spiritual organization), and Reshad Feild. On the second course they were joined by
David Spangler from Findhorn, Maung Maung Ji and Bruce
MacManaway, the healer.

Summer 1971 was the final one at Attingham and inevitably contained many farewells; they were made without regret. The governors
gave George permission to have a family party there in mid-July. It was
a very joyful and memorable occasion. George's nephew, Peter
Trevelyan, the heir to the baronetcy, spoke about his involvement with
a new organization known as Friends of the Earth. This was a moment
of great harmony for the Trevelyan family: ecology, of course, was
high on Sir George's list of priorities too. The final summer school
came at the end of month. It was The Doors of Perception, with fine
speakers and a final production of *Persephone*, a legend of light
descending into dark and balancing it. This was a symbolic drama for
George to set out on his world-wide lecturing programme. In his closing words the next day, George spoke of the work as "the greatest
adventure of man ever," saying that all concerned should thank God for
the privilege of being involved. He said, "we are called on a journey
into the spirit," and observed that leaving Attingham was a watershed
in his life. He might not shed a tear, but must show he could give up
what had meant so much to him with joy, to allow room for something
greater.

And then it really was the final curtain. On Saturday, 28 August,
1971, celebrations for 350 people were held in two giant marquees.
The college at Attingham was to continue under Geoffrey Toms;
George and others had created the Wrekin Trust, an organization dedicated to continuing the esoteric teaching and lecturing programme
peripatetically. The marquee at the front of the house was packed

with people, the front row filled with VIPs, including the Secretary for Education for the County. George came out of the front door, a red rose in his buttonhole. He entered the marquee, paused to acknowledge applause, then gave a marvellous speech, finishing, "in my end is my beginning." The day's events were harmonious and various, and at one point spectacular. In the middle of the afternoon a hot air balloon flew George above Attingham on a tether, so that he could see the house from far above. His own physical capacity was so limited by arthritis that Roger Orgill had to lift him into the balloon basket. Roger Orgill had not seen George for a few years and was appalled by the deterioration his condition. "George was as light as a feather," he remembers, "even with the cumbersome callipers on his legs." Then there was supper, a concert, punch and fireworks — and a surprise. George and Helen had been asked to appear on the front colonnade in warm clothes. A horse and trap with a coachman and pillion rider in eighteenth century costume came trotting round the corner of the house, George and Helen climbed in, and they set off down the drive. George loved it! Next morning he was back to give his final Attingham service. He drew on the works of Steiner, Teilhard and Tudor Pole, and quoted Aurobindo: "It is a beginning ... an adventure absolutely unexpected, and unforeseeable ... What will happen tomorrow I do not know; you must leave behind whatever has been foreseen, whatever has been designed, whatever has been built up, and then on the march into the unknown come what may." This was George and Helen's departure after 23 years, for George to set up the Trust and continue his work and his adventure elsewhere. The postscript for adult education Attingham is less happy.

Due to the withdrawal of public finance, Attingham College was closed at the end of November 1975. Geoffrey Toms said that everything possible had been done to keep it open and one academic commentator described the closure as happening by default. Geoffrey Toms had re-established a successful, conventional curriculum, and a record number of courses was being attended by the largest number of students the college had ever seen. A new bedroom wing had been added, bringing Attingham's capacity to 70 beds compared with an average of 40 in most other adult residential colleges. However, members of the local council had put forward objections to the college on grounds of élitism, and local gossip about hippies did the rest. It could have been terrible for George to see all that he had built up come to an end, but he wrote to Ruth Bell: "We have wound up Attingham. It was certainly a tremendous final day. First, the great concert, then the Greek course for which, after Geoffrey's closing lecture, I gave him a vote of thanks which reduced many to tears and I was able to include Plato's prayer to Pan ... Finally, at the end of the afternoon/evening event, I got the chance of a farewell oration which was designed to give a lift and was followed by the Trumpet Voluntary. Everyone went away with some sense of triumph in the heart." George looked at what had been achieved, not at what had been lost. Geoffrey Toms said, "His great achievement was to make it from nothing. That and his charismatic leadership, and the fact that he got the right tutors, represent a tremendous life achievement."

Why did the college at Attingham close? Surely not just because of the gossip? Perhaps the cultural experiences that were offered, such as music and plays, became more generally accessible than they had been. Perhaps participation in these spheres is less attractive than it was; perhaps the fiercest post-war cultural hunger was assuaged. Nowadays residential courses are more usually concerned with professional interest groups or in-service training and there is broader provision for adult learning within local authority evening classes. There is a still an adult residential sector, but its functions have shifted. There is greater emphasis on learning for the sake of career advancement, less on learning for its own sake. But whatever the current situation, and whatever factors brought it about, the work at Attingham Park represents an extraordinary chapter in the history of adult education, and post-war Britain benefited from it in other ways than those which are quantifiable. Sir George strode through it in a typically inspired, inspiring, theatrical way, and many people gained hugely from his presence there.

CHAPTER 5

Findhorn and the New Age

All are but parts of one stupendous whole
Whose body nature is, and God the soul.
Alexander Pope

Sir George Trevelyan played a part in many idealistic and spiritual concerns during the last thirty years of his life. His primary work was with the Wrekin Trust, which he formed on leaving Attingham. Outside the Trust probably no other enterprise was as important to him as the Findhorn community, on the north east coast of Scotland. George inspired the founders and early members of it, and was in turn inspired by their effort and example. He was a constant source of ideas and practical help; they were a purposeful reminder of ideal in action. They exemplified George Trevelyan's favourite notion: the *living idea*. The community practised the everyday reality of living proposed in the burgeoning New Age conferences and literature; thus George often spoke about it on platforms and in meeting places where he had gone in his capacity as head of the Wrekin Trust. At this time, the term New Age was coming into use as an umbrella for what are now more commonly called alternative ideas. It covered different kinds of spiritual exploration, different styles of living and sharing means and ideas, different perceptions of nature and of the right relationship to it of human beings, different styles of health care, both physical and psychological. The term refers to the New Age of Aquarius, with itsshift towards the imaginative and the intuitive, away from the rational and material. It is concerned with change both internal and external, with social transition and spiritual transformation.

The Findhorn community had been founded by Eileen and Peter Caddy, with their friend Dorothy Maclean, in November, 1962. They had all moved to the inhospitable caravan site when Peter Caddy was dismissed from managing the Cluny Hill Hotel a few miles away. Their aspirations as an innovative spiritual and ecological community were entirely harmonious with those of George Trevelyan. What George taught, whether at Attingham or for the Wrekin Trust, was realized practically at Findhorn, where the work was respectful of the natural environment and of all living creatures. Great as was George's fascination with organic husbandry and the emphasis on spiritual effort, his fascination with the experiment in egalitarian group living was its equal. His friendship with both Caddys was deep and intense, although Eileen Caddy remembers it as being stronger between the men. She says that from the moment Peter Caddy met George Trevelyan at Attingham, "they were deep friends. George's relationship was mostly with Peter, they worked in parallel." Straight away George brought in influential people to help bring the Findhorn community into the public domain; later he taught Peter Caddy to project his voice for public speaking so that he could also reach more people. Findhorn-dweller Nick Rose observes of the influence of the early group: "He and Peter Caddy and Tom Welch — they *were* the New Age. They were trustees of everything." He recalls a style similarity too. "They all had big sweaters, they even all looked the same."

The Findhorn community gave George a special proximity to nature. His own theories about plants were related to the ideas of Goethe and to Gaia theory. The Gaia notion was becoming very popular. Scientists such as James Lovelock proposed that because of the self-regulatory system of earth's atmosphere and temperature it is reasonable to perceive the planet as a living organism; this notion couples with a Greek creation myth concerning the goddess Gaia's dance. Such theories found many supporters at Findhorn, and seemed to be practically proved by the record-breaking garden produce there. Roger Doudna, an early community member, has another interpretation of the attraction of Findhorn for George Trevelyan. He says, "Sir George always craved what Steiner called 'knowledge of higher worlds'. At Findhorn, those worlds are a bit closer." George took part in a great number of New Age associations; he opened many spiritual centres and endorsed many publications; he held honorary positions with groups and often gave their keynote speeches. But Findhorn represented the largest commitment of his time and energy, and is offered as the example of the way he helped and inspired organizations other than his own.

George Trevelyan first heard of the three adults and three children living in the corner of a caravan park near Elgin when Peter Caddy turned up uninvited at Attingham in the late summer of 1965 for a weekend course on The Significance of the Group in the New Age. Caddy was an ex-RAF Officer, caterer and hotel-keeper. He claimed to work only in accordance with guidance received from God by his wife, Eileen, and he turned out to be the participant with the greatest practical expertise in the subject of the course. By that time, the tiny Findhorn community had lived for three years in a windswept part of northern Scotland where they were growing unaccountably abundant trees, vegetables, fruits and flowers on bare sand dunes, using very little compost. Their neighbours, meanwhile, did poorly. The community explained their success by saying they were consciously co-operating with nature spirits. The notion of a spiritual element within all life forms, including plants, was one with which George Trevelyan was sympathetic. After the course he wrote to Peter Caddy:

> Let me say how deeply I enjoyed your visit and value the
> contact with you. We have just finished a conference with the
> Soil Association, and I spoke to them about you and the work
> you are doing in plant growth. This is to warn you that some
> of them may approach you to know more about it.[1]

For George Trevelyan it was the start of another enthusiastic, personal PR effort, bringing influential people to Findhorn to take in for themselves the wonder of what was being done there. For the fledgling community this interest created the practical challenge of finding proper accommodation for the guests. It also crystallized something which had been in Peter Caddy's mind for a while: the need to make their work more widely known. George himself, however, was not able to visit the Findhorn community until three years after his first meeting with Peter Caddy. It was Easter 1968 before he finally arrived there, by which time the original group of six had become much larger. He returned to Shropshire full of admiration for the whole thing. Peter Caddy wrote, "The timing of his visit was perfect in every way, for there was sufficient development in the garden for him to see the results of what I'd been speaking about in theory...he remarked that we were ... in the world but not of it, and we were completely free to devote ourselves to God's Will. His visit was a great tonic for all of us." Afterwards George wrote to him:

> You will have realised that I was thrilled. What is happening
> is important beyond all words. I realise that in the general

pattern of a God-guided group, you are in a position to show
us a prototype pattern. People are rarely in a position to "go
it" as completely as you do, but all of us can be inspired by
the example, and many will in the coming times find, with
joy, that this is the way.

It was characteristic of George Trevelyan when he felt enthusiastic
about something that he made sure to tell everyone else; and since his
enthusiasm was tremendously infectious, it had a tremendous effect.
His letter to Lady Eve Balfour, founder and president of the Soil
Association, sowed the seeds for a productive co-operation.

At Easter I stayed with Peter Caddy, who lives with a small
group of friends on the caravan site on Findhorn Bay, in
Morayshire. The caravans are surrounded by a lovely garden.
There were daffodils and narcissi, as beautiful and large as I
have ever seen, growing in beds crowded with other flowers. I
was fed on the best vegetables I have ever tasted. A young
chestnut tree, eight feet high, stood as a central feature, bursting
with astonishing power and vigour. Fruit trees of all sorts were
in blossom — in short one of the most vigorous and productive
small gardens I have ever seen, with a quality of taste and
colour unsurpassed. Many species of broad leaved trees and
shrubs are planted and thriving, yet the caravan site is on the
landward slope of the dunes. The soil is simply sand and gravel
on which grows spiky grass. Exactly opposite them is Culbin
Sands where after 50 years of growing, conifers have rooted
and held the dunes so that tough new grass can begin now to
root. Other folk on the caravan site, seeing the lovely
burgeoning around their neighbours' caravans, put in cabbages
and daffodils which come up as miserable specimens.

Along with the Soil Association George brought in the Biodynamic
Association and there was a special conference, which was considered
very useful, and coincidentally illustrated the conference principle that
the total value of the individual contributions is greater than the sum of
them. Mari Hollander, a long-term Findhorn dweller and now its management team co-ordinator, says, "George Trevelyan's interest made a
difference, gave authenticity. His endorsement was very useful." Eileen
Caddy's biographer, Liza Hollingshead, says, "He put Findhorn on the

map," observing that, "Sir George captured the vision of Findhorn before they were doing anything significant." As a tribute to one putting new ideas into the public domain, Brian Nobbs, another early community member, gave George a line drawing of an oak tree with a wise old face in the detail of its trunk. It was intended to represent the Attingham oak and was called the Ancient of Days.

Tom Welch was an early community member, and a trustee. He saw another useful result of George's interest. "He helped to bridge Findhorn into more conventional education. Through his long experience of running spiritual courses at Attingham, and also very traditional ones, he brought a different discipline." There were unexpected benefits from the presence of George as a guest of the community. "He was extraordinarily good at arts and drama; he made us aware of Shakespeare and hidden meanings." The academic Roger Doudna recalls that when he himself joined the community he brought with him "more erudition than most" in the philosophical subjects he had studied, but was frequently told, "wait 'til you hear Sir George!" He says, "Happily I didn't have to wait long before Sir George made one of his increasingly regular visits. He spoke at the first conference on World Crisis and the Wholeness of Life, and I enjoyed hearing him very much, as everyone did. In his speaking he shared his most intimate thoughts and concerns. I think he enjoyed coming to Findhorn because he knew he was going to be in the company of kindred souls. He had a continually active mind. He brought a renewed appreciation for the power of what he called *the living word*, and also — perhaps equally significantly — the pregnant pause. He did so because he came from an old school of classical education in which rhetoric played an important role, as indeed it did in the classical curriculum. He could speak easily about all the formative philosophical figures, such as Plato and Aristotle. I always envied his capacity to put very substantial thoughts into such a moving oratorical flow."

The community was impressed not only by the power of George's speaking but by how inspiring and engaging was the man himself, and many testify to the lightening of the atmosphere when he visited. Everyone looked forward to it. The extremity of his aristocratic elocution was also a source of amusement and apparently many of the community members did very adequate George impressions at their Friday night community dinners. Tom Welch believes that George's aristocratic quality was useful to the organization of Findhorn, which he describes as having been "somewhat chaotic." Fortunately, he says,

George, "could communicate with the establishment." It is a matter of record that George could communicate with everyone, like Sir Charles before him.

George was also very attractive to women, and an accomplished flirt. "He loved all the young ladies in rainbow sweaters putting their arms round him," says Nick Rose. Tom Welch says, "he played up to women who fancied him, but in a harmless way. He didn't expect people to think they could get into a total relationship. Many thought they were special. Many wanted more than there was." George Trevelyan loved female company and had many close platonic relationships, although Tom Welch is not alone in observing that George did not always make his meaning as clear as he might have done. This magnetism lasted all his life. According to a much younger Findhorn-dweller, George on his last visit (aged 87) in 1994 was supported everywhere he went by no fewer than four young women. This man said that he decided there and then that whoever George was, and whatever he done in his life, he was to become his role-model.

One at least knew she was special but did not want more than there was: all other considerations apart there was more than fifty years separating them. This was Elisabeth Tønsberg, who went to live at Findhorn largely because of Sir George's association with it. Roger Doudna says of George's presence: "every time Sir George visited we all experienced it as a real blessing," and Elisabeth Tønsberg says, "he made you feel more than you commonly were. He inspired living with a purpose: he expressed somebody who lived as though there was something better." She first heard him speak in 1985, when she was in her early twenties and newly arrived from Denmark to study George's own first discipline, the Alexander Technique. "In walked this beautiful, charismatic figure — who knew it, by the way! He had white hair, radiant blue eyes. He started talking. I'd brought a dictionary but I gave up quite soon. My English then was a good school English, but not fluent." She says she was spellbound. "For the next couple of years I talked about this amazing experience, he made such a strong impression." Three years later she met him properly, at a weekend seminar on complementary medicine. He invited her to hear him speak at the Friends' Meeting House in St Martin's Lane in central London, and afterwards they went to dinner. "I was burning with questions and I had to shout them, because of the noise in the restaurant and because he was deaf. I was dying with embarrassment! They were big questions. *What is God for you? What is meditation?* People in the restaurant were turning their heads — they didn't hear his answers because he spoke softly." Afterwards, "We wrote lovely letters. He sent lovely Christmas presents — a silk scarf, a pendant."

Elisabeth Tønsberg says that she has never had an inclination for a guru, but Sir George Trevelyan was the greatest source of inspiration of her adult life. "George understood human excellence, like F. M. Alexander. Doing things in a non-doing way, with much more grace and less effort. Alexander is a mental thing, you have to think your way in. If he had captured Sir George's mind, perhaps that's where an enormous reassessment began for him." She continues to be fascinated by George as an example of living one's beliefs. "He took risks," she says. And of the man himself, she remembers with a private smile that, "he held himself like a knight!" George's nobility, in the original sense of the word — not a worldly embellishment but an essential refinement, perhaps even a refinement of essence — is often mentioned by those who remember him well.

Marion Leigh met him in the mid-1970s and remained in contact with him until his last visit in 1994, not least because she used to prescribe flower remedies for him. (Flower remedies mirror the mood or physical state of the patient, and balance negative aspects.) Her patient records show that on 9 May, 1994, she made him a sycamore remedy, sensing him to be exhausted. She remembers that when in 1972 the group legally became the Findhorn Foundation, he became a trustee. "Mostly, people hear about his gifts as a poet and a speaker, but he was a definite influence during the great expansion here. As a trustee, he was aware of all the decisions. That early trustees' group was very powerful; he influenced it and he was an inspiration to the community."

Miraculously, George appears to have accomplished much of this influential trustee work asleep, often dozing off during the meetings. Nick Rose recalls, "He'd fall asleep, then you'd say something to him and he'd wake up and summarize it perfectly." He ponders this for a moment. "Possibly he wasn't really asleep?" But no, because, "he snored!" This recollection of George sleeping his way through conferences, meetings, or lectures, is often repeated, and always with the same ending. On waking up he could give a precise account of the proceedings, indeed a much better one than the people who had been awake throughout them could have done. Many Mystics and Scientists' members recall the phenomenon with equal amazement.

The leadership of Peter and Eileen Caddy was the main feature of the early Findhorn community but the work which came from the collaboration of Peter and George was hugely influential. Marion Leigh sees George's contribution to the Findhorn mix as a human one. "There was much strong will energy, which had been necessary to get it going. George balanced it — he had the more visible love aspect. I believe Peter and George recognized each other. They were both initiates. For me, there's no doubt that George's presence is still here — for me he was one of the founders. Peter is also still around." (Peter Caddy died in 1995, but many Findhorn community dwellers consider that his essential influence is still present.)

Balance is an important concept at Findhorn. The balance of nature, the balance of relationships, the balance of body, mind and spirit, are constantly under review. Intuition is another. Eileen Caddy refers to it as *guidance*, and believes it comes to her directly from God. For many years she had long nocturnal meditation sessions, when the channel of communication with the divinity is said to be clearest. She shared with Peter Caddy and George Trevelyan the belief that, "the key to your happiness and contentment lies deep within each one of you, within your own hearts and minds."[2] She is similarly convinced of the value of meditation. She asks: "How do you start each day? Try to start with inner peace and contentment, by taking time to be still, and allowing that peace to infill and enfold you." The original community was the product of the practical efforts and abilities of Peter Caddy and the inspirations of Eileen Caddy. Neither Peter Caddy nor Sir George Trevelyan had what was called "the sight," and both of them minded it very much, perhaps especially George. With or without this form of intuitive reception it is very much part of the Findhorn way of life to meditate daily, and one of the earliest facilities to be set up there, other than the caravans for living in, was the Sanctuary.

The value system within the community was harmonious with the outlook of contemporary thinkers on ecology and human-scale values, such as that of E.F. Schumacher. In putting forward his big idea in *Small Is Beautiful*, Schumacher rejected large-scale production and consumption, which he saw as destructive of physical, mental and spiritual health. He quoted The Limits to Growth pollution report, noting, however, that it omitted any reference to "pollutants entering the human mind or soul." He criticized the effects of the industrial society on not only the green environment but also the quality of human existence. He proposed a Buddhist economic outlook instead. "Since consumption is merely a means to human wellbeing, the aim should be to

obtain the maximum of wellbeing with the minimum of consumption."
He questioned the modern equation of standard of living with quality
of life, and quoted the French political philosopher Bertrand de
Juvenal speaking of Western man: "He tends to count nothing as an
expenditure, other than human effort; he does not seem to mind how
much living matter he destroys."

Disenchantment with the limitations of materialism was widespread
during the 1970s, and alternative communities such as the one at
Findhorn were being established not only in the British Isles but also
in other parts of the western world. People were no longer satisfied
with the definition of real life as leisure, and of leisure as consumption.
The emerging understanding of the disastrously polluting effects of
over-production and large-scale economics on the human participants
and the natural environment brought a reaction. George Trevelyan
found these ideas very much to his taste, and whole-heartedly endorsed
the idea of green, local production and simple living. (It seems fair to
mention, however, that when he went up to Findhorn he always stayed
at the Cluny Hill Hotel, and never in any of the caravans. A couple of
years after Peter Caddy's dismissal from its management, a twist of
fate had brought the hotel back into the ownership of the Findhorn
community.)

Disaffection for what was regarded as the tunnel vision of scientists
was accompanied by a belief in the fundamental accuracy of intuition
and a new emphasis on extra-sensory perception. At Findhorn, beliefs
concerning nature spirits, devas, and the souls of plants are central to
the community's relationship with its environment and the way produce is grown. Each plant is believed to have a spirit which can be
addressed directly. Sir George suggested that devas and all other ele-
mentals under any other name could be seen as metaphors if preferred.
Within the community, however, they are believed to be real. Dorothy
Maclean spoke often about her contacts with devas, which she
describes as "a sister evolution to the human on Earth."[3] She noted that
the word deva is Sanskrit, meaning "shining one," and she considered
the deva entities to be the architects and life force of all plant forms,
holding the archetypal pattern and plan for all forms around us. She
understood the devic kingdom to say, "We do not see things as you do,
in their solid, outer materializations, but rather in their inner, life-giving
state ... What we see is different forms of light." This definition endows
all life forms with divinity. Kirlian photography, which records the
luminescence given off by matter, supports it. Brian Nobbs believes

that George Trevelyan, "possibly had some information about devas
through his Alice Bailey interest." The spiritual and occult philosopher
Alice Bailey founded the Arcane School. She postulated a small but
growing minority of people she called intellectual mystics, knowers of
reality, belonging to no single religion or organization but regarding
themselves as members of the Church universal and "members one of
another."

Whatever George's personal position on devas, he was definite on
nature. "The Romantic poets knew that ultimately nature is not fulfilled until humanity takes a step in consciousness to blend with nature.
Humanity is integrally part of nature, not an observer of it," he said. He
would quote Pope, and speak of the Living Whole. He would recall the
creation story in the Book of Genesis, which says that God made each
life-form — animals, plants, birds — *after their kind*. This phrase must
mean, said George, that God created the archetype for each kind of living being. Current developments in genome research which point to
the notion that all cell forms are essentially the same might support
this. In his *God's Grandeur* video George explained that Goethe had
answered a question about the secret of life: "That which the plant does
unconsciously, do consciously." George Trevelyan loved to illustrate
Goethe's explanation of plant development by taking the leaves off the
stem of a plant and laying them down in order. "Nature created the
dynamic and evolving form which flows through the plant," he said.
"Groping for an understanding of the archetypal plant, working back
until we can discover the archetypal idea in the mind of God, we can
start with the leaf." Looking at the leaves laid out, he would explain
that each leaf contained everything needed for the plant, and at the
same time showed the circle of life and the principle of metamorphosis. "The plant is all one organ," he said. The leaf was the same as the
petal, and contained a stem in the form of a spine. A petal was a metamorphosed leaf, as was a stamen. "The leaf can metamorphose down
into earth, or it can metamorphose up into the corolla," he said. Then
— a miracle! — "it transforms itself" (George took a petal) "into a new
realm of colour!" Observing that, "the seed contains matter returned to
total formlessness," he said one could hold in the hand the seed of an
oak tree or a rose and see that they were "archetypes outside the realm
of sense." Thus, "The whole plant is leaf." After making the petals, it
contracts itself through the pollen-bearing organ, expands into fruit,
contracts into seed. The seed "is matter chaoticized!" Hence, continued George, it could be seen that all life was part of an idea in the mind

of God, and thus it was possible to make the essential bridge between scientific and spiritual thinking.

Sir George Trevelyan's was one of many voices during the 1970s and 1980s to speak of changing the individual in order to bring about change for the many. He was speaking not of psychological change only, but of the essential metamorphosis of the human spirit. The new relationships between people would be built, not on ownership, obligation, or attachment, but on a highly developed, spiritual love for humankind. This quality of love would be attained through spiritual practice such as meditation. "By each meditation, we align with a universal process," said George. "The thinking of the heart is the field of action for the Higher Self ... The whole reclaims the particle and reunites it in its attunement with the world." It was the grand scale objective. "Change man and you change society." Satish Kumar, director of programmes at Schumacher College, says, "We have to live in a small community if we want to have organic relationships where men and women and children and older people are part of an organic family, where everybody understands each other, helps each other and needs each other... The most important change starts in our mind, in our heart, and in our consciousness... Fixed mind is a stiff mind. Stiff mind is a dead mind, like dead wood. Flexible mind is a living mind like a living tree."[4] To this he adds another comment. "When we want to change ourselves we need to look out of the window at the world. The self is part of the universal force, it is not singular."

In keeping with the aspiration towards the ideal, organic family in which everyone helps each other, the community at Findhorn is cooperative and non-hierarchical. The capacities of the individual members are recognized and used; they are also stretched to include more exacting and unusual tasks. At the same time, the everyday maintenance work of the community is carefully organized on rotas. Food is prepared joyfully, mealtimes are strictly kept and meals are cleared up on time, caravans are immaculate, and the concept of practical spiritual service is a component in all activity. Before meals, everyone in the dining room joins hands and one of the kitchen team blesses the food. The influence of Peter Caddy's catering career in the private world of the hotel and the public one of the armed forces, is visible in the disciplined attitude to domestic work at Findhorn. He would have enjoyed watching Elisabeth Tønsberg briefing a cleaning team. Towards the end of each sojourn on the camp site, a note appears in the guests' caravans asking them to strip their beds and take out rubbish when they leave. On the Saturday mornings of her supervision duties, Elisabeth Tønsberg would remind the cleaning team members to clean behind the 'fridges and inside the cookers, to wash the floors carefully and get into all the corners. They were asked to do these things with love. The Caddy mantra, "love the place you are in, the people you are with, and the work you do," was repeated. To send them off Elisabeth Tønsberg would say to the cleaning rota, "Work is love in action — have fun doing it!" and the team would quickly scatter to its allotted tasks. The result is that guests arrive to a warm and pristine caravan with beds made up with laundered linen, fresh whole food in the cupboard, organic fruit in a bowl, dairy products and fruit juice in the 'fridge, and a note of welcome. Many of the caravans are 40 years old but they are all kept as clean as a pin, and have as calm and hospitable an atmosphere as a good country hotel.

Other aspects of the community are similarly pleasing. The Phoenix Community Store is housed in a huge hut, and has a wonderful variety of organic fruit and vegetables, fruit juices, cheeses, tofu, breads, birthday cards, books, music, periodicals and soap, and inevitably, tie-dye t-shirts, leather sandals, Spiritual Sky incense, and *Positive News*, a journal mostly devoted to ecological news. The shop is clean and tidy and the service is smiling; they boast an annual turnover in excess of £1m and are in the process of becoming a co-operative. It should perhaps go without saying that the quality and condition of the produce is outstanding. Bach Flower Remedies and homeopathy are popular in the community (and have their many expert exponents) as are many other alternative and complementary therapies, and astrology, and quasi-mystical tools such as tarot cards. At Findhorn in many ways it is forever 1975; perhaps part of the charm of visiting is the sense of being in another, and perhaps more innocent, time. In the Universal Café Cat Stevens is played on a continuous loop; by staying in the community for even a couple of days a guest may involuntarily learn six songs from Teaser and the Firecat. The community constantly takes its own spiritual and emotional pulse, for which there are meetings, meditations, therapy groups.

Whenever Sir George Trevelyan visited the community Findhorn its members experienced a rush of energy. His eager question to everyone he met was, "What are you doing?" Spoken in his much imitated aristocratic pronunciation, and with his enthusiastic curiosity, this conveyed interest rather than inquisition. If the person replied what activity they were undertaking he would repeat the question, smiling more. "No! Not that! I mean what are you *doing?*" The question implied, where are your inner efforts taking you? His presence was always a tonic. Tom Welch believes, "everything in Findhorn is George — and in the people he has inspired and enabled to be slightly braver, recognizing a deeper side to themselves than otherwise." George Trevelyan and Tom Welch corresponded frequently, and Tom Welch treasures a letter George wrote in May, 1980, which expresses his romanticism. It was written on heavily decorated writing paper.

> My dear Tom,
> This theme deserves the Celtic paper.
> Now, my feeling is frankly that the world is so bloody nasty that it is well worth while backing any flame of romance and adventure in quest of something better. Our moderately well educated minds cannot quite rule this all out as nonsense ... Thank God for unsolved mysteries —and for the adventurers who are prepared to risk everything for them. Rider Haggard still fires the boy in us all. ("High in the branches of my green tree is a wild bird singing...")
> Lets get all the fun we can out of New Age adventure in these benighted days. The adventure itself is worth while, just as Bonnie Prince Charlie's escape through the Highlands did more for reviving the broken folk soul of Scotland than his mad-cap attempt at invasion.
> If you attempt to join him, the more enchanted I shall be... "I am certain of nothing but the holiness of the hearts affection and the truth of imagination!"
> So there. Send a copy of this to dear Victor, who at heart is still a boy..
> Love
> George

"So there!" is very George; it is determined, defiant, and slightly ironic, and is intended to pre-empt riposte. The emphasis on adventure, imagination, quest, and mystery is also characteristic. And there is a straight line linking all this with his Northumbrian boyhood, roaming over the hills, hearing stories, learning poems by heart.

George used to discuss his inner journey with Eileen Caddy, who says of him, "Sir George always spent a little time with me when he came here. I'm everybody's mother, everybody's grandmother." When he arrived in Scotland, "I used to put him on my bed to rest." Perhaps surprisingly, she says that he "had a lot of doubts and fears. I used to write him affirmations and he had his own way of doing them." (Affirmations are a means of concentrating and focusing the mind on aspects of a person's life which they wish to improve. The basis of the theory can be summarized as *energy follows thought*.) Eileen Caddy says, "I had a real love for Sir George. I loved him and respected him, not just admired him. His enthusiasm! He used to say, 'Splendid! Splendid! Splendid!'" The memory of Sir George's great optimism and vigour is common to practically everyone who knew him. Eileen Caddy says, "We just adored him!"

Craig Gibsone was brought up in Australia and joined the community in 1968. He met Sir George in the early 1970s and describes him as, "a key figure in the pantheon of enlightened souls who helped put Findhorn on the map. His open acknowledgement of the spiritual worlds is a strong memory for me; he was a pioneer in acknowledging the diversity of spiritual realms. He epitomized the ideal of the Knights Templars, the human quest (in the patriarchal model). He was a humble, yet proud representative of that. And he was so eloquent, and elegant! He always maintained his bearing. He embodied the Arthurian archetype, yet he never wore his 'Sir George' on his sleeve. I believe the nobility have preserved aspects of Britain despised or ignored by others. When I came here I didn't know there was a Western Mystery tradition; Sir George brought it alive, he was the major voice of his time. His qualities of nobility, beauty, integrity — they were strongest. And he spoke about the tradition in a way that made it accessible. He lifted me out of the wild colonial boy into something that was my next frontier."

These are memories which are repeated in different forms by most of the people who met Sir George Trevelyan. He made them feel in some way greater than they had felt up to that moment, more capable, more in touch with themselves. Craig Gibsone says that he, "gave sense to that meaning of the search for the Holy Grail: my encrusted heart. The other part of that is that he helped me to see humanity as a collective expression of divinity; that we have a future that is connected to this planet." Craig Gibsone has a strong interest in songs and music, and for him, the understanding of a collective expression of divinity was mostly achieved through the medium of the Power of the Living Word courses. He recalls George, "patiently and lovingly working with someone on a stanza, going into the inner meaning. He was so far in front in his visions." He concludes his appraisal. *"Beautiful man!"* he says.

Nowadays the Findhorn community includes not only different kinds of dwelling place but also a different kind of dweller, with less direct involvement in communal life. Eco-houses are built for purchase by individual families, which means that not everyone lives in a communally owned caravan or prefabricated house, or even a whisky barrel. (The huge wooden whisky barrels were bought in the mid-1980s when local distillers switched from oak to steel vats, and are lived in very happily by several Findhorn families including that of Craig Gibsone. Roger Doudna was instrumental doing in the deal; he lives in one himself, and says they are extraordinarily warm.) Not all of the 150 members use the communal dining room; perhaps not all of them even use the Phoenix Community Store, which is in the process of becoming independent and collectively-owned. The Findhorn Press, which was set up to publish books pertaining to the interests of the community, has been the subject of a management buyout and has moved most of its operations to Florida. Few of today's Findhorn dwellers even know the name of Sir George Trevelyan, much less what he stands for, even though a portrait of him still hangs in the Universal Hall where they hold their big meetings. So what, after all, remains of him in the changing community?

Mari Hollander has been associated with Findhorn since her arrival in autumn, 1976, for a One Earth conference on sustainability. "My parents are Dutch, I grew up in the USA and came to the UK from there," she says. "At the conference I danced with Sir George, and it felt very old world and grand. I was soaking all of it up: it was all new to me. My lasting impression from my first visits to the community was of a substantial group of middle-aged Brits doing white magic." She defines "white magic" as spiritual work. "I came for that. I came for the eccentrics and I saw real people, working at a way of life that was alive with meaning and respect. The energy of community life impelled me to come back a few months later and I have stayed in the energy field ever since. Sir George had a vital role in linking the original little group at Findhorn with the growing number of groups in the south. His interest made a difference, gave authenticity. George's endorsement was very useful. He drew people here."

So, he helped to put the community on the map. He also inspired it, excited it, taught it, brought it his poetry and his delighted enthusiasm. Everyone who met him says the place was different for his presence;

in some sense it could be said that he helped to maintain its integrity. Elisabeth Tønsberg's observation gives another clue. "He believed deeply in living with a purpose. At one of the very last conferences, the person introducing him said, 'When I went to pick up Sir George from the hotel and asked for him, the little boy there said, Where has Saint George gone?— Now, please welcome a saint in training!' That is actually what exuded from him, he was transmitting the holiest of holy. In his presence you were aware of questions — *Who are we? What is God? How do we live our purpose?* The deepest questions of existence, he demanded that we ask them."

CHAPTER 6

The Wrekin Trust: Spreading the Word

If thou couldst empty all thyself of self
Like to a shell dishabited
Then might He find thee on an ocean shelf
And say: This is not dead,
And fill thee with Himself instead.
T.E. Brown

George Trevelyan and Ruth Bell had the idea for the Wrekin Trust in the spring of 1970, eighteen months before leaving Attingham, and much later it was named for the famous beacon hill called the Wrekin that could be seen from the house. One afternoon, not long before his time there was due to end, he and Ruth Bell were gazing out of an upstairs window contemplating their departure, and wondering about the future. Suddenly George said, "I've got it! The Wrekin Trust!" and the name was settled (it became colloquially known as the *Wrecking Trust*, which George enjoyed.) George said he wished to "light spiritual bonfires on the crown of the holy hills of England." The word *bonfire* means good fire; bonfires were used by the Celts to represent the sun in their seasonal ceremonies. Wrekin Hill is on a ley line. All of which was significant for the anticipated work.

He would have remembered, too, his great-great-uncle, Lord Macaulay, describing the signal fires leaping from hill to hill to warn of the approaching Armada:

All night from tower to tower they sprang, they sprang from hill to hill,
Till the proud Peak the flag unfurled o'er Darwin's rocky dales,
Till like volcanoes flared to heaven the stormy hills of Wales
Till twelve fair counties saw the flame from Malvern's lonely height.

George loved this sort of excitement; especially with hills and mountains playing the leading role. He often quoted the Psalmist, "I will lift
up mine eyes unto the hills, from whence cometh my help."

The founders of the Wrekin Trust defined it as, "an educational
charity concerned with the spiritual nature of Man and the Universe,"
an undertaking on the most magnificent scale. During his years as
Warden of Attingham Park Sir George Trevelyan's spiritual interests
had grown exponentially, and he had found that when he put on esoteric courses they were oversubscribed. This, added to the expansion of
the Findhorn community, seemed to him to provide enough evidence
of a growing interest in the new ideas to indicate the need for a forum
in which to explore them. At the time there was little outlet for such
concerns. Courses and conferences were few, and the New Age bookshops which can now be found in many towns were still to come.

The premise of the Trust, George said, was, "All life is of God and
everything is of Divine origin," or, "The whole Cosmos is in very truth
shot through with creative intelligence and spirit from which all physical substance is derived." The material world was understood as an
aspect of the divine. Science was another facet of the divine, rather
than proof its non-existence. Whatever lines of investigation are followed by contributors to the work of the Trust, this belief is fundamental. Retrospectively, George said: "I created the Wrekin Trust to
educate people, and to create groups." Of the need for a new vision he
said succinctly, "There is too much emphasis on war and money!"
Alice Friend, who knew him for the last 25 years of his life, says, "we
keep teaching what we most need to learn ourselves," and recalls that
he had two main obsessions: the unity of god, and *living ideas*. The
unity of god (as the notion that the concept has no division) is matched
by the George Trevelyan assumption that all religious teachings are in
essence the same thing.

The Wrekin Trust began to establish the germ of a lifetime's programme of study towards inner, spiritual wisdom. Wisdom, and the
Western Wisdom tradition, is based on the regeneration of the inner
life, of the meditative, contemplative, spiritual being who would live in
harmony with the earth and the seasons. Seekers hoped to find a peaceful, creative existence focused in a different direction from the mainstream dependence on material props and exterior rules. The Trust had
the objective of helping people to find the doctrine most suited to them
through lectures and workshops on a broad range of subjects.
Ultimately it was to be a University of the Spirit, the continuation of

the medieval concept of university. The founders spoke of Universus, meaning "turned to the One," recalling that the early universities had been founded for the purpose of spiritual endeavour. George Trevelyan emphasised experiment. "Take the idea. Try it out. Live with it. Because ideas are living beings they draw conviction towards them!" For himself, he found great delight in this activity. His lifelong pursuit was developing insights gained through study, observation, meditation and illness, and considering mythological interpretations of the universe. It was his good fortune to possess intellectual independence. His mental freedom from conventional doctrine was matched by his aristocratic freedom from conventional material concerns, the compulsions of those with money to make and status to attain.

Throughout his later life, George Trevelyan continued to deepen his own understanding of Christianity. In his lecture on The Cosmic Christ in the New Age he said:

> The name 'the Christos' is the Greek for this Exalted Being of the Spiritual Sun. The worship of the Spirit of Light and Truth is common to all the great religions, which acknowledged his approach to the Earth for the redemption of mankind ... To Christians he is the Christ, but clearly the present vision would lift us far above the sectarian conflicts... We are dealing with concepts which would renew and widen Christianity so that veritably the coming of the New Age would be seen to include and express the Christ Impulse for all mankind.

A key concern for George was planetary pollution. In his taste for belief systems that encompassed the wellbeing of the planet in harmony with that of the human race he was highly contemporary. In his New Pilgrimage lecture he observed:

> We enter the last decades of the twentieth century and stand on the threshold of the Aquarian Age, when energies for the cleansing of the planet are flooding through the Earth. We all know that if mankind continues in his folly, greed and ignorance, the living Earth of which he is the errant steward, will react against him in earth changes, earthquakes, storms and floods. On the deeper level we must recognize that our own wrong doing and faulty thinking is a factor in causing these great disturbances which threaten us.

Apocalypse was a term in frequent use about the man-made natural disasters that were believed to be imminent. Books were published along the same lines. George's leaflet *Apocalypse Now* (1974) said, "Many have foreseen breakdown in our economy, since a great technology obsessed with getting rich quickly is too clumsy and top heavy, altogether too inhuman in its values ... Values must change." Anxiety about pollution and industrialization accelerated, the increasing power of international corporations was seen as aggressive and damaging. To counteract the doomsday feeling, green groups were formed. The logical consequence of accepting the George Trevelyan statement, "Mankind is steward of the planet," was acceptance of the obligation to take proper responsibility. "The human race is seen as one of the great experiments of God in evolving a being ... who can learn to carry the divine gift of free-will and become in time a co-creator with God." The thoughts and aspirations of many people were beginning to move in a similar direction. The key word was holism, combining all-encompassing definitions of wholeness with existing concepts of holiness.

In addition to poetic vision, George Trevelyan brought to his spiritual life his considerable experience of the natural world, experience with its roots in his country childhood and at Findhorn. He could blend his pantheistic love of rocks, trees and landscape with poetry, his personal vision of the unified Christ energy, and his understanding of the guiding principle of unifying, universal love. Many other people were beginning to see the natural world as something to be cherished rather than mastered. Harmony with nature, and a more personal spiritual understanding, were sought together.

The musicologist Mary Firth was the first Wrekin trustee and there is poetic symmetry in that too, since she and her husband Dr George Firth had played a key part in George's move to Attingham. Mary Firth thinks her appointment to the position of trustee probably had something to do with the fact that she lived in Scotland: her geographical and perhaps also emotional distance would enable her to be more objective — and reassure the others that she wouldn't be able to get in the way. It is also true that they wanted someone sympathetic, and George trusted her absolutely. Ruth Nesfield-Cookson (then Bell) says, "Few could equal Mary's clarity and purity of thought. She looked at things spiritual in the same way as George, but she had greater clarity for understanding others and for business affairs."

In the first programme for the Wrekin Trust, George wrote:

Above: This look-out hut was built by George and some Gordonstoun schoolboys. The pupils today still do Coastguard duty.

Below: Oak table built by George and some boys from Gordonstoun School, which is still in use, and its inscription.

Above left: *George was one of the earliest campaigners for archeological and architectural conservation.*

Above right: *George with Eileen Caddy, one of the founders of the Findhorn Community*

Left: *George Trevelyan was an accomplished mountaineer*

Opposite: *Sir George Trevelyan prepared books and lectures working in his study.*

Above: George's parents, Charles and Molly, with their six surviving children. From left to right: Patricia, Kitty, George, Geoffrey, Pauline and Margery.
Below: George enjoyed outdoor challenges and gained much inspiration there. Right: George on the Wrekin.

Above: Sir Charles and Lady Trevelyan on the occasion of their Golden Wedding, 1953.
Left: George with his sister Margery.
Below left: George did a craft apprenticeship in the Waals furniture-making workshop at Chalford in Gloucestershire, working with Oliver Morel.
Below: Sir George Trevelyan with Roger Orgill, MBE, in the latter's Herefordshire garden.

Attingham Park housed an extraordinary adult education college, of which George Trevelyan was the warden.

Outside Attingham: A round table group that included Bruce and Patricia Macmanaway, Karl and Betty Abraham, Father Andrew Glazewski, Dr Kenneth Cuming, Ludi Howe, Lavender Dower, Theodore Gimbel, Rosemary Russell, Reshad Feild and Rev. Robert Whitfield.

Sir George's remarkable gift for oratory was a matter of legend.

George's athleticism took many forms, often involving water.

A portrait of George Lowthian Trevelyan as a young man.

Many people nowadays are fundamentally dissatisfied with
the materialistic outlook on life. There is a quest in many
minds, both young and old, for a world-picture which
includes the spirit as a primary creative force. Those who
discover for themselves the reality of higher worlds of spirit
are finding a new sense of meaning. A flood of spiritual
knowledge has entered the thinking of our time. It is in a true
sense a recovery of ancient wisdom, but couched in terms
acceptable to our intellectual and scientific minds.

This is to be seen not as a religious revival, but as a
spiritual awakening. There is no dogma, nothing sectarian,
since every creed can find its relation to the vision of
wholeness offered by this world view.

The activities of the Wrekin Trust will take their place in
the educational aspect of the new understanding, chiefly
presenting and introducing the broad picture without
commitment to any particular doctrine or school of thought.

The idea was to organize residential conferences and one-day meetings
related to all aspects of the emerging understanding. Some would be
large, and held in universities and colleges; others would be smaller,
and held in conference houses and retreat centres. They would be at
different levels of attainment and in different parts of the country.
George was clear that he wanted a mailing list rather than membership
for the Trust. He wished to establish that he did not want followers, but
the opportunity to present ideas. He also rather relished the prospect of
travelling to speak to people: he started every expedition with a sense
of adventure. However, this peripatetic lifestyle did nothing to help
harmonize the Trevelyan home life and tended to perpetuate the communication difficulties already established.

To the early programme was added over time a number of activities
which became equally important. They included pilgrimages to sacred
sites, silent retreats for meditation and study, and the holding of ancient
ceremonies at locations such as rocks and mountains and ley lines
which were believed to possess particular earth-energies. None of
these activities was placed higher than another, there was to be no hierarchy of means, only a general effort towards understanding. It was
central to the Wrekin outlook that the planet was no longer to be seen
as something to be subdued by the master species man, but as a living
entity to be respected in its own right.

A few days after the retirement celebrations at Attingham, George and Helen Trevelyan moved to a cottage a few miles north of Shrewsbury and Ruth Bell to a small house which also contained the Trust offices. George was semi-mobile with arthritis at the time, and Ruth also fairly unfit, but both were keen to start. They felt they had an obligation to the 1,500 people already on the Attingham mailing list. In the event, everything fell into place quite easily. There was no start-up capital but the founders, imbued with the Findhorn concept of manifestation, believed that the necessary funding would come. (The manifestation principle proposes that the means for achieving a purpose will present themselves if the purpose be clear enough.) The staff was joined by a full-time person to help with bookings, with several part-time helpers from the village. There were good auguries in the form of gifts. The previous summer they had received a first donation for £1,000 from Cynthia, Lady Sandys. A house had been bought by the Scottish businessman Andrew Wilson and leased to the Trust for three years. A connection of Ruth's gave £3,000 which enabled university and college accommodation to be booked. Small gifts and profits from courses seemed to be assured, and funds for specific projects seemed miraculously to turn up. Thus they were independent, with the freedom to be indiscriminate and to present an eclectic programme.

The early courses had been planned while George and Ruth were still at Attingham, something which was necessary not only financially but also to maintain the momentum. The first Wrekin Trust open course was held in November, the first of the meetings known as the Round Table of Group Leaders having already been held in a place described by Ruth Bell as, "a lovely little conference house run by nuns at Acton Burnell, in Shropshire." The purpose of the Round Table was to draw together leading figures in the New Age movement to exchange ideas and experiences. George promoted, "the strength of an organically united group. 'Unity in Diversity' is the true note. We must support each other in all ways possible but chiefly in thought and intent." Many strong connections were already in place, notably with the Sufi adept Pir Vilayat Khan, and Satish Kumar, editor of *Resurgence* magazine. A similar gathering for people working in the field of complementary medicine had been set up the previous November, prompted by seeing many practitioners who thought they were the only ones doing non-orthodox healing work.

A vital function of the Trust was this one of bringing together people who up to then had had no means of meeting, and who sought not only teaching but also fellowship. Janice Dolley, who now runs it, recalls, "It seemed as though a number of people in different and often quite isolated settings were waking up. This was my experience, but whenever I tried to describe it to others — especially those in the local parish church — it was dismissed as being quite outwith an orthodox religious faith." To create the University of the Spirit, there must be a network of co-operation between people and organizations. Public courses were held approximately every fortnight for groups of between 20 and 500 people. The smaller ones often involved personal help with meditation and similar questions. Mrs Dolley recalls, "Imagine my delight when I attended my first Wrekin Trust weekend and, with about 60 others, listened to the assured inspiration of a white haired and poetic man who not only glimpsed the growing reality of which I was as yet only dimly aware, but knew it well and could expound on how the myths and fairy tales, Shakespeare and many poets, architecture and landscape had enshrined the truths we were rediscovering for ourselves. Notions such as reincarnation, angelic beings, the soul as living reality, were no longer closet thoughts voiced only to a few."

The establishment of the Trust brought a shift of emphasis from the Attingham arrangement: courses were no longer seen as reflections of George Trevelyan. Nor did he attend them all personally. Close friends such as Father Andrew Glazewski, Bruce MacManaway and the Reverend Gordon Barker taught the programme, with Ruth Bell in the role of hostess/administrator. The growth of the number and range of courses was matched by a growth in George's personal popularity, and he accepted more invitations to lecture in places other than those organized by the Trust. Such engagements were seen as stepping stones towards the wider development of his work. The first Wrekin Trust open course was held in Derbyshire in November, 1971, and was attended by nearly 200 people. The teaching team included Father Andrew Glazewski, the healer Bruce MacManaway, and the mystic and Sufi Reshad Feild, to talk once again about Death and Becoming: the Joyous Adventure, a subject close to George's heart. George Trevelyan was always happy to talk about relinquishing joyfully attachments within the material world, and the freedom it brought. "We see that the life in each of us is eternal as all life is eternal. We must each clear from our hearts any vestige of fear of extinction, realizing that the gateway of death opens through to a realm of ever widening consciousness," he said, and, "Death from the viewpoint of soul and spirit must be seen as a beautiful and solemn birth into light ... we enter into endless realms of creative possibility." To Sir George Trevelyan, this journey promised one more, infinitely more exciting, exploration. He spoke of seers of the age, and the rediscovery of eso- teric teachings of Rosicrucians and Knights Templars. "The core of man is seen as an imperishable spiritual entity, a droplet of the Divine source. As such it cannot be extinguished. It is eternal as all life is eter- nal." The atmosphere at the first Wrekin day course is recorded as hav- ing been joyful; one commentator observed happily that the emerging group had re-created the harmony remembered from Attingham. Optimism was George's cornerstone. He was certain that it could be maintained as a matter of will. He brought his own optimism into the communal effort and from his personal position of exemplary courage following bereavement and serious illness he was in a position to say, "we have no right to despair." Like all great orators and actors he gained energy from the response of his audience; for this he was some- times accused of egotism.

A series on Developing the Inner Senses was planned, to be run by Father Andrew Glazewski, a mystic, theologian, physicist and musi- cian. He was keen on telepathic communication and spoke of some- thing he called psycho-physics, and of training the inner sense, which he regarded as many times more accurate than the five senses in daily use. In this he was at one with George Trevelyan, who loved to quote from 'The Cage,' a poem by Martin Armstrong:

> Man, afraid to be alive
> Shuts his soul in senses five,
> From fields of uncreated light
> Into the crystal tower of sight.[1]

Andrew Glazewski would quote Steiner: "arrogance and impatience are the main obstacles to our development of the inner senses ... In order to communicate you have to listen ... Let us train our inner ears to hear, and then telepathy will not be a mystery but an everyday expe- rience." Another strong theme for Father Glazewski was his Light- Love Technique, the ability to call down the Christ Light and transmute it into love in the heart, sending it out again to other people and trou- bled places.

Developing the inner senses relates directly to meditation, wherein the communication is with the inner self, or inner being. Bruce MacManaway ran weekends on Meditation in Everyday Life, often in retreat centres. George Trevelyan also led groups on the same subject. His Rainbow Meditation, focusing the seven colours of the rainbow on the seven major chakras (energy centres) within the body, was especially loved. In his lecture Meditation and its Purpose, George spoke of, "the art and practice of creating an inner centre of quiet and stillness within the self and then allowing it to be flooded with light from the higher planes." Reverend Gordon Barker researched meditation and healing. He believed that the healing of the male/female relationship was the key to inner harmony. This relationship could be perceived as essential balance exemplified in universal phenomena: dark/light, winter/summer, inner/outer. Gordon Barker also set up and ran the Family Crisis Counselling Service.

George was strongly aware of the Christian festivals. At the 1972 Easter Retreat, hosted by the nuns of Acton Burnell, he asked that light be directed to the divided city of Jerusalem and trouble spots throughout the world. The retreat was held in silence except for his talks, and on Saturday evening there was a deep meditation, George having linked the lighted candle with the Lamplighter Movement by reading his own dedication. The harmonious aspiration of meditation groups is seen to have an effect upon the rest of the world. On Sunday the group attended Eucharist in the local church and George read the lesson. This sort of concentrated service was a frequent element in the life of the Wrekin Trust and something which the New Age brought into the lives of many more people. Other important courses during that year included Spiritual Awakening in Our Time; an early conference was Community Living in the New Age. At the conferences it began to be noticed that ideas seemed to be generated by the act of group discussion, ideas that no single member had thought up on the day or even brought with them. The joint effort was seen to create more than the sum of its parts.

For his loyalty to conventional Christianity George Trevelyan attracted criticism among New Age people; for his New Age associations he troubled the minds of conventional Christians. For George himself, the Christian inspiration was esoteric, rather than exoteric:

> The entry of the Cosmic Christ for all men relates
> Christianity to the other great religions. The recognition of
> Jesus as the vehicle of the Christ places Him in His true
> relation to the other prophets. The Buddha prepared the way
> 600 years before the Event of Golgotha, by showing the path
> to enlightenment. Six hundred years after it Mohammed

made his revelations of the One God... The Master Jesus is
ever present with us as leader of the group of the great
spiritual Masters. Thus this concept of the Cosmic Christ
helps us to lift clear of the apparent contradictions between
the religions and points the way to a vision which unites all
men who have found their way to the health-giving power of
the Christ Impulse. What name we give does not matter. We
are united in recognition and worship of the Lord of Light.

One of George's guiding principles was that religious difference could
be dissolved and all people be illuminated and inspired by a simple,
refocusing motive, that of realizing the deity within.

The geographical reach of the Trust's conference programme was
determined by practicalities: the conferences had to be held in pleas-
ant, affordable places which were accessible to speakers and had
enough potential students to make them financially viable. Effectively
this often meant the southern half of England, although George's
Scottish and Northumbrian associations sometimes took them north. In
May 1972 George and Ruth travelled to Scotland for a course on The
Cosmic Future with Father Andrew Glazewski, Bruce MacManaway
and Ogilvie Crombie. Robert Ogilvie Crombie (Roc) was an early
member of the Findhorn community. He was a pianist, actor and scientist, he had a close rapport with nature, and was said to be able to see
Pan, and to communicate with nature spirits. It was as George was
leaving for this event that he first met Rod Friend, on whom he made
a lasting impression. Rod Friend recalls him standing on the steps of
Hawkwood College in a typically theatrical cloak and a deerstalker hat,
crying: "Onward to Iona!"

The Cosmic Future course brought the opportunity for a visit to
Findhorn. George loved being driven through his beloved northern
mountains and never complained that he could no longer climb them.
When they reached the island, Father Glazewski administered the
Roman Catholic Mass in George's room, and Ruth Bell recorded that
it seemed like a Teilhardian Mass on the World, with the Sound and the
mountains of Mull visible through the great picture windows. Peter
Caddy wrote of the island of Iona:

There is something unique in the atmosphere, a quality that
sets it apart as a spiritual oasis, just as geologically it is
separated by tens of thousands of years from neighbouring

islands of the Inner Hebrides. There is a sparkling clarity to
its light... on most days the sun miraculously breaks through
to bathe Iona in light, seeming even brighter against the
sombre unlit hills on the opposite shore. Thousands of people
are drawn to this place of pilgrimage each summer.[2]

The first conference on Health and Healing, the brainchild of Bruce
MacManaway, was held in July at the University of Surrey in
Guildford. It was almost certainly the first public conference on non-
orthodox healing, drawing speakers from disciplines such as nature-
cure, homeopathy and radionics. Healing was also under consideration
as a means towards spiritual understanding. Some 500 people attended
and a similar number were turned away, an encouraging response for
the first Wrekin Trust effort on such a large-scale project. It was felt to
be indicative of strong interest in the full spread of the new possibilities. In 1972 the phrase "complementary medicine" was next to
unknown, and this conference made a long step towards awareness of
it. The understanding of participants was deepened: a Wrekin intention
regardless of subject matter. One said, "I have never in my life been so
aware of Christ's presence as during the last three days." George was
encouraged, and directly afterwards returned in celebratory mood to
his roots, spending a week at Wallington, where the Attingham
Summer School for American Art and Architectural Historians gave a
great dinner for the Trevelyan family. The Trust had also held a
Spiritual Springs of Architecture event that year, and with it the opportunity for George to observe, as he loved to do, that the layout of all
the great gothic cathedrals matched the plan of the chakra system of
energy centres within the human body.

What are Life and Death All About? was next, a summer school at
Killerton House in Devon with Clarice Toyne and the Rev. Tony
Duncan. Killerton belongs to the National Trust and provided a glori-
ous setting in which students could feel a close link with nature.
George Trevelyan had high aspirations for universal contacts to be
forged at these summer schools, contacts between teachers and students, between human beings and the natural world, between life on
earth and life in other dimensions. He believed that such links could be
more perfectly realized in beautiful surroundings such as in Devon, at
Attingham, and from time to time Wallington. However, not everything
they did took place in the rural setting. After Devon George went to
Birmingham University to lecture to some 500 followers of the

Maharishi. There he mentioned that Birmingham Extra-Mural Department had been telling him for 25 years that his spiritual ideas were not valid education (as they probably still would today).

Wallington was soon back in the frame, this time for proximity to the College of Education at Ponteland for The Inward Journey with Marabel Gardiner, Theo Gimbel and Mary Swainson. The hostess on this course was Norah Cornwell, who wrote, "Our visit gave us a magical day, walking through the lovely house and woods and having tea at the clock tower." The beautiful setting nurtured drama in the way it had been realized at Attingham. George wrote, "In support of my lectures on the deeper significance of the *Odyssey* and other great myths, Marabel Gardiner swept most of the group into improvized dance and drama ... Such creative activity is a very important adjunct to the lift given by lectures." Norah Cornwell saw that George could bring together poet and peasant as equals, meeting in full acceptance. She wrote, "the drama... became a thing of beauty, a joy to watch and to take part in. The elderly ladies became young and beautiful, the men became Grecian Gods, and the hero, Odysseus, was a triumph. Audience and cast were drawn together as a family." George Trevelyan had always had enormous adherence to the expressive power of drama. His daughter, Catriona Tyson, says, "George loved acting. [At Attingham] we often did the *Dream* and *Twelfth Night*. George usually played Malvolio. Very well, I seem to remember."

George summarized the Wrekin Trust's first year: "First, we saw that our very first course had been at Swanwick on What are Life and Death All About? and this series of summer schools was giving the answers. In a way, Killerton had been the prelude to Ponteland, linking us with the nature forces. Odysseus at Ponteland had portrayed the launching of western thinking, of the birth of modern consciousness. Parsifal at Beshara would give the union between western thinking and the thinking of the east. All is one continuity." He observed, "love has to be lifted beyond the personal. It has to be transmuted into universal love and sympathy. Parsifal finding the way is the completion of Odysseus launching the modern scientific ego-consciousness which needs to be Christ-ened and lifted into higher thinking."

He continued, "in the trip to Wallington I had come to my own home country. This was magical, the highlight being when my sister Patricia, and Old Jack (long associated with Wallington), played the pipes to us after our tea, ending with, 'Will ye nae come back again'. This was so moving that many were in tears and all joined in the singing." He wrote, "throughout the drama there was the theme of kingship. It seemed relevant that Wallington and Attingham had now been triumphantly relinquished so that I can move light into the New Age. The king must be crowned and the crown given back." Dinah Molloy, a student, wrote, "I do not know whether it is me who is changing or that each course *is* more beautiful than the last. I think the latter." Another student, Ishbel McGain, described the group on the east lawn, with George on a seat, "and all of us on the grass at his feet hearing the history of the house and hilarious stories about Sir Walter Blackett's (supposed) short-horned cattle. This is Wallington with a voice." A traditionally aristocratic perception of continuity had been shown to be once again capable of transformation for the sake of its own survival.

Thus the mode of working was established. It was a sort of peripatetic, spiritually adventuring Attingham, engaging speakers from different viewpoints and using various means towards understanding. So it continued for several years, with the mailing list growing steadily. George began to write books to spread the teaching and even make a little money. He called this marketing. His books are characteristically scholarly, bright, readable, energetic: they are also more or less transcripts of his talks. The teacher and poet in George Trevelyan makes very difficult ideas accessible and his conviction is clear in every line, although he often stops to say, "Make your own mind up." His publisher, Alick Bartholomew, says that unlike the authors on his list, "I didn't feel comfortable with editing his thoughts." Like so many others he recalls George as a speaker. "He was an inspired orator; he had an inner spirit connection which enabled a high degree of communication. Good writers, in my experience, are not necessarily good speakers, and the same holds in the other direction. George's books were basically his lectures; however his greatest lectures, in my view, were given in the 1970s, which was the time he was writing." None of the books is still in print but they can sometimes be found in second-hand bookshops.

In the light of all this activity it is surprising that Sir George Trevelyan's diary had any space left at all, but in fact there were not only New Age concerns. Back home in Shropshire, as chairman of the local branch of the Civic Society, he presided over the unveiling of the restored Bear Steps Cottages and Hall in Shrewsbury by Sir Clough Williams-Ellis, creator of the fantastical seaside village of Portmeirion, on the coast of North Wales. Bear Steps was the first major project achieved by the Civic Society. The preservation of historic buildings and an involvement with local matters were still dear to George's heart. Friends also recall happy social visits, although usually with a local teaching purpose. He never arrived at households where there were children without bringing very good quality toy animals, such as bears or pandas. Apparently he bought these at craft fairs whenever he happened to see them, and always had a stock at home to take as presents. Children remember him as a story-teller, and a lively speaker of poems. Adults say he was a delightful guest, always good-humoured, "wonderful to listen to and spouting phenomenal poetry *even at breakfast!*" There were also exploits with mountains, although by this time Sir George sometimes had to be pushed up them, and to make the descents backwards.

How someone with George's serious illness could so eagerly and energetically carry on with so much activity has been variously explained. Some say the naturopathic diet kept him functioning, others that it was more or less faith alone. He himself believed he had a mission to continue teaching, and a huge enthusiasm for it. His determination and positive outlook did not allow him to regret lost abilities or waste time considering the loss of mountaineering or running. In every day there was too much to do that was exciting and vital for George to allow himself to become tangled up by the pain or nuisance of his physical difficulties. When he needed to go somewhere to speak, generally someone would drive him. When he needed to climb stairs or steps someone might have to push him to the top. Much more often, however, he would force himself to do things unaided. The determination that characterized the last part of his life is another aspect of the George Trevelyan legend. Nothing short of death itself could stop his effort, and in some people's minds, not even that. There is another important factor. People engaged in work which comes under the heading of healing, in however broad a definition of the word, are energized by it. People who work with audiences are energized by that: actors and comedians receive in attention and applause some of the energy they have given out as entertainment. George gained vitality from all of his efforts, since effort creates energy for further effort.

The synthesis of legend with various mystery traditions increasingly found expression in Wrekin programmes. At a course on Michael, Easter, and the Quest for the Grail with The Christian Community in Bristol, George took the Parsifal story forward, linking Parsifal with the Arthurian knights and with Archangel Michael.

George had emphasised that the motto of the Grail Knight is, "Work upon yourself and save the world," and he had a renewed certainty that although it was right to co-operate with the Sufis and with all religions (they have much to teach), "it is Anthroposophy and the Cosmic Christ that is what we are about. What is happening is a Cosmic Christ process but is not bound to any religion. We can no longer be tied to sects and religions."

In March 1973 he ran a course on Eastern Wisdom and Western Spiritual Science, with Francis Edmunds of Emerson College, and Reshad Feild. At The Cosmic Christ conference run by Canon Spink of Coventry Cathedral on Iona, George was the main lecturer. In July came The Concept of the Cosmic Christ in the New Age at Nottingham University. George lectured with Russell Evans and Dr Thomas Weihs, two prominent students of Rudolf Steiner's Spiritual Science. Numbers began to increase for the esoteric subjects: 400 people came to the public meeting on Spiritual Awakening in Our Time. The same year took in another Death and Becoming, the Sufi mystic Reshad Feild on the esoteric stream of Islam, a weekend on Developing the Inner Senses, Keith Critchlow on the big questions of Sacred Geometry, and two which were designed specially for younger people and went under the general heading Living in a Changing World.

In November 1973 Father Andrew Glazewski gave the opening session on a Wrekin Trust course at Hawkwood College, and then, in the presence of Gordon Barker and Bernard Nesfield-Cookson, quite suddenly he died. Gordon and Bernard continued his course and its participants reported that they were constantly aware of his presence among them. Andrew Glazewski had long wanted to see the foundation of a University of the Spirit; some time after his death the idea metamorphosed into the Scientific and Medical Network. George felt that his death strengthened the whole movement, in that he could be expected to have a greater input from the spiritual worlds than he could when he was in his earthly body. George talked of Andrew Glazewski on the final day, giving a summary of what he saw was happening and of Andrew's part in it.

The movement, if that is the correct description of this disparate effort, reassessed itself constantly. During its first few years the Wrekin Trust had struggled to its feet, getting by on gifts and willing help. George took no lecture fee and other lecturers often worked for reduced fees. The Trust made available the best possible facilities to the greatest number of people, reducing their charges to less well-off people and asking only for an annual subscription of £3. (Financially, the organization was flying by the seat of its pants. In July, the AGM noted that the Easter Retreat had made a profit of £29.40 and the course on The Arts as Gateway for the Spirit had lost 60p.) The Newsletter published cheering information about the successes of people doing similar work or investigating similar subjects. It also discussed the skills of running groups. George said, "I stress the profound importance of the making of groups and centres across the country." He believed the new thinking, the new, positive mental energy, needed new channels through which to flow.

The Newsletter reviewed books in the subject area and in 1973 reported that Magnus Magnusson had made a film for Scottish Television about Findhorn, and the community's involvement with devas and nature spirits. Summarizing the first three Wrekin Trust years, although Sir George believed, "this may well be the apocalypse," he also recorded: "Many go away from our weekends bold in heart and joyful of soul." In those early years the Trust had put on 78 courses, about 29 a year: a sturdy start, to say the least. The programme continued in similar vein. In a couple of years, George determined that he wanted to write and do lecture tours instead of organizing courses, and he handed over the administration. In time he visited many parts of Europe, Scandinavia, the USA and South Africa. He generally had someone to help him on these tours, often Rhoda Cowen or Geseke Clark.

In January, 1974, George had to have an operation in Reading Hospital. He was fit long before his doctors had expected and returned to work with new strength and determination, and a greater clarity of mind. As always, he made use of an enforced time of withdrawal. He found such periods away from his working environment invaluable for meditation and review, and for receiving intuitive information about his next moves. This period of illness had prepared him to partially free himself from the Wrekin Trust and he felt ready to do more, to travel and lecture more widely. In the coming years he would make many tours throughout Europe, in America and in South Africa, and when the time came, he was able to let the Wrekin Trust go, just as he had let go of Wallington and Attingham.

In March there was an important course at Reading University on The Polluted Planet and the Living Spirit with Lady Eve Balfour, Dr E.F. Schumacher, Ralph Verney, Ogilvie Crombie, John Soper, Lady Chance and George Trevelyan. At the time it was unusual to link the fields of ecology and spiritual awakening but ever since the Soil Association conferences at Attingham, George had been as convinced as his friends Eve Balfour and Cynthia Chance that it must be done. He said, "if man could learn to co-operate with spiritual energies and higher intelligence, there is great hope that pollution could be overcome and the planet regenerated." Therefore he drew together speakers who represented a deep understanding of the practical situation and those seeing it as a spiritual challenge to all the people of the world.

Three years after the foundation of the Trust, with the mailing list standing at 3,000, a new figure entered it who was to have a profound effect on its direction. This was Malcolm Lazarus, whom Sir George Trevelyan first encountered on 23 July, 1974, at a conference at St John's, Smith Square in London. George said that he noticed in the audience during the afternoon someone he was sure had not been there in the morning, "bearded, in jeans, with an aureole of long dark hair. I sought him out in the tea break... I asked him, 'What are you doing tomorrow?' and he replied, 'Coming to see you'." There seemed to be an immediate bond between the two men. Malcolm Lazarus had been a designer and a Fellow of the Royal Society of Arts and was at that time at something of a loose end. A couple of months later he went to Shropshire to see George, the Wrekin Trust team and the office, and within a short while he had moved into the offices and was involving himself with the work. Over time it became clear to George that Malcolm Lazarus would be able to help take the Trust into a wider sphere. He had a real grasp of business, as well as knowledge of the fields in which the Trust was active and an ability to attract well-known speakers to it. George was aware that his own work was lecturing. His physical and mental energy seemed to be improving by leaps and bounds; he had been back up to Northumberland where he had excelled himself with enthusiasm and contacts with people. He was more than happy to hand over the business side to Malcolm Lazarus, who had a much greater flair for it. Hertha Larive, who had joined the Wrekin Trust mailing list a while earlier, noticed a difference. "Malcolm Lazarus brought a professional standard in," she says, "important names, known speakers. He must have done a good deal of homework to get them. They got big audiences, they became financially secure. He was constantly introducing new people, new ideas. They were very successful until the regional groups started, sort of mini-Wrekins, which tended to cut down attendances at the main events."

George was concerned about the importance to the work of the Trust of the healthy growth of local groups, and wrote about it in the Newsletter. "I stress again the profound importance now of the linking of groups and centres across the country. The invisible but palpable pressure of the Coming Light needs channels through which it can flow." He was also concerned about the importance of the setting in which these efforts took place. "Every Wrekin Trust conference or meeting is to be seen as a focal point in which the worlds, visible and invisible, can blend together." He spoke frequently of angelic worlds and of the need to provide hospitable environments in which they could work.

For the Michaelmas Festival in September, A Pilgrimage to Cornwall was advertised; the first on a Wrekin Trust programme. George Trevelyan was aware of the significance of pilgrimages to *centres of power*, by which is meant places where the focus of earth energies are believed to connect, not only with each other, but also with power sources beyond. He was among the first to recognize that the relationship between human beings and the planet on which they live needed to be harmonized, and he saw pilgrimage as a means to provide simultaneously a spiritual experience. The West Country is famous for its extensive mythology, which is linked with that of Brittany. The history of the Knights Templar, mystical Celtic legends and ceremonies, the presence of ley lines, testify to extraordinary magnetic activity.

Ley lines are aligned to movements of the sun and were used in Celtic times and before to calculate dates. One of the most important runs from the centre of power at St Michael's Mount to that in Bury St Edmunds, in East Anglia. There is also a link between St Michael's Mount and Mont St Michel in Brittany. Many Michaelmas pilgrimages concentrate on the links between three landscape temples: Glastonbury Zodiac, Dartingon, and Land's End. Landscape temples were described by George as, "vortices of power and light which mark where Heaven and Earth meet, where ethereal space unites with the field of gravity... it reaches out to Infinity." Cornwall was thus a clear choice for pilgrimage even without George's Trevelyan family connection, although George additionally had strong sense of relationship with his roots. He wrote in the programme, "The Archangel Michael, Lord of the Cosmic Intelligence, is the Regent of the Forces of Light in this age. The Festival of Michael now holds a new relevance for mankind," and, "Michaelmas is a festival for the future. We are called to bring it to birth in our own initiative."

Reclamation of some of the means of approaching ancient wisdom is another vital element in the work of the Wrekin Trust. George wrote, "We may (indeed must) begin *consciously* to move in the landscape with our psychic feelers out. There is Being in everything. The elemental world is there in every aspect of the nature kingdoms. We may look beyond the usual aspects of nature-study to 'see' with the eye of the mind the life within trees, plants, rocks, birds, clouds, mountains. Look into the hill and feel the response stirring in your own soul, which is really the dormant Being of the Hill stirring at the contact of your consciousness, the touch of your thought-beam." His notion of the life-force within every part of creation is one which some find difficult to grasp, but is essential to at least one interpretation of Gaia theory.

George made a report of this pilgrimage.

Human initiative is essential if the Michaelic thinker is to flower in our lives, for Michael will do nothing to interfere with human freedom as man learns to become a creative co-worker with the Divine Power. Thus we can recognize that if we can generate soul courage, joy and tranquillity, lifting towards imaginative and intuitive knowledge, we shall be supported and strengthened by the Power of Michael, the Great Mediator of the Christ Power. But for this to happen we must first awaken to the reality of this great Archangelic Being and learn to invoke his help. He is the Patron Saint of Cornwall and St Michael's Mount is his chief shrine among the many sacred points dedicated to him. Thus we took our pilgrimage to Marazion opposite the Mount. The first day we made our pilgrimage up the Mount and took part in the Harvest Festival service in the chapel. In a series of lectures I discussed the meaning of Michaelmas and of the Michael Impulse in our time in relation to the Cosmic Christ and the meaning of the Coming of Arthur.

In this context the significance of Michaelmas was concerned with the dedication of the lives of all the pilgrims to the service of God, for Michael and Jesus. The Mount itself is regarded as a huge energy vortex for the country and for Europe. Archangel Michael is said to have been seen on it; there is even a legend that Joseph of Arimathea visited it. Irish pilgrims used to stop there on their way to the sacred places in Brittany; other travelling pilgrims traded in Cornish cream and tin for their journeys. Even people with no perception of sacred sites realize that St Michael's Mount is an extraordinary and power- ful place.

The pilgrimage included lectures, a walk to St Michael's Mount, and a pilgrimage up Chapel Caen Brea led by the Bishop of Truro. Beth Holman now leads the local pilgrimages and used to host the ones led by Sir George. She says of the climb: "I have felt the energy of the Divine come down and smite the mountain and ricochet through the country. You are aware of the Light, and of the huge energy with which it comes. You can send it to wherever it is needed." Pilgrims have dif- ferent expectations. Rosemary Warner says, "I just listen to what might be told to my unconscious mind. Some people go instead with a par- ticular purpose. You feel the need to do it, and it does have an effect. The intention is the healing of the landscape; stone circles may have had this function. Sir George was one of the early thinkers in these areas. It has a profound effect on me, and it may change much bigger things."

Participants, perhaps especially Sir George himself, say that they are re-energized by doing this work. Archangel Michael is invoked, who in mythology led the other angels against evil and now exorcises evil influence and fear. Many practices that survived into the Christian church such as Harvest Festival, as well as hymns in the vein of *We plough the fields and scatter*, recall earlier observations such as thank- ing the pagan gods and blessing the ground before planting. Some of them are still observed in country places, with or without New Age input.

At the end of the first pilgrimage to St Michael's Mount, a poetry recital and meditation were given at the superb little Minack Theatre which perches on the clifftop above the sea, a setting reminiscent of ancient Greece. The stones to build it were carried up singly from the beach by Rowena Cade; she is remembered for her total dedication to the task. On such occasions Sir George would give speeches from *The Tempest* and *The Merchant of Venice*, always ending with "Ye hosts angelic." It is a powerful picture, the vigorous, aging aristocrat with the perfect voice, giving, "The quality of mercy is not strained," or perhaps:

... I have bedimm'd
The noontide sun, call'd forth the mutinous winds,
And twixt the green sea and the azured vault
Set roaring war: to the dread rattling thunder
Have I given fire and rifted Jove's stout oak
With his own bolt; the strong-based promontory
Have I made shake and by the spurs pluck'd up
The pine and cedar: graves at my command
Have waked their sleepers, oped, and let 'em forth
By my so potent art.

In closing the first Wrekin pilgrimage, George celebrated not only the place but also the memory of the founder of the Lamplighter Movement and the Chalice Well Trust. "I would close in doing honour to our friend Wellesley Tudor Pole, that great servant of Michael and the Christ, who in his writings urged us to revive a pilgrimage whenever we visited our Cathedrals and holy places and above all to recognize that Cornwall, as the great area in Britain dedicated to Michael, may once again become a great source for the spreading of the light and power of the Revealer of the Word."

Of pilgrimage itself Sir George Trevelyan spoke often: "Tourism has debased pilgrimage in an age which is largely agnostic and on the quest for pleasure and diversion. This is a picture of our state of consciousness. But that consciousness is undergoing the most notable change which is truly epoch-making in its significance. The Holistic World View is emerging in our generation, a veritable reversal of the materialistic, mechanistic and reductionist picture of the universe discovered by our grandfathers ... [giving] place to a revival of the Ancient Wisdom, which grasped that the Universe is an affair of Mind, a vast, harmonious continuance of Thought poured out from the mind of the Creator." One of Sir George's central tenets was: "The Whole is Holy."

He also believed, "we are rediscovering the Holy Mountains and the Landscape Temples. By Temple we mean a structure which enables a Divine Being to operate in the heavier density of the Earth plane ... The Egyptian Temple has clearly the same pattern of chakras as is found in the human body, and the same is true of the Gothic Cathedral ... We see that the human body with its psychic centres is truly a temple into which the Divine Spark of the immortal, imperishable Ego can descend to operate with creative will on earth." (The term Ego when used by adherents to Rudolf Steiner means the inner person, not, as more commonly, the outer personality.)

Sir George had much to say on the importance of place to the total effort. "Every Wrekin Trust conference or meeting is to be seen as a focal point in which the worlds, visible and invisible, can blend together. Those whose faculties of vision are developed can often bear out that the conferences draw down many beings from the angelic worlds and from our friends now sojourning on higher places. Such contact is vitally important. We have to raise our vibrations."

CHAPTER 7

Last Years

Never the spirit was born; the spirit shall cease to be never,
Never was time it was not; end and beginning are dreams.
Bhagavad Gita

In early February, 1975, two big steps were made. George made a four-day tour of the south of England and talked to about a thousand people, and the Reverend Peter Dewey set up the Bridge Trust, to try to make New Age groups and interests comprehensible to the conventional world. Initially it had forty members, of whom Janice Dolley was one. She recalls, "a small association that was bringing some of the ideas into practical action, recognizing perhaps that things like meditation, organic food and farming, group endeavour and community living needed to become part of every day." George's tour was made in the missionary spirit of reaching as large an audience as possible and it came as the Trust was showing signs of needing change. The three-year lease of the first premises was expiring and Lady Trevelyan wanted to move to Ross-on-Wye to be near their daughter, since George was away from home so much. Malcolm Lazarus could move anywhere; Ruth Bell was no longer well enough for full-time work. It was time for a reshuffle.

The situation was resolved by moving the Trust and George to Herefordshire, and Ruth Bell leaving to join the Findhorn Community. George and Helen moved into May Tree Cottage, in the village of Upton Bishop, near Ross-on-Wye in Herefordshire. The Wrekin Trust appointed the astrologer Edward Matchett to the position of co-director. With Sir George, he wrote *Twelve Seats at the Round Table.*[1]

This mystical appreciation of the zodiac drew on the imagery of the legendary Round Table of King Arthur and related it to the rose windows of the Christian cathedrals and abbeys, especially those in France, where the Grail legends originate. It provided meditations and exercises for self and group development. It offers a rare example of

George collaborating on a book: he wrote with Pir Vilayat Khan on occasion, but was more often a lone writer. *Twelve Seats at the Round Table* is no longer in print, but its perception of the twelve seats corresponding with the signs of the zodiac and their karmic progress is insightful and unusual. There are esoteric exercises for each star sign. Subjects of Pisces, for example, are characterized as Oneness Re-established after the Duality of the Beginning of Creation, and their life's work defined as, "to ensure that thought and action is sufficiently mature and strong."

Otherwise the year was concerned as usual with furthering existing efforts and broadening them. *Subtle Attunement of the Senses, Whole Food for Health, Releasing the Self* (an introduction to transpersonal psychology) were among the offerings on the programme. There was also a new symbol for the Wrekin Trust: a three-dimensional version of the Celtic cross of the risen Christ. This re-interpretation, known as the Cosmic Cross,was understood by Sir George Trevelyan to extend the original meaning to include light emanating from the heart chakra throughout each human being and out to wherever it was needed. At the same time, the Round Table meetings concerned themselves with the heart of the organization, its essence, its purpose, and what should be radiating from it. More than a policy-creating body, this group was set up to maintain integrity. Their prayer and intention was: "lift our understanding through thoughts [lectures], our imagination through music, poetry and the visual image, our hearts through good companionship."

So far the work of the Trust had become known within a fairly closed circuit; gathering subscribers to the mailing list and generating interest within the existing coterie. The tours, pilgrimages, conferences and sacred journeys had spoken to the converted. Single day events began to be organized by local groups; there was a conference at Findhorn. For Janice Dolley and others with family obligations, events such as these could only be attended once a year, but Mrs Dolley says, "Frequently those of us listening felt uplifted in thought and inspiration. At one weekend a few of us around the dinner table shared the need for small centres of light to be linked together. The idea of networking was just beginning." It was defined as meeting people to discover new insights through conversation and activity, also meeting psychically in a sort of mental network. (A more traditional description might be a community of prayer.) In the Newsletter of August, 1974, Sir George had written: "I stress again the profound importance now of the linking of groups and centres across the country. The invisible but palpable pressure of the Coming Light needs channels through which it can flow." The subscription list expanded, the local groups and links between them continued as George wished, and after another year, the whole thing began to go public.

In 1976 the first Mind, Body and Spirit Festival was held at Olympia in west London, and George and his friends were energetic movers behind it. Olympia is one of the largest exhibition halls in the country and the Festival's existence there acknowledged a huge expansion of interest in the ideas and products of what became abbreviated to MBS (initials applied to publishing, and alternative therapeutic practices and products). At last, they were on general release. For this first Mind, Body and Spirit Festival George gave a rousing opening speech, rallying the people with his insistence on wakefulness in an era of unprecedented upheaval. "There is such a short time and so very much to be done," was his cry, and: "the forces of integration are also very much at work ... they need to be fed with the involvement of each one of us ... society is being transformed from within by an evolutionary change that is taking place within the individual ... a quantum leap in consciousness becomes possible, a rebirth through which we may become *homo-universalis.*" As always, people who heard him testify to the extraordinary force of his delivery and to the marvellous, powerful blue of his eyes. He thought the Festival offered, "a chance for ordinary people to transform themselves into extraordinary people by discovering their true selves," and to see that "life on earth is truly a sacred adventure."

The sacred adventure could be said to have continued at Findhorn, with David Spangler talking on Aquarian Age Self-Consciousness; and elsewhere with the Trust's first conferences on Reincarnation; and on Astrology and Psychology, which were increasingly being linked. Other notable conferences that year included The Art of Living Spirit in Action; and The Higher Vibrational Experience. These were terms and topics which had been thriving among members of the alternative society, just waiting to break the surface. In the mid-1970s, events such as the Mind Body and Spirit Festival and the work of the newly visible Findhorn Foundation were bringing them to public attention.

Thus passed the first five years of the Wrekin Trust. Organizations with similar aspirations had joined the field, but the Trust was still by far the most comprehensive. Its pool of high-minded new thinkers, scientists, artists, healers and meditators was increasing. Their work

combined for the purpose of creating George's quantum leap in consciousness, a leap which appeared to require only adjustments to previous assumptions, and yet carried massive implications. Accepting,
for example, the George dictum, "we are all a droplet of God" — a
pretty notion — brought responsibility for excellence in thought,
word and deed. Taking proper responsibility for the natural environment meant altering lifelong assumptions about personal consumption
and consequently about ambition and aspiration. Responsibility for the
physical and emotional health not only of the individual but also of the
rest of the world places a massively different demand upon people
brought up to see themselves as individual competitors within it.
George asked for nothing less than total dedication to ideal.

In January 1977, he went with Peter Caddy to California. The two
men had been invited as guest lecturers to the annual convention of the
International Co-operation Council, an association of New Age organizations. George wrote, "[we] addressed a number of meetings and
seminars in which we found that Peter and I made a good and complementary team, he talking about Findhorn and I setting it in the broad
context of a new age vision ... We also flew to San Francisco for a
weekend mounted by David Spangler and the Lorian Association with
audiences of over 1,000." George wrote, "It was an experience to realize how much is bursting out in California." Why the West Coast of
America was — and remains — so entranced with New Age ideas is
not really known. On that occasion at any rate there must have been
some piquancy in the prospect of an aged English aristocrat being the
bearer of such revolutionary tidings.

The same year he published, with Belle Valerie Gaunt, *A Tent in
which to pass a Winter's Night*, which prefigured *Magic Casements* in
its treatment of the importance of poetry to intuitive, mystical and esoteric understanding. There were several lecture tours, including to the
Midlands and Edinburgh. As George was setting up his south of
England series he happened to visit Rhoda Cowen. New Age people
believe there is no such thing as chance, everything is foreordained and
happens at the time it is meant to, but coincidence or fate, this was a
particularly happy meeting. George had planned to drive for ten days
along the south coast from Chichester to Dover, lecturing in different
towns, and staying with different friends. When he explained this to
Mrs Cowen she said impulsively, "But you can't do this alone — driving all day, and speaking every night — and what happens if the car
breaks down?" Apparently he shrugged and said there was no one to

help. The two consulted their diaries and found that Rhoda Cowen could manage the same period. In the event they took a fortnight, and stayed in the big houses of the localities. She loved their journeys. "Great fun! George was so excited, we said we'd drive the whole of the south of England! Each place was different. He talked to groups collected by local people and there was always a bigger crowd assembled than the room could take... All these hostesses who had arranged it were longing to talk to George, waiting for him to arrive. Instead, they got great slabs of me! My job was to give him a chance to rest before he spoke so I did everything I could to get him some peace; I helped them cook the supper, I cut up vegetables, and I simply babbled away, so he could get away upstairs and change. It was hard work doing all that every night. We always stayed with people socially — and they always had their own poetry they wanted him to read.

"In point of fact, I don't think he could have done it without me! Every five minutes people wanted to come and see him, and I tried to extricate him to have a swim or get some exercise. All the hazards of travel became quite tiring at times, the car broke down, and so forth, and we had to hire another. It was really a wonderful experience for us both. I found it stimulating, for what he talked about was precisely the ideas that were fermenting in the 1960s — fresh concepts that fascinated and startled me... I think the strongest thing that came through his speaking was his total sincerity. I had a first cousin, a very high-up civil servant, very good brain, and I told him how George spoke. Ronald came to hear George and was flabbergasted at the power and flow. He said, 'This is *extraordinary*!' From him, that was quite a tribute."

Mrs Cowen's cousin Ronald was one of many. It is impossible to say often enough how powerful was George's lecturing, or to convey by listing the elements that composed it, how compelling was the totality of the experience for so many people. George was aware of it, and enjoyed and cherished it as a wonderful gift. Mrs Cowen says, "I look back on him not as a writer, but as a lecturer, as his lectures were so intensely alive." Nick Rose, once a Findhorn resident, attended many of Sir George's talks. "He took his world with him," he says, and not only to the homes of well-off acquaintances, but everywhere. "He recreated it in some dreary little spots, and with struggling little groups, his arrival always brought a spark. He was uplifting, he had time for everybody, he was so supportive."

For the best part of the next twenty years, George lectured, and went on speaking tours and dedicated pilgrimages. The familiar places were regularly visited, Findhorn high on the list, but new arenas in Europe and elsewhere were important too. In time they included several Scandinavian countries and France, where the significant sacred sites include many associated with Cathars and Rosicrucians. He tended to go to places of spiritual significance, such as ley lines. He spoke at gatherings, he wrote books, he led meditations, and he chaired conferences. He did it all from a profound sense of vocation.

With Rhoda Cowen Sir George made two visits to South Africa, spoke to many groups, and somehow, to the wonder of all who witnessed it, managed an impossible climb. "He started to do speaking tours and I went on trips abroad with him, listened twice a day sometimes to what he had to say," says Mrs Cowen. "At first I thought, shall I take some knitting to fend off boredom? — but he always brought a different spark. No matter how often I heard him, there was something new to listen to. There's no doubt that George opened the doors of perception for hundreds of people — thousands!" In time, says Mrs Cowen, they went to "Norway, Sweden, Denmark — not much France, a lot in Germany." She testifies to the richness of the experience for both of them, as well as for the people who were entranced by the blend of traditional, aristocratic English gentleman with humble spiritual guide and seer.

Back in Britain, people around the country who had heard George Trevelyan or who had an association with him began to form small spiritually oriented groups. This was something George had been keen on for some time, partly because of the difficulty of people travelling distances to attend Wrekin events, partly because he believed that much of the work of the new awakening had to be done individually and constantly, with only occasional input from external stimuli. However, the forming of separate groups all over the country also caused some fragmentation of the original association. Many of them still continue. Among them is one which is run by Geseke Clark. She describes her Centre for Spiritual Education as a bridge: — for people; between old and new ideas; and between England and Germany. Mrs Clark advises people who wish to set up such a group to have enthusiasm and a light-hearted attitude because things don't always go according to plan; she recommends personal approaches to speakers, the use of a big front room or a village hall, and the advantages of working with other local groups. Sir George himself opened her house as a spiritual centre in 1991 and often visited it, and she remembers how well he communicated with her groups of young German students. She says, "You couldn't ignore the fact that George had a good education — nor could you ignore his teaching. He had such a good touch across all classes. Many people of the middle classes, academia and so on, would talk about the New Age as nebulous, possibly even occult. What he did was make it respectable. He made it so people of education or upbringing could listen. He had a pioneering quality, the same as his father."

It wasn't always serious, however. One supper time, for the sake of international understanding, Mrs Clark offered a group of German visitors a traditional English Christmas pudding. It was not Christmas but the pudding was a fine one that she had in her cupboard, and she explained its origin and symbolism, the making of it and the ingredients. Then she lit the brandy, flamed the pudding and sent the portions round. For fun, Geseke Clark passed a note to her neighbour George which said, "between you and me, this pudding is two-and-a-half years old." Christmas pudding, of course, is practically immortal. The meal continued, and after a time, a young German girl sitting opposite her looked up and said, "Geseke, what does it mean, 'between you and me'?" George had passed the note to his neighbour and it had travelled halfway round the table. He could never resist a tease. Mrs Clark loved the naughty side of Sir George as well as the serious, ethereal side. "He was fun," she says, "he brought lightness always."

A couple of years after the first Mind Body and Spirit Festival came the first Mystics and Scientists conference, masterminded by Malcolm Lazarus and George Trevelyan. The first programme proclaimed: "the scientific mind can pass through the door of the infinitesimal into the infinite. The mystic by going within and entering a state of sense-free perception can discover that he is part of all that is. The sub-atomic physicist using methods of observation that go beyond ordinary perception, experiences reality as a harmonious organic whole." Furthermore, "the importance of this scientific breakthrough into a model of reality that is essentially spiritual in nature cannot be overstressed." Five main areas of investigation were identified: cosmology, physics, biology and the Gaia hypothesis, consciousness and psychology, mysticism and spirituality. Notable conferences considered music and mathematics, the evolution of consciousness, unification and the search for wholeness. In time the event was taken over by the Scientific and Medical Network, and organized by David Lorimer, an academic and an old Etonian with a background similar to that of Sir George.

David Lorimer taught at Winchester College, then received inspiration which made him change direction towards the investigation of the interplay between the material and spiritual worlds. The intention is to discover the common ground between rational and intuitive perception; longer term there is an aspiration towards synthesis.

The Wrekin Trust's report of its first twelve years describes the Mystics and Scientists Conference: "Its purpose is to work towards developing a more complete model of the nature of reality out of which it is hoped that man's relationship to himself and his planet will fundamentally change." Malcolm Lazarus noted that, "George Trevelyan was fond of saying that political change only scraped the surface and that the only change of real value was an inner willed change in consciousness. I saw ... that a new rationale for experiencing ourselves through the exploration of mystical, scientific and artistic experience could contribute to such a change. For myself, the Mystics and Scientists conferences became increasingly intellectually challenging... Stretching my mind to embrace concepts that were being articulated by some of the great minds of our time was a spiritual discipline in itself." The inner willed change in consciousness was to come from synthesis, a different quality of comprehension, a different perception of material and other worlds.

In their annual weekend conference they may consider topics such as the relationship between art and physics; dreams and visions; parapsychology; the symbolism of medieval religious art; and the contrast between the tasks of reading (sequential, scientific) with interpreting pictorially based information. Scientists of the calibre of Sir John Eccles, who talks about consciousness; and Richard Gregory, who discusses the occasional failure of the intelligent creation of the external world, with its implication that phenomenology, or what is seen, is not always adequate in science, consider the boundaries of scientific understanding. Others may look at extended, intuitively perceived possibilities within events and phenomena which have a culturally accepted meaning. Much of this has a clear relationship with George's own observations, for example in his book *The Active Eye in Architecture*, which was published in the '70s. Like Goethe, George Trevelyan saw sacred architecture as a growing organism, transcending solidity and soaring into lightness and transparency. James Lovelock, Frederick Hoyle, and Bede Griffiths, are among the many luminaries who spoke at such events.

Of the Mystics and Scientists synthesis George wrote in the Wrekin Newsletter:

> The joining of these twin streams of human experience will
> have a profound effect ... We are witnessing the breakdown
> of a culture based on the Newtonian concept of the
> materialistic nature of matter and the re-emergence of the
> essential spiritual vision held by mystics. A vision
> strengthened and confirmed by the findings of sub-nuclear
> physicists who experience reality as a harmonious organic
> whole ... For those who hold a spiritual viewpoint it is
> tremendously heartening to find that several aspects of its
> deeper truths are now scientifically provable and this ...
> points the way to the development of a society based on a
> more realistic understanding of human life.

Further efforts at the end of the first decade of George's hyperactive
retirement included the publication of *Magic Casements*, a beautiful
collection of poems and commentary. George always knew that poetry
could express far more than prose, bearing subliminal sense beyond the
beauty of the words. In his own superb rendition of famous poems he
brought the realization of this thought into the minds of his listeners.
Magic Casements summarized his perception:

> In 1987, two days after Christmas, the Christ impulse simply
> plummeted into me. It was the Power of Love. I discovered
> then the simple recipe that I try to teach people, that one can
> jettison from the vocabulary all wor ds of criticism negativity,
> dislike, fear, scandal. Just drop a third of the vocabulary. This
> does not mean that one automatically has all positive qualities
> but it does mean that the negative moods are likely to go and
> find somebody else, because they get rather bored. I don't think
> I have said any word of criticism against anybody since 1987.
> That has changed my life: forgiveness comes with it. Also, that
> change creates a vehicle into which the Christ light can come.
> It is an insult to invite Him to come and then be negative
> towards anybody else. The Inner King, which is Christ, could
> never enter the inner castle if there was any space for nasty
> thoughts about other people. (*Kindred Spirit*)

George defined once more what he meant by the Cosmic Christ. "The
Cosmic Christ, the heart principle of Divinity, chose to enter the prepared vehicle of Jesus at the baptism in Jordan. In the following years

it was no longer Jesus speaking but the Christ speaking... What is happeningnow is that once again the Christ, the Cosmic Christ, the heart Power of God, is being released on Earth ... It is time to claim our Christhood."

The 1980s: back to the Cotswolds

The new decade brought a change of focus and of location for George and Helen. In 1981, Helen Trevelyan found that since George's lecture programme took him away from home for much of the time, she wished to move back to the Cotswolds, nearer their daughter Catriona. George said that he did not want to run courses any more, so he stopped doing it. They moved. This time George and Helen had part of Catriona's huge, beautiful Cotswold vicarage, and filled it with many beautiful pieces of furniture of George's own manufacture or design. The way to George's room was past a five-foot mosaic of a unicorn. George remarked to a magazine interviewer, "Do you see in our national coat of arms, his crown has fallen around his neck? Now, we should re-crown him, because we're becoming a unicorn nation — the courage of the rampant lion must be transmuted by the purified intelligence and spiritual vision of the unicorn." The large upstairs writing room contained not only all his books and papers but also his walnut desk and chairs, and an octagonal book table made by Eric Sharpe, also of the Gimson workshop. There was a stained glass angel in the window pane, made by the artist Jasper Kettlewell.

Coincidentally, this move brought him back in touch with Ruth Bell, who in 1977 had married the lately widowed Bernard Nesfield-Cookson and was running Hawkwood College with him. (George had been a Hawkwood trustee since Bernard and his wife Eileen arrived there in 1970.) Catriona was married and had a son called Jack, with whom George formed a great friendship, often reading stories to him at night-time before going out to lecture, and occasionally returning to find Jack still engrossed in reading or sometimes re-telling the tales himself. His mother remembers, "a little boy with big eyes" waiting for George to come home again. Apparently if she told Jack it was time to go to sleep he would reply that he still had something to talk to George about, and naturally when George reappeared from speaking, he would back him up.

In the year of his move back to the Cotswolds, George Trevelyan came into direct contact with one or two people of high spiritual importance, among them the Dalai Llama, with whom he had an audience on July 1st. Of this period in his life George said that although he was too old to do any organization he could say, "Give me an audience of any size and the energy flows." The early eighties saw many more people attracted to the New Age movement, and increasing international recognition. In 1983 Sir George Trevelyan with Malcolm Lazarus travelled to Sweden to accept the Right Livelihood Award on behalf of the Wrekin Trust, for "work forming an essential contribution to making life more whole, healing our planet and uplifting humanity." This award is known as the alternative Nobel Prize and is given to organizations and not individuals, however the panel referred to Sir George's contribution to "educating the adult spiritto a new non-materialistic vision of human nature." At the ceremony the originator of the award, Jakob von Uexkull, said, "The movement towards a more complete vision of reality and human nature is the fastest growing development in the world today. At the crest of this wave stands Sir George Trevelyan and the Wrekin Trust, one of the major influences in the revolution of thinking which is beginning to enlighten the world."

In that year's summer Newsletter, George referred to the transformational journey necessary for the survival of mankind, and said that the Trust need no longer put on introductory and general courses but should develop a series of seminars to "start people working at their own transformation." He called this phase three, phase one having been Attingham, two early Wrekin, and three later Wrekin. The Transformational Journey courses that were part of the consequence of this change were organized and conducted by Malcolm Lazarus. They were intense and complex, preparing participants for "the exploration of their psychological and spiritual potential and the development of higher states of awareness." Much of the work was based upon myth. The story of Icarus, for example, popularly interpreted as a simple warning against trying to fly too high and thus falling and drowning (pride comes before a fall), would be seen as an event demonstrating the necessity for spirit (celestial, elevated) to rediscover the material world (the sea of the unconscious mind) in order to balance the two. The use of metaphor for the participants' individual efforts offered opportunities for deep investigation. Malcolm Lazarus regards psycho spiritual experience as, "something to do with tapping inner knowledge which leads to psychological understanding. Spiritual knowledge unrelated to psychological understanding is incomplete, and vice versa." He speaks of the importance of "achieving a state of consciousness usually cut off by the personality — getting yourself out of the way." In terms of the development of the work of the Wrekin Trust, Malcolm Lazarus recalls that he wrote "all sorts of letters" on behalf of Sir George, who had said to him, "Use my name as much as you like." The second decade brought in broader influences and better-known speakers, and, for a time, attendances rose. Hertha Larive, a Wrekin trustee since 1981, says that during this time the quality of the lecturing improved and for a while the Trust was also financially successful.

One of George's most notable tours was to South Africa in 1983, accompanied by Rhoda Cowen, who was free to travel since her husband had died two years before. According to custom, George spoke to and inspired many interested people, mostly in universities. Mrs Cowen enjoyed the travelling a great deal, and wrote:

> From Johannesburg we had a glimpse into the Drakensburg
> mountains, then full of flowers, and later camped in a game
> reserve where lions were often around our hut, and we saw,
> quite close, zebra, giraffe, elephant and rhinoceros roaming
> around, and the very dangerous white rhino ... Over the
> camp-fire in the hot close night we listened to the stillness
> and many wild animal calls, while the game warden and
> George shared their favourite poetry quotations.[2]

They were away for three weeks and Rhoda had anticipated boredom from listening to George once or twice a day, but says, "each time was different and like meeting a different person." Of his fabled speaking powers she wrote:

And what extraordinary oratory it was! An hour without notes, his ideas bubbling and sparkling, and carried ... into different fields by constant quotations ... The bigger the audiences the greater the challenge to him, and he loved to raise his powerful actor's voice to reach the very back row. Or we might travel a long way only to find a handful, when he spoke just as faithfully and with as much vigour.

The suggestion that he only spoke to the white population is only marginally refuted by a talk organized by the Emissaries of Divine Light of Johannesburg group. Katherine Ingles was there and says there were possibly no more than about twelve people. "They absolutely revered him," she says. "They felt that he was a wise man, and they were incredibly interested. There was great respect." She first heard him on his first visit to South Africa in 1972 and says she was, "instantly hooked. I heard about Findhorn, the people there getting guidance, and it was working." The concentration on white audiences was not because of any preference of George's, rather because of the difficulties of the times and a too great cultural divide. Mrs Cowen said, "Perhaps he was not the right person to appeal to the blacks: he could not change his approach."

He spoke on large topics such as Living into Change or A Vision of Hope in an Age of Turmoil. Living into Change appears in *A Vision of the Aquarian Age*:

> Our world view, as we have seen, includes the principle of the Higher Self. Each of us has this 'utterly trustworthy parental being', to use the Huna phrase, who is part of the super-conscious world and a counterpart to our subconscious mind. Psychology as yet is only beginning to recognize this all-important factor in our being, though it appears to be the source of many of the creative impulses in our conduct previously explained as sublimation of the sexual drive. What we are really working with are higher 'drives,' issuing from the light-filled plane of the superconscious.[3]

George often touched upon the new perceptions of psychology which included and encompassed spiritual perception. In *Operation Redemption*, subtitled *A Vision of Hope in an Age of Turmoil*, he spoke of, "an attempt to play with certain big thoughts and ideas. Play, indeed, light-heartedly — the heart filled with light, to dance with great Ideas ... to Think Big Thoughts."[4] Often in his speaking there was a rallying cry, an almost Shakespearean raising of the standard for the excitement of battle. The over-simplified message of a George Trevelyan evening might be rendered *Get On With It!*

Mrs Cowen recalls her own part in these journeys as seeing that everything went smoothly, making space for George Trevelyan to see people, rest or get fresh air and exercise; and to protect him from over-eager hostesses. People often wanted to show him their poems, and to read them aloud, something he did at Findhorn. She remembers how hard they both worked, how tired they both became — and how little they spoke. George was very deaf and could not hear while they were travelling. However, for herself she says, "I did not do this only to help George, or for the trip. It was much more from a conviction that these lectures and meetings were bringing a powerful spirituality to so many people, with quite another approach, a paradigm shift, a spark of life and meaning, and a wider perspective and inspiration, which felt of such vital importance that it was a delight and privilege to help in such a work of enlightenment."

George Trevelyan retired as a Wrekin trustee during the Spring of 1986, his eightieth year. This was the year in which for the first time the educational programme was presented as a formal curriculum rather than a calendar of events. George defined a new social class: self-explorers (exploration was constant theme with him) and published *Summons to a High Crusade*, a summary of some of his best Findhorn lectures. It speaks of "that peak experience when the human being breaks through from normal separative self-consciousness into cosmic consciousness... reality as a great oneness. We are all reaching the threshold where we overcome the limitations of sense-bound, brain-bound consciousness, when mind in us unites with Universal Mind." He remarks characteristically, "This is the immense excitement of the time we live in."[5]

Many parties were held when George Trevelyan reached his eightieth birthday in November. One was at Hawkwood College, where a house full of people came together to celebrate. In the middle of it George turned to Ruth Nesfield-Cookson and said, "I have fallen deeply in love ..." She waited expectantly and he concluded, "with *everybody*!" Another was arranged by David Lorimer and Serge Beddington-Behrens at Imperial College in London. A huge number of people seemed to want to pay a spoken tribute to the venerable teacher from whom they felt they had learned so much: the final tally was more than 800. Serge Beddington-Behrens says, "More and more people began to say they were coming, and having booked a small hall, too many wanted to come. We got a last minute cancellation of a larger hall.

"The keynote was a celebration. Sir George embodied a higher celebration of life; he praised and raised life. We saw him as an agent for evaluation of life in situations and people. You were conscious of a deep spirit of goodness in him: one felt him not quite of this world, he walked more with the angels. George was a descender — he came down from above with a message to tell people how it was up there so they could ascend." There were many such tributes. Hertha Larive recalls that about fifteen people spoke under various headings. She herself spoke first of the growing network of people and ideas that derived from George's efforts, next of the value of George himself and of his work. Then she received an inspirational message: that everyone in the room was becoming the messenger. Serge Beddington-Behrens asked for silence at the end of her speech, to absorb it, and the people remained silent for two minutes. The speakers also included Frédéric Lionel, Pir Vilayat Khan, and many of the luminaries of George's Wrekin years. George enjoyed it all hugely.

Two years later, George attended Frédéric Lionel's own 80th birthday celebrations in Switzerland. Frédéric Lionel was a teacher and writer trained in an esoteric school in the Pythagorean tradition. He was also expert in the tarot, and he spoke beautiful, precise English in a rhythmical cadence which was remembered by all who heard it. During the Second World War, M. Lionel had served in the French Resistance. He recorded that after the party the two men sat in silence for a time beside Lake Geneva. Eventually, George spoke. "I mentioned this morning the importance of reaching a turning point because I realized on my own 80th birthday that it could be compared with a threshold," he said "Behind us loom all our experiences. I say 'loom' because time and time again I have realized that I may have missed an opportunity or, over-enthusiastically, ended in a dead alley ... one of the most important aspects of self-realization is to discover the error wherever it hides, so as to see the Truth ... [instead of doing this] we cling to our errors. That is why we turn our back to Happiness and to the Joy of Living. That is what I am now hoping to be able to communicate to all my friends all over the world." A George Trevelyan perception that equates Truth with Happiness, and observes that illusion is addictive.

Meanwhile the Wrekin Trust broadened its reach, using ever more exciting means to attract and inspire people. Malcolm Lazarus is especially proud of the weekend they held in September, 1987, called The Secret Heart of Music, subtitled "an exploration into the power of music to change consciousness." The publicity leaflet said, "This unique gathering has been arranged to help restore music to a central place in our culture as a unifying and transcendent force. It will bring together from many parts of the world musicians and music lovers both amateur and professional who are awakening to a spiritual reality." The event was headlined by Van Morrison, whose inspiration it had been, and who played on the Friday night. He had attended a Wrekin conference on Matter & Sound, Music & Consciousness, and been inspired to take it further. Other musicians included Robin Williamson of the Incredible String Band, Derek Bell of the Chieftains, and Nishat Khan, who plays the sitar. Pir Vilayat Khan spoke on Music and the Chakras, and led a meditation. The topics included Music as a Force in Spiritual Development. There may have been some affinity with Attingham, where people came for the purpose of learning, whether music or drama or pottery-making, and through it gained access to deeper insights.

George continued to teach well into his eighties, although as time passed he was less physically capable and in the later years his memory was less certain. He travelled a great deal in Western Europe, notably in Holland with Peter Dawkins, who remembers a ten-day tour which included The Hague and Amsterdam and hospitality in a castle from a Dutch aristocrat, with whom, apparently, George got on especially well. With Peter Dawkins and others he went for long study weeks for about ten years to Le Plan, in Provence, a holiday home of George's good friend Lorna St Aubyn. It had once been a nunnery, still had a chapel, and became a centre for spiritually oriented courses and discussion groups. They investigated aspects of different wisdom teachings with an informality which is recalled as being in delightful contrast with other conferences. Both George Trevelyan and Peter Dawkins were able to visit there for holidays as well.

In 1987, George travelled to Germany for the first of several lecture tours in which Geseke Clark translated for him. The first time she heard him lecture he quoted Goethe in German, and she thought his accent so good that she asked where he had learned it. He explained that he had spent time in Germany during his youth; she said that she was impressed by how well he had retained his command of the language. Nevertheless when he spoke to German groups George was often translated by Mrs Clark; who had to do some homework on the more esoteric phrases that he used. Here are some of them:

— Metamorphosed: *verwandelt*
— Enriched knowledge: *mit bereichertem Wissen*
— No hurt — no sin: *keine Verletzung — keine Sünde*
— A setting in which the nascent impulse of Christianity could find nourishment: *Ein Rahmen in dem der Impuls der werdenden Christenheit Nahrung finden konnte.*

"He was a great soul," says Mrs Clark. "A Universal soul. He understood the German soul, the German spirit. That is why he was so keen on Steiner." Aspects of the German soul that were close to George's being included the close, perhaps even symbiotic relationship with natural phenomena such as forests and rocks. "He wanted very much to visit big rocks, the Externsteine," says Geseke Clark. "He said, 'I must go and visit this, because Steiner thinks it is very important'." The place has a mythological significance as powerful as that of Stonehenge or any of the English stone barrows and circles that he loved. He visited them also with Mrs Cowen, and wrote:

> In the forest of Northern Germany to the west of Hanover stands an astonishing outcrop of sandstone towers, six of them in a row emerging from a geological fault and soaring 200 ft above the trees. The Externsteine have been carved into chambers, steps and grottoes and have, of course, become a well-known tourist attraction. But for us they are something much more.
>
> Archaeologists date the workings with the Pyramids and Stonehenge. When Steiner visited them, he declared that this was the centre for the Germanic Folk-Soul ...
>
> This centre must surely be a key point in the ley line network over Europe. Perhaps it will prove to be linked with that great landscape temple from the Mediterranean to Ben More Assynt near Cape Wrath.
>
> Rhoda Cowen was with me, she also came to Skellig Michel, that remarkable temple centre five miles off the south west corner of Ireland. The rock pyramid 700 feet high, tip of a drowned mountain, rises above the Atlantic. Steps are carved which lead up to a monastery 100 feet below the summit. Six tiny beehive huts, with a chapel, comprise the monastery. It was occupied from 700 ad until the twelfth century ... I submit that these two astonishing sites might be linked into the great structure of light centres across Europe. (*Gatekeeper News*)

The poet and philosopher Goethe alluded to the folk-soul (*Volkseele*) as did many writers, including Grimm. It influenced the Romantic music of the eighteenth and nineteenth centuries; in a grotesquely perverted form it was part of the basis of Nazism; it remains a huge influence upon the nation. The *Volkseele* is central to the German notion of nationhood and self. Many German folk stories deal with the intense natural environment, in particular with rocks, mountains and forests:

forests full of animals, where it is possible to get lost for days. Fear of the forest, real and symbolic, is a typically German emotion. The ideal-ist philosophers proposed something called *Weltseele* — a world soul, or oversoul. German idealistic philosophy has unity. George Trevelyan had a lifelong feeling for similar notions of the significance of landscape; and a relationship going back to the seminal Stein lecture in 1942 with German interpretations of the concept of soul — oversoul — folk-soul. He shared another powerful facet of Teutonic understanding: forests symbolizing the unconscious mind in myth, fairy tale and dreams. Hence a landscape temple such as Externsteine would be profoundly important to him, both as a natural phenomenon and as a symbol.

After his journey to Scandinavia in the following year he wrote to his Findhorn friend, Elisabeth Tønsberg.

25 May 88

O dear, my dear dear Elisabeth, I have failed so badly in not replying to your letters. But I rejoiced to hear of you back in our lovely Findhorn. I *was* so glad to hear from you. I am just back from a week of lecturing in Gothenburg, Stockholm and Oslo. This was exciting. I'd wanted to see a stave church and the old wooden buildings. And I go on being interested in finding how to speak to overseas audiences. Germany is next — a week near Hanover and on to Berlin. But this coming weekend (is) the London Festival of Body Mind Spirit.

And writing goes on, and the inner change (in me). And I get closer and more full of love and affection for so many — so many. But among them the Specials — of which you are one. And underlying all, the *knowledge* that Alexander is really about the human individual learning to stop and control reaction, break the circuit of habitual & instant response to stimuli. And when this is achieved, so simple & so difficult, it is a *release into freedom*. We are no longer possessed by the reflex pattern on the animal level.

Thus in his 82nd year, George Trevelyan was still finding fascination in his explorations into the human condition, and within Europe.

He had affinity with Germany all his life and the following year travelled there again with Geseke Clark. Afterwards he wrote:

My dear Geseke,

A note to thank you so much for all you did. I liked our partnership! Don't you feel it was growing into a creative act? I found this interesting and satisfactory. The lady who took over in Berlin, though adequate, had no sense of the dramatic, and so merely repeated my words, dully.

But the whole Bad Pyrmont experience was admirable. So thanks for yr very real contribution.

Berlin was very well worth while.

A *very* good *young* group for the main lecture, & a small seminar, which was very good practice. And we crossed the Wall & got back again, having seen the Pergamon Altar in the great museum.

Altogether I was well pleased and learned a lot.

Love and blessings

George

The handwriting in this letter is still clear and bears the characteristics of the fine copperplate that he wrote all his life, though it is a little shaky. His 83-year-old hands were horribly twisted by arthritis. His earlier script almost looked like a calligrapher's: beautifully formed strokes written with a square-ended pen. A handwriting analyst might notice that the upward strokes are of more or less equal length with the downward strokes, denoting a balance between the outer and inner self, and the direction is slightly forwards, a mark of optimism. Of the note itself, it is typical of George's charm that in thanking his sympathetic translator he elevated her contribution to the talks almost to equal status.

Legend and myth, as in the German tour, were constantly important to Sir George Trevelyan. At midsummer that year he gave *Brewer's Dictionary of Phrase and Fable* to Rod and Alice Friend. The inscription in the fly leaf, in a hand just as well-shaped as for the letter to Geseke Clark, was characteristically definite:

I declare that every interesting and intelligent family should
keep this amazing book in their dining room! George Trevelyan

And a year later, at 84, having suffered from dreadful arthritis for 25 years, he could still say, "My real pleasure is to do what I can in lecturing and writing. My craft is lecturing and I can go on

improving it." Some people believed that he fed his ego on his audience, others that the enthusiasm of his audiences energized him to
carry on. Perhaps both interpretations are true.

On his 85th birthday in November 1991, George had to take part in
an event which he thought was the closing of the Wrekin Trust (it
turned out to be a period of dormancy, rather than closure.) Rhoda
Cowen said that at a conference on near death experiences held on the
Trust's twentieth birthday, George stood up and said, "I wish it to be
closed." He felt that it had fulfilled its task, and that many other organizations were taking over aspects of the role for which it had been set
up. Mrs Cowen said there was an extraordinary atmosphere. Those
present believed that, since it did not seem possible for it to continue
in its current form, it seemed right that it should cease activities sooner
than drift into extinction. For a couple of years some of its activities
were carried on independently by various key members, then it rose
again like the phoenix and now continues differently, under the guiding hand of Janice Dolley and others. For Sir George Trevelyan it more
or less ceased when he was 85.

George still worked long hours on his own behalf, buoyed up by
his vocation and the enthusiasm with which he and his lectures were
received. He often had to drive himself to appointments, and he
sometimes did so when he was too tired. Returning from a lecture
one evening in the following year he fell asleep at the wheel, ran his
car into a bollard, and was injured. He spent time in hospital and
returned home with a new perspective. Some revelations had come to
him: the most important was that he must never again say or think
anything negative. In particular, he believed that troubled close relationships could be healed by positive thought, by the discipline of
accepting into the mind only that which was joyful. He expressed this
thought often during his later years, although as he had never had a
critical or an unkind word to say about anyone, people around him
claim not to have been able to notice a difference. George was interested in the notion that we can control our thoughts. By doing so we
affect not only our own destinies. We alter our effect upon other people through thought as well as word and deed, and hence their
reflected effect upon us.

In his increasingly frail old age, George metamorphosed yet again. He
smiled more, and he became much gentler. Those who knew him then
say he was happier to contemplate human qualities such as kindness and
simple gifts, happier with the everyday world, less concerned with

intellectual activity. He talked a great deal about his furniture and recalled in detail the making or designing of every piece. He often showed photographs to visitors, a truthful honouring of a great skill and the beauty of its realization. David Lorimer says, "light and love emanated from him in the last few years of his life. You could feel he'd experienced a bliss, and a light. Something was coming from him that was beyond charisma." Many people have made similar comments, to the effect that it seemed that George was surrounded by an aura of pure, non-egotistical simplicity.

By the time George was 87 he had begun to be forgetful, sometimes to talk for too long, occasionally to repeat himself. It fell to Geseke Clark to suggest that he alter the pattern of his lectures. She did it delicately, in a letter dated 11 January, 1994, 7am.

> Dearest George,
>
> I would very much like to talk to you about future lecturing. People have said to me that they want to see you and be with you, not necessarily because they want to hear the things that they could read in your books but to feel your presence and your vibrations.
>
> ... Perhaps a shorter talk and longer question and answer sessions? Because you do that very well and I, as your loving assistant, can keep you focused ... You still have so much to say, and in a way, no one else can. Please go on giving talks, but let me help you.
>
> You are a great Soul
> I feel so privileged to be your Friend and truly loving
> Geseke

George accepted this. He had gone beyond the ego reaction to what might have seemed like criticism; he could see that his powers were not as they had been. He carried on speaking, but less often. Later that year he was to be found back at his alma mater, Sidcot School, Somerset, which he had left 70 years earlier to go up to Cambridge. Afterwards Geseke Clark received a thank-you letter from the headmaster: "I feel the event was a great success ... I have written to Sir George separately to express our appreciation." By this time she was having to nudge him back into line from time to time. She had to push him to do his research for a particular poetry session and he was so contrite that he gave her a written undertaking, in a hand grown very shaky. It read:

A Committal

I AM resolved to do my homework on my Poetry Session on Sat morn between 10 & 1230 and shall thereby lift these pages into The Living Word that we may together achieve an awakening & lifting of consciousness in our audiences/victims.

George Trevelyan (affirmation)

There!

The last word (underlined twice) is characteristic of the man: determination with a seasoning of naughty defiance that allows the word *so* to be understood before the word *there*! The word *victims* bracketed with *audiences* is also typical George.

There were several visits during the year — to Scotland, to the Lake District, to Somerset. By this time George was being nursed and accompanied everywhere by Anna Benita, a nurse whom his daughter Catriona Tyson had found to help him and Helen in their final years. She was an ideal companion, being both practical and spiritual, able to understand and sympathize with George's vision and also maintain him through the everyday problems of survival in an increasingly frail body. It was Anna Benita who drove George on his last tour around the country. In the Lake District he visited his old university friend, Gurney McInnes, with whom he had so often climbed in younger days. Gurney McInnes was tall and slim like George: unlike him he was still very fit. They reminisced and laughed together, then George went to Seatoller where the Trevelyan Man Hunt had been (and, thanks to George, continued), and to Wallington again, and thence to the Findhorn community for the last time.

He did all this without regret. It seems possible that the visit to Findhorn may have been more of a trial for the people there, for whom George had been such an inspiration, than it was for him. However, one man who had not previously met him commented that during the several days of the visit he never saw the fabled Sir George Trevelyan without two lovely women supporting him, and he said that if he found himself in such a position at such an age he believed he might not mind too much. Or for that matter, if he found himself in such a position at any age. With Anna Benita and others to help him, George took tea once more with Eileen Caddy, who apparently looked at him with great affection and kept repeating, "*Dear* George! *Dear* George!"

Elisabeth Tønsberg had known him for years and says that his interest in Findhorn was one of the reasons that she went to live there. She says, "Sir George wanted to do a farewell round of Britain. He was staying in Cluny [the Findhorn community's hotel]. His carer drove him to the front entrance, they arrived and he was sitting in the car. A cunning look came on his face. He said, 'This is not an ordinary hotel'. I said, 'Sir George, welcome!' He said innocently, 'Thank you, who are you?' There was no recognition, but he had a Christ-like innocence. Ten minutes later he said, 'What's your name again? Elisabeth? *Splendid!*' It was heartbreaking — but he was so present."

Sir George's memory was fragile but his old magnetism was intact. A big farewell celebration dinner was given for him, at which all the old-time members of the community got up and paid homage to him. It was a great adulation. At the end, says Elisabeth Tønsberg, he indicated that he would like to express his gratitude. Anna Benita was nervous. "I said, George can get lost and go off track, but the atmosphere enlivened him. He sat on the edge of the table, legs crossed, and delivered the most wonderful talk from some deep reservoir of his being. I was completely amazed." He spoke for about a quarter of an hour and everyone who heard him says it seemed as though twenty years had fallen from him. He was eloquent, poetic, graceful, magnetic, charismatic, compelling: he held his audience in the palm of his hand with the skill of a fine actor and the power of a classical orator. It was just like the old days.

At the end of this impromptu speech there was a stunned silence, then the room erupted into applause. Anna Benita, who had spent many months with him, was awestruck. She said, "I didn't know who I was nursing." This was the George whom everyone had found so inspiring, the George who had excited the minds, the creativity, the imagination and aspiration of so many, the George who had brought to Findhorn and to so many places a joyful spirit that had galvanized people into positive activity. He was aware of it as he acknowledged his applause. "That wasn't bad, was it?" he said. But leaving the room, he turned to Anna Benita to ask what the occasion had been. It was as though the old George had returned for positively the last appearance before his best Scottish audience, so that the very ancient George might finally leave Findhorn.

Sir George and Lady Trevelyan had another year together after that, and a lifetime's differences were harmonized. Their daughter Mrs Tyson says, "They had an up-and-down relationship but at the end they were very sweet together. They read poetry and they acted in plays, and George could always come up with a poem, whatever the cause. When she was getting quite old, my mother made a decision about the parts she would play. She said, 'I've told George I'm not going to play any of those soppy heroines any more, I'm only going to be old hags and witches!'" It was a peaceful twilight. Anna Benita nursed them both, and drove them to see people and places, and acted as the sensitive intermediary between them and their visitors. "I came in when George was getting frail," she says. "I lived with him and Helen for a year, then with him for the last eighteen months while he petered out. He was an enigma, he was not an ordinary person. He had appalling arthritis which would have finished most people off. Because of the Alexander Technique he could stay mobile, he knew how to move. He never ever complained, he was not embittered by it. He was exceptional, and still had the power to inspire people."

George's memory had become that of a very old man and he generally forgot what had happened the day before. When Lady Trevelyan died of a stroke in the autumn of 1994 he was utterly disconsolate, to the point of wandering in the garden looking for her. All the same, many of the people who visited him towards the end of his life remark on what a fine experience it was. Among them were Rod and Alice Friend, who lived quite near him. Alice Friend in particular was close to George in his last months. She says: "For years George came to me every three months, for my work as a medium. George had faith without having what he called 'the sight', but it pained him that he didn't have it. Not many people saw him late in his life. I used to sit with him in peace; there was a quiet knowing; communication happened wordlessly. Anna sometimes put him in the car and drove him round to us, and the last time he was in our house was quite near the end. We spoke to George down on the road, in the car, then we decided they could stay for supper. George got out of the car, without his sticks, and walked up the steps [the steps to the Friends' Gloucestershire home are many and steep, the climb would have been akin to a mountain for George]. He was very crippled in his legs by that time and he did it by sheer will power. His will power was extraordinary." Anna Benita recalls that Lois Atherden, a climbing companion of George's youth, sat with him and was a great comfort to him. Peter Dawkins remembers that throughout his last illness George refused drugs because, "he wanted to experience everything. He wanted to explore the dark spaces." His publisher Alick Bartholomew says, "I sat with him at the end. One was aware of a great sense of peace: I regarded it as an honour. He was thoroughly prepared, with his whole being. He was already halfway there, and there was almost a sense of rejoicing."

Yet, according to Catriona Tyson, "when it came to the point of dying, George couldn't let go. We waited and waited for him to go. During the last eighteen months of his life his mind went and he was lonely. He believed that no one visited him, which wasn't at all true. He said, 'no one's been to see me'. How he died was strange: he just refused to get up. I think he decided to die." He was often visited by his New Age friends who brought love and alternative healing, and prayed and chanted for him. On one occasion Alice Friend gently massaged his arthritic old legs and arms and hands, to the point that they relaxed and the fingers unfurled once more. His family and visitors respected his frequently stated wish to experience everything fully, to participate in the passage from one world to the next, even in its physical pain. Yet strangely enough, he who had been looking forward to this journey for so long seemed, at the point of embarkation, reluctant to make it. Finally, in his ninetieth year, towards midnight on the night of 7 February, 1996, Anna Benita heard a great cry from George's room. She went to him. Catriona Tyson was already there. For a couple of weeks the two women had been sharing the nursing rota so that one or other was awake to hear him at night. It was appropriate that it should have been Catriona who reached him first on the great cry that he made, before he, in his own words, "embarked upon the great adventure"; or in the New Age description, "left the body." By both of their accounts, it was a cry of triumph.

And afterwards

There were many celebrations of George Trevelyan's life at the time of his passing, and there have been many more, in different forms, ever since. The family funeral at Hawkesbury was beautifully organized, a wonderful, harmonious gathering, remembered by those who attended, according to Peter Dawkins, with something akin to joy. Then there was a memorial service at St James's Piccadilly and a Wrekin Trust gathering at Hawkwood College. The service at St James's was conducted by the Rev Donald Reeves, who blessed a commemorative yew tree given by David Lorimer. Afterwards Roger Orgill suggested that the tree be planted at Attingham and undertook to arrange it with the National Trust. The planting eventually took place on the banks of the river Tern, looking across the Deer Park. The work of the adult college is also commemorated within the house. Among many memorials to the inspiration given by Sir George Trevelyan is the empty chair left for him at all Wrekin Trust meetings, so that his presence will bless the proceedings.

CHAPTER 8

Legacy

George's contribution, according to many people who heard him, learned from him, worked with him, read his books, walked and climbed with him, listened to him recite poetry, or spent any time at all with him, was to enable people to look at matters spiritual *first*. George Trevelyan understood early the huge implications of the twentieth century movement known first as the Aquarian Age, then as the New Age. Under whatever name, a perception which includes imagination and intuitive, non-sensory perception, was coming into sharper focus. It has many dimensions. In the Western world we have clung to the idea that knowledge is power; but the Western definition of knowledge in recent centuries has been science. Although for many people looking at spiritual matters first may be some way off, a different view is nevertheless filtering through many long-held assumptions. Perhaps science does not after all encapsulate all knowledge, is one of the thoughts. It is beginning to be widely acknowledged that changing the way we see the world, and hence our priorities, could be vital to survival. Sir George Trevelyan was one of the first to raise his voice to let this be known. That the exceptional power of that voice and the beauty of its communication are still present in so many minds is testament to the quality of the man.

The ecologists' view is that the power we have wielded by the use of unfettered, unmoderated technology has done great, even untold damage. They say that without a transformed understanding of the status of the human species as simply one aspect of the living world, there is a real danger of self-destruction. This apocalyptic interpretation could be written off as part of the doomsday thinking of the 1970s and 1980s, but the fact that not all the predicted catastrophes have happened yet should not obscure the disasters that are happening already. Atmospheric pollution, nuclear accidents, climate change, accelerated extinction of natural species, and the many recent food scares, are only a few.

Many of the material and technical systems which have supported human life and civilizations are also breaking down. For the better part of a century there has been confusion, to say the least, about the most effective way of providing the world with nourishing food and clean drinking water, and of running the world economy. Leaving politics to one side, in astrological terms this can be accounted for by the shift from the age of Pisces to the age of Aquarius which is taking place at the end of a 2,000-year cycle. Some say that unspeakable inequities happen because we have not the will to change them. Some say they happen because we have not the imagination to see ourselves as part of the whole, each of us microcosmically responsible for the totality. However it is, we are clearly adrift, with one set of assumptions appearing hopelessly inadequate and no other ready to take its place. We continue to cling to the known even when it no longer serves any purpose.

George Trevelyan knew that the world was a living collection of living things, seen and unseen, that do not submit to exclusively scientific analysis. He knew that the mind that is causal for the material world is the divine mind. This is not to succumb to the temptation of careering off in the opposite direction and saying the rational viewpoint has no validity. It is to say that rationality must be seen as only a part of the picture, to be balanced with other kinds of understanding. In the New Age perception, material phenomena come second, not first. It follows that the logical mind is only a tool. Sir George was ready to consider ideas that came to him from almost any source, however improbable, and this quality often brought the charge of lack of discrimination. On the contrary, it was the genuinely objective attitude promoted at least nominally by the scientific community. George made his choices only after considering things in a genuinely uncritical spirit, and weighing and testing them with a sharp, trained intellect and a highly developed intuition.

Alick Bartholomew was George Trevelyan's publisher from the early 1970s, at the beginning of the Wrekin Trust. He says, "I was very struck — and moved — by how much George would go into difficult areas of thinking, extraordinary experiments. I also remember how he always saw the best of what people were doing. His own vision was incredible, it was overlaid by Blake, Goethe, Wordsworth, and so on. He was really a pioneer, and he was so clear, so focused. He saw no evil in anyone. In this he was really a pure spirit. His was an extraordinary contribution; I really think that without him what is called the New Age movement would not have been so coherent." Alick

Bartholomew acknowledges that most of George Trevelyan's books were little more than transcripts of his lectures, but says that George was the only author he worked with who he felt should not be edited. The thoughts in the books were extraordinarily powerful, and powerfully expressed. George also recorded many of his ideas on tapes, which are still published by Conference Cassettes.

Alongside the apocalyptic vision, George held Rudolf Steiner's belief that: "We are only at the beginning of Christian evolution." He said, "Christ being everywhere is like water which could flood into any space open to it; this could lead to an atmosphere of forgiveness and goodwill to all neighbours the world over, and this in turn could lead to great changes in all spheres of life, including politics and economics, education and culture." He saw the possibility of overcoming the problems of the era, and frequently concluded talks by saying delightedly, "There never *was* such a time to be alive!"

The legacy of George Trevelyan exists not only in the people who remember him and perpetuate his vision and aspiration, but also in the many specialist libraries, associations and groups which continue aspects of his work. His interests and activities were so many that no single one of them could be regarded as a direct successor to him.[1]

In his later lifetime, George Trevelyan was so famous in New Age circles that he was often asked to write introductions to people's books, and during the 1970s and 1980s it sometimes seemed as though few such books were published that did *not* have an enthusiastic endorsement by Sir George Trevelyan. In the same way, he would champion the work of small associations of greater or lesser authenticity. All this brought further charges of lack of discrimination, in this case perhaps more justified. But the fact that George was at the hub of a wheel with so many spokes testifies to his indefatigable energy, his inspiring enthusiasm. His response to so many propositions, efforts, ideas was, "Wonderful!" — unless, for a change, it might be "Splendid!" How much he gave in the way of excitement to fire people up in their creative efforts, to boost their imaginative exploits, how much he encouraged, excited, enthralled, how much he got things moving, must also come into a consideration of his legacy, for some of that energy is around even now.

To try to sum up George's personal ethos in a paragraph or even a book is to risk a ridiculous simplification. Something about the continuity of pure aristocracy is important, but the definition of aristocracy has to return to an original sense of refinement of essence and connection with the land. Something about the deep understanding of stewardship, of looking after one's neighbours, taking responsibility for one's community, extends into the larger perception that one is part of the whole of creation and must play one's proper part in it. This implies never shirking one's duties and obligations.

Earth as a training ground for souls is a notion shared by many belief systems. In George Trevelyan's it took a Gnostic form, relating to his taste for visionary, intuitive knowledge. He believed that real wisdom went beyond the rational and towards symbolism, rather than literalism. This linked with his knowledge of poetry: the beautiful, rational mind at work conveying and interpreting abstract thought or even spiritual perception. Karma, the understanding of cause and effect, is a concept within several religious disciplines, even if the same word is not used. Sir George Trevelyan understood the events and circumstances of his life and birth to be significant in the working out of the deeds of his aristocratic family and in turn for the fate of England itself. The relationship between these observations and the Western Mystical Tradition with which he was concerned is complex, and perhaps encompasses the Trevelyan proximity to legendary Britain, and the deeply symbiotic relationship between aristocracy and myth.

George Trevelyan undertook his own spiritual life eagerly. It was a continuous quest, as vital to him as breathing. Every event which might have been regarded as a disaster was understood by him as a lesson, and since he believed that all lessons came from the divine source, was accepted joyfully. This idea is not new, but is one that George held very dear. His question to people when he met them was often, "What are you *doing*?" and it meant, "what are you doing *internally*?" In his famous Rainbow Meditation he refers to the space for discovery within each person, which he perceived was infinitely greater than the space for discovery in the outer, visible, material world.[2]

However, the practical realization of some of the spiritual theories in George's personal life was not always so successful. The psychologist Serge Beddington-Behrens, who first met him at a Wrekin lecture in 1974, observes, "It is possible to be a remarkable person without having got one's personal life in order. Personal life was not what he was about." Serge Beddington-Behrens read English Literature at Oxford University but says he only began truly to understand the spirit of literature, and in particular of Shakespeare, through George. Like many others he says, "He was a pivotal figure in awakening my intellect and my spirit." However, on the question of George's effectiveness at an intimate level he remarks, "He was all right in the public eye, but did he know how to love?" The answer to that might well be, in the abstract, large, universal sense, yes he did. At the intimate level there may still be a question mark.

To try to sum up the key themes of George's life is to court dispute; all the same, here are seven of them:

— The essential idea of One-ness
— The being within form
— Earth as a living creature
— Ideas as divine, with lives of their own
— The current, massive shift of consciousness
— Reincarnation
— The crucial importance of engaging with a spiritual perception

Many people in many countries recall the extraordinary influence of Sir George, the energy, enthusiasm and purity of the man, the quality of the ideas he brought and the way he transformed their lives. All the same, he had better conclude this account himself. The final chapter of *A Vision of the Aquarian Age* is entitled: Man Attuned — the Hope for the Future. In it, George Trevelyan wrote:

> The transformation of man begins in ourselves and no one is too small or unimportant. The thinking of the heart is the field of action for the Higher Self ...
>
> Change man and you change society. Try to change society without the inner change in man, and confusion will be the sole result. And each conscious individual is solely responsible for making changes in himself. One basic spiritual law is that for each step into higher knowledge, a man should take three steps in development of his own character.
>
> Lovingness, the power of spirit, can never stagnate. The heart, lighted by love, will radiate outwards and the light will unite with itself in others. With joy, recognition will ensue ... There is no bond like that of spiritual understanding, for it unites people of every type and age. It is the real social solvent.[3]

Sources

Chapter 1

1. *Wallington,* Raleigh Trevelyan, National Trust, 1994.
2. *Twelve Seats at the Round Table,* Edward Matchett and George Trevelyan, Neville Spearman (Jersey), 1976.
3. *Fool in Love,* Katharine Trevelyan, Gollancz, 1962.
4. *C.P. Trevelyan 1870-1958: Portrait of a Radical,* A.J.A. Morris, Blackstaff Press, 1977.
5. *The Gold and Silver Threads, A Memoir of Life in the Twentieth Century,* Rhoda Cowen, Alan Sutton Publishing, 1994

Chapter 2

1. *The Roof-Climber's Guide to Trinity,* Geoffrey Winthrop-Young, W.P. Spalding, Cambridge 1899.
2. *The Philosopher's Stone, Diaries of Lessons with F. Matthias Alexander,* ed. Jean M.O. Fischer, Mouritz Press, London 1998.
3. *The Gold and Silver Threads,* Rhoda Cowen (see above).
4. *George's observations on the art of looking were outlined in The Active Eye in Architecture,* The Wrekin Trust, 1977 (out of print).
5. *The Synthetic Vision of Walter Gropius,* Gilbert Herbert, Witwatersrand University Press, Johannesburg 1959.
6. *Gimson and the Barnsleys,* Mary Comino, Evans Bros, 1980.
7. *Kurt Hahn,* H. Röhrs and H. Tunstall-Behrens, Routledge & Kegan Paul, 1970.
8. *Unfolding Character, the Impact of Gordonstoun,* Adam Arnold-Brown, Routledge & Kegan Paul, 1962.
9. *Gordonstoun, Ancient Estate and Modern School,* Henry L. Brereton, W. & R. Chambers, 1968.

Chapter 3

1. *The Philosopher's Stone,* ed. Jean Fischer (see above).
2. *Exploration into God,* George Trevelyan, Gateway Books, 1991.
3. *Operation Redemption,* George Trevelyan, Turnstone Press Ltd, 1981.
4. Quoted in *Magic Casements,* George Trevelyan, Coventure, 1980; Gateway Books, 1996.
5. *The New Age, An Anthology of Essential Writings,* ed. William Bloom, Rider, 1991.
6. *Operation Redemption,* George Trevelyan (op.cit.)

Chapter 4

1. *The Gold and Silver Threads,* Rhoda Cowen (see above).
2. *Exploration into God,* George Trevelyan (see above).
3. *C.P. Trevelyan, Portrait of a Radical,* A.J.A. Morris (see above).

Chapter 5

1. *In Perfect Timing, Memoirs of a Man for the New Millennium,* Peter Caddy, Findhorn Press, 1995.
2. *The New Age,* ed. William Bloom (see above.)
3. *The New Age,* ed. William Bloom (see above.)
4. *The Best of Resurgence, selection from the first 25 years,* edited by John Button, Green Books, 1991.

Chapter 6

1. *Quoted in Magic Casements,* George Trevelyan, Coventure, 1980; Gateway Books, 1996.
2. *In Perfect Timing,* Peter Caddy (see above).

Chapter 7

1. *Twelve Seats at the Round Table,* George Trevelyan with Edward Matchett (see above).
2. *The Gold and Silver Threads,* Rhoda Cowen (see above).
3. *A Vision of the Aquarian Age, the emerging spiritual world view,* George Trevelyan, Gateway Books, 1994.
4. *Operation Redemption,* George Trevelyan (see above).
5. *Summons to a High Crusade,* The Findhorn Press, 1986.

Chapter 8

1. For those who wish to investigate further aspects of the George Trevelyan legacy, contacts are given in an Appendix.
2. *Introduction to Meditation/The Rainbow Meditation,* Sir George Trevelyan, produced for the Wrekin Trust by Conference Cassettes.
3. *A Vision of the Aquarian Age,* George Trevelyan (see above).

Bibliography

Sir George Trevelyan's books are no longer in print, though they can be obtained through second-hand book sources or searches. The following titles, together with articles and lectures, are available for downloading or reading offline through the Sir George Trevelyan website (for further information, see Contacts and Organizations below).

Books

Exploration into God: A Personal Quest for Spiritual Unity
*Magic Casements: The Use of Poetry in the Expanding of
    Consciousness*
*The Active Eye in Architecture: An approach to dynamic and
    imaginative looking*
A Vision of the Aquarian Age: The Emerging Spiritual World View
Operation Redemption: A Vision of Hope in an Age of Turmoil

Articles and lectures

The Emergence of the New Humanity
Landscape Temples
Stewards of the Planet
Meditation and its Purpose
Thoughts on Childbirth
Retirement and Old Age
Death — the Great Adventure
Prototypes of Holistic Achievement
The Living Word
Something of an Autobiography
Autumn Letter to Lamplighters
Missionaries for the Cosmic Christ
The Cosmic Christ in the New Age

Contacts and organizations

George Trevelyan's interests and activities were so many that no single person or association could be regarded as a successor to him. His legacy exists in all those people who remember him and perpetuate his vision and aspiration and also in the many specialist libraries, associations and groups which continue aspects of his work. Those mentioned here are intended as a cross-section of the kind of activities in which he was involved. The list is by no means comprehensive but it can lead to further investigation.

For details of George Trevelyan's teachings and publications, as well as contributions from people in related spheres of activity around the world, see the Sir George Trevelyan Website at www.sirgeorgetrevelyan.org.uk.

This website was built by Palden Jenkins, and both welcomes authentic memories and anecdotes, transcripts of George Trevelyan's speeches, or any printed or written material, such as letters, which could add to the fund of information.

Anthroposophical Society

35 Park Road, London, NW1 6XT. Tel. 020-7723 4400

Rudolf Steiner, the originator of anthroposophy, was a seminal influence on Sir George Trevelyan, who often quoted Steiner's definition: "A path of knowledge leading the spiritual in man to the spiritual in the Universe." Steiner's scientific training was complemented by a knowledge of literature, especially the poetic and scientific works of Goethe, and by many clairvoyant experiences. These elements were synthesised to form a new perception of the way in which thought affects spiritual comprehension and development. For a time Steiner studied theosophy, then he moved away to form the Anthroposophical Society. The word was coined from the Greek *anthropos*, meaning man, and *sophia*, meaning wisdom. The all-important principle is that everything has its origin in living spirit; this is coupled with a perception of Christianity as a mystical system.

Avalon Library

2-4 High Street, Glastonbury, BA6 9DU. Tel. 01458-832 759

After considerable thought and negotiation, George Trevelyan donated much of his personal collection of New Age books to the Avalon Library. Books in other categories are in private hands, many of them still those of his daughter. The Avalon librarians are happy to help with research projects and advise on material relating to George's New Age work. Glastonbury itself was very important to George for its mystical associations and the community of New Age people which was forming there.

Conference Cassettes

13 Piccadilly Mill, Lower St, Stroud, GL5 2HT.
Tel.01453-766 411.

Philip Royall runs this company, which was formed to produce and sell tapes of Sir George Trevelyan's speeches and meditations on behalf of the Wrekin Trust. It is represented at many events and exhibitions. The publications list can be obtained by sending a stamped addressed envelope. The range of Sir George Trevelyan's work is remarkable, and something of the experience of hearing him speak in person can be obtained from listening to the tapes.

Among the most notable productions are: Introduction to Meditation; Thoughts on Holism — the Illusion of Separation and the Return to Wholeness; The Metamorphosis of Forms and the Archetypal Patterns in Nature (with meditation); Psychology and Spirituality; The Convergence between Science, Religion and Spiritual Knowledge; Exhortation — Summons to a High Crusade; Grounding the Spirit in Creative Action; Poetry as Gateway to the Invisible Worlds.

Chalice Well

Chilkwell Street, Glastonbury, BA6 8DD. Tel. 01458-831 154

George Trevelyan became a member of the Chalice Well Committee to further the aims of Tudor Wellesley Pole, whose inter-level (between spirit and matter) work he admired. The Chalice Well and the Healing Spa Pool are said to have healing properties. The pool is called the ancient red spring of Avalon, a mythical place with which George Trevelyan had a particular relationship as it relates to the story of King Arthur and the Knights of the Round Table. Glastonbury has many associations with the Arthurian court.

Taras Pringle of the Growing Needs Bookshop in Glastonbury was a custodian of the Well from 1980–87. He remembers Sir George as charismatic, dynamic, and compassionate. "He remembered us after a gap of four years, and what we had been doing at Findhorn, conversations we'd had, things we'd said — he just bounded into the shop and started talking," he says. Rod and Alice Friend recalled Sir George bringing water from the Well for their daughter's sore throat, which they say was cured by it.

College of Psychic Studies

16 Queensberry Place, London, SW7 2EB. Tel. 020-7589 3292

The College works in a wide spiritual field, including psychic experience — or "guidance" — from people who have passed on and are understood to be able to communicate with those living in the physical world. There are courses and lectures on practices such as relaxation and meditation, and subjects such as dreams, altered consciousness, all with the object of teaching "how to listen for and become obedient to a wiser inner self." There are also activities concerned with tuning to the spirit world. This is the location for different kinds of healing work which involve the use of psychic energy and avoid artificial interventions.

Among many eminent teachers and practitioners who work at the College are Tony and Ann Neate, who were close friends of George Trevelyan. They used to run a Cancer Help Centre in Cheltenham and also co-founded the College of Healing. Their early association with the Wrekin Trust came through a Findhorn connection. They were instrumental in setting up alternative healing lectures during the first year of the Trust's existence.

Findhorn Foundation

The Park, Forres, Scotland, OYL OT2. Tel. 01309-690 311

George was a trustee of the Findhorn Foundation for many years, helping to set the parameters of its early efforts. Its work of living New Age ideals and continuing to explore and disseminate them is still a beacon for the whole movement. Members of the community are concerned with living harmoniously with the earth and all things in and on it. The practical application of this principle involves inhabitants and guests in activities concerned with every activity associated with organic husbandry and spiritual endeavour, using methods such as meditation. Emphasis is placed on intuitive insight and the work of the group. Individual efforts are seen to be important simultaneously to the community members making them and to the community as a whole. The Foundation hosts conferences and events under headings such as Spirit in Education, Global Harmony, Organic Farming, Ecological Survival. It publishes books and leaflets, and is represented at conferences throughout the world.

The original caravan site is now augmented by some fixed houses and more are being built. The Cluny Hill Hotel was bought by the Foundation and its accommodation is used as a conference centre and for visitors: Sir George Trevelyan always stayed there. Since the Findhorn philosophy includes the notion that one activity can subsidize another, the Findhorn Community has an additional caravan site which is let commercially.

Foundation for Outdoor Adventure

33 King Street, London, WC2E 8JD

The Foundation was established in 1994 and sets out to be a catalyst for change, providing "development opportunities for all young people through outdoor adventure and challenge." This is something which was advocated by Sir George Trevelyan all his life. The Foundation is chaired by Roger Orgill, whose long career in the sphere of outdoor education is largely attributable to George's influence and practical help. Opportunities for the philosophical and esoteric exploration are sought in Roger Orgill's extensive outdoor adventure work with young people, both students and leaders.

The Foundation was formed as the result of a consultation called in 1986 by the Royal Geographical Society at St George's House, Windsor Castle. This consultation was set up by Lord Hunt and Lord Shackleton, and of the 34 attendees, many had explored their own challenges in mountains, polar regions and deserts. The resulting study evolved into the manifesto statement, prepared by Roger Orgill with Lord Hunt. They defined the purpose: "to explore the nature of outdoor education and adventure training and their potential for recovering the sense of conscience and commitment in society."

The manifesto statement, which was endorsed by public figures and government ministers, recognizes that, "in an attempt to better understand themselves, others and the changing context of their lives, all young people are engaged, consciously or unconsciously, in what it is to be human. This is in essence a spiritual journey, in which young people come to terms with the mysteries and uncertainties of existence, establish standards and values by which to live and work; identify worthwhile goals; and develop the understanding and life skills through which these may be achieved."

The purpose of the Foundation is: "to encourage self-realization through right relationship with the natural world, build self-confidence through outdoor pursuits, and recognize the essential spiritual dimension of young people's development within adventure activity." Responsible use of and a respectful attitude to the countryside are aspects of this. In 1989, just before standing down from chairing the National Association for Outdoor Education, Roger Orgill received an MBE in recognition of work for young people. In congratulating him, George Trevelyan observed wryly that he himself had not had to work for his honour, which had come easily as it had been inherited.

Francis Bacon Research Trust

Roses Farmhouse, Epwell Rd, Tysoe, Warwick, CV35 0TN.
Tel. 01295-688 185

Peter Dawkins believes that Francis Bacon was the real author of the works attributed to William Shakespeare, and so did Sir George Trevelyan. The Trust sets out, "to research and make known the lives, philosophy, and wisdom teachings of Francis Bacon, Shakespeare, the Rosicrucians and others." The esoteric meanings within the works of Shakespeare, infinitely more extraordinary than the meanings more generally understood, are a crucial aspect of this work.

In *The Wisdom of Shakespeare* series, Peter Dawkins has published commentaries on four plays: As You Like It, The Merchant of Venice, Julius Caesar, and The Tempest. They draw on alchemy, astrology, and other forms of ancient wisdom. In his notes on The Tempest, Peter Dawkins says the play, "is remarkable in depicting virtually the whole spectrum of human development in an archetypal way, from human grossness to the exaltation of the human spirit. the four basic stages of every life cycle are symbolized by the four alchemical elements, earth-water-air-fire, depicting how life transforms itself in both nature and mankind with the eventual aim of manifesting light (æther) the quintessence." *(The Wisdom of Shakespeare in The Tempest*, Peter Dawkins, IC Media Publications, 2000.) This kind of analysis is very much on Sir George Trevelyan's wavelength. The explanation of the parallel between the alchemical cycle of the seasons and the life process (Earth/Winter/Seed — Water/Spring/Bud — Air/Summer/Flower — Fire/Autumn/Fruit) concludes, "Knowledge is derived from the result of the action, which we can choose to learn from or not."

Mark Rylance is artistic director of the Globe Theatre in London. He recalls a talk given by Peter Dawkins at a gathering where George Trevelyan was also present. "Sir George, who had demanded many years before that Peter spoke about Shakespeare in front of people, would fall asleep after lunch next to Peter, wake with a start, and immediately fire off some of the best acting of Shakespeare I have had the privilege to hear ... the love and enquiry into Shakespeare was deeper than I had ever encountered in any rehearsal room." Peter Dawkins believes George "gave power to people." He enabled Dawkins, "to be the person I almost didn't yet know I was. He was an inspirer; he had an extraordinary ability to see what was in people and draw it out. He got me to read Shakespeare with him and he taught me how to speak it. In effect, he also taught me how to teach. I think his legacy is in the people he gave power to, the power to be who they really are."

Gatekeeper Trust

c/o Richard Douglas, 154 South Park Road, London, SW19 8TA.
Tel. 020-8540 3684

The concern of the Gatekeeper Trust is, "the art of pilgrimage and its potential for personal and planetary healing." The Trust seeks to recover the human ability to be in tune with landscape, and its members believe that many have forgotten how to walk on the earth in a simple, sacred, aware manner. They believe they contribute to the healing of their own inner selves and of the landscape, and to universal harmony. Pilgrimage walks can include ley lines, sun lines, and lines that connect different faiths, such as Michael–Apollo, through mystical-magical sites and sanctuaries. The Trust's general programme may include equinox celebrations, and observation of ancient festivals.

Sir George, from his lifelong relationship with mountainous regions and caves, was very keen on all this. He often led sacred walks and conducted ceremonies, read poetry, lit bonfires, connected ley lines. Attingham, Wallington and the Scottish islands were key places for such work but there were many others. Once, he led pilgrimages to sites all around the British Isles, making connections between them. Peter Dawkins says that George's historical family relationship with St Michael's Mount and the allegory of the original Sir Trevillian, leaving the sea (representing a lower state of life), on a white horse (the higher mind), moving into air (the higher consciousness), and on to the dry land (the material world), occupied him throughout his life.

Lamplighter Movement

George Trevelyan was entrusted by Wellesley Tudor Pole to create this movement as a successor to the Silent Minute observed during the Second World War at the time of the BBC Home Service nine o'clock news. It was acknowledged to be very powerful (see Attingham). The first lamp was lit in an upper window of Attingham Park in 1964, and George asked for amber sanctified lamps to be lit with dedicated intent. The Movement ceased in November, 1991, but the Silent Minute is still observed by some people.

Resurgence

Ford House, Hartland, Bideford, EX39 6EE. Tel. 01237-441 293

A key ecological and spiritual publication, *Resurgence* magazine is edited by Satish Kumar, who is also programme director at Schumacher College. Both the College and the publication set out to broaden the concept of spirituality to include matters concerning society and the environment. The magazine looks at spiritual and ecological topics, new economics, new education, the arts of the imagination, mythology, native cultures, and traditional wisdom. It is an advocate of green thinking and a forum for the discussion of the causes of what it calls "our current industrial and materialistic crisis." A key aspect of the theories of Schumacher is the proposition, "Small is beautiful" — the observation that the scale of larger concerns automatically dehumanizes. This is a notion very much in line with Sir George Trevelyan's thinking. Satish Kumar sees Sir George Trevelyan's contribution as, "bringing back a sense of community of the spirit, rather than community of economy. He saw that we are joined together through spirit. It is a broader view."

Scientific and Medical Network

Gibliston Mill, Colinsburgh, Leven, KY9 1JS.
Tel. 01333-340 490

This group was founded in 1973 and its 2,000-strong membership is made up mostly of doctors, engineers, psychologists and other scientists from more than fifty countries in the English-speaking world. Its purpose is, "to question the assumptions of contemporary scientific and medical thinking, so often limited by exclusively materialistic reasoning" ; and this objective is to be achieved thus: "By remaining open to intuitive and spiritual insights, it fosters a climate in which science as a whole can adopt a more comprehensive and sensitive approach." Sir George was a great supporter of the Network from the beginning, and in 1978 he opened the first Mystics and Scientists Conference, which it partly sponsors. With Malcolm Lazarus he had organized the first conference, and he gave the introductory addresses until he handed over to David Lorimer, its director from 1986 to 2000.

During the 20 or so years of the conference, seminal thinkers have considered contemporary questions of great complexity. They have included Jim Lovelock, Sir Fred Hoyle, Sir John Eccles and Bede Griffiths. In the preface to *The Spirit of Science*, an anthology of Mystics and Scientists Conference contributions (Floris Books 1998), David Lorimer mentions, "a high point with Karl Pribram and Charles Tart coming over from the States to join Glen Schaefer, The Ven Sumedho and Warren Kenton ... Glen, Professor of Ecological Physics at Cranfield, received a standing ovation after his talk on the necessity for a holistic philosophy of nature and the failure of chemical warfare on insects. He outlined several inconsistencies in evolutionary theory and spoke of the delicate balance on which the created world depends." This took place at the fourth Mystics and Scientists Conference in 1982: there have been many other such moments.

David Lorimer first encountered Sir George Trevelyan at an early Mystics and Scientists conference but says they met properly at Winchester College, where Lorimer was teaching. He found Sir George's ideas fascinating. "In 1983 I invited him to lecture at the Toynbee Society on Spiritual Awakening. It was quite daring: I didn't know how it would go down with the boys. There must have been 70 or 80 there. In fact, he was spellbinding. I was quite apprehensive, but he pitched it to stretch their minds and there were good questions. Afterwards at dinner at my house some of the boys were also invited, and they asked excellent, exploratory questions. They were interested in the ideas and wanted to clarify them. The note in the visitors' book was about the new holistic world view. George said things in public, in his particular style, that I would have had to put more cautiously because I was teaching at Winchester. I joined the Network in 1983, and two years later, when I was thinking of leaving Winchester, I was offered a job by Malcolm Lazarus. I wanted to take on something nearer the centre of my interest."

The Scientific and Medical Network took over responsibility for the Mystics and Scientists conferences in 1992. The Network aims to deepen understanding in science, medicine and education by fostering both rational analysis and intuitive insights. It questions contemporary scientific and medical assumptions, and by remaining open to intuitive and spiritual insights, fosters a climate in which science can adopt a more comprehensive and sensitive approach.

The first two themes in 1992 considered the nature of the self and of transformation. Subsequent topics included the nature of light, and the life of the heart. In 2001, the theme for the 24th Conference was Trees of Life, subtitled Humanity and the Harmony of Nature. The lecture titles included many that would have greatly appealed to Sir George Trevelyan: Does Nature Have Sacred Depths? The Tree of Life: an Inner and Outer Journey; Sacred Trees in Indigenous Wisdom Traditions.

David Lorimer's personal interest in Death and Becoming research has led him into many areas of inquiry of great significance to Sir George Trevelyan. Of the relationship of their work, he says, "I think I'm carrying on a part of a spiritual impulse, but we're different generations. The 'Spiritual Awakening' — his phrase — I'm very happy with it. I can connect it with esoteric Christianity. He was more pro-Steiner, I'm more Peter Deunov, but we are in the same stream. I think his legacy is the influence he had on people, and the encouragement he gave for them to continue their work. When I remember him I recall four words he used very often: energy, enthusiasm, encouragement and excitement. Do you know the derivation of enthusiasm, a quality I associate particularly with George? It's really two Greek words, *en*, which means within, and *theos*, which means god. The god within. I think that sums him up. That, and his great sense of joy."

Soil Association

Bristol House, 40–56 Victoria Street, Bristol, BS1 6BY.
Tel. 0117-929 0661

One of George's favourite concerns, the Association is still researching the condition of the soil of Great Britain and now more than ever is involved with the organic movement. Contemporary concern about land use and farming methods is rendering Soil Association research and data more relevant than ever. Sir George was one of its earliest champions, against the prevailing thinking, and regularly brought speakers on subjects related to organic farming to Attingham Park.

Theosophical Society

50 Gloucester Place, London, W1H 3HJ. Tel. 020-7935 9261

Theosophy was the original inspiration for Rudolf Steiner, whose theories George studied and followed from the moment he came across them at the age of 42. Theosophy declares that it is concerned with "the laws of nature and of man's being, physical, mental and spiritual; and that man is essentially a spirit, a unit of the all pervading spirit which energizes all matter." It declares that all existence is governed by invariable laws which are cyclic and harmonious, and that being alternates with non-being accordingly. It accepts the principle of reincarnation. It gives as its objects:

1. to form a nucleus of the universal brotherhood of humanity without distinction of race, creed, sex, caste or colour.
2. to encourage the study of comparative religion, philosophy and science.
3. to investigate unexplained laws of nature and the powers latent in man.

The Society provides lectures, seminars and courses covering the field of spiritual unfoldment. Many of these are parallel with the topics considered by the Wrekin Trust. The Path of Light— Personality and Soul; and The Joy of Meditation are only two examples.

Wrekin Trust

Mellow Farm, Hawcross, Redmarley, Gloucester, GL19 3JQ
Email: info@wrekintrust.org

Writing about the closing event of the Wrekin Trust in November 1991, twenty years after its inception, Sir George quoted Goethe: "If you have not got this, this Dying and Becoming, you are only a dull guest in a dark world." So, briefly, Wrekin allowed itself to die in the form it had been, while many of the strands of work it had initiated were taken up in new ways. Six years later, the Trustees met to discuss whether the time was yet ripe to further the Trust's original mission, "to explore the spiritual dimension of ourselves and the world in which we live." It seemed that the will was there to move forward again in ways that both resembled and were different from those of the previous decades.

A part-time executive director was appointed, and a small office established. The first Sir George Trevelyan Memorial Lecture was given in London by David Lorimer, chair of trustees, in October, 1998. The title was Spiritual Education for the Twenty-First Century. Subsequent lectures have included Soil, Soul, Society, given by Satish Kumar; Living in a Sacred Way, by Ravi Ravindra; and The Spiritual Destiny of Britain, given by Peter Dawkins. A small programme of weekends on themes such as Awakening to the Spirit of Learning, and Exploring Spiritual Paths through the Great Traditions has been started, and some local groups established.

At first, the Trust encouraged other developments through a programme of small grants, towards — for example — a course participant on Reclaiming our Culture: Redesigning a University at Schumacher College; the Soul in Education conference at Findhorn; and the development and publication of The Quest, an open learning programme for personal and spiritual development. Next, there emerged a vision for a University of the Spirit. This was a response to the impulse to move away from the exploration of the outer and physical world that had characterized the second millennium, towards an exploration of our inner and spiritual world in the third. It had been foreseen by Sir George in 1981. He wrote, "many minds are now questing for deeper meaning and a new understanding of the great oneness of life." He saw the need to restore the original definition of a university as, "universitas — turned towards the One." He also saw the need for an educational programme that would, "help people develop as conscious instruments for creative change." He believed there was, "theoretically absolutely no limit to the human potential ... as we see the coming of a consciousness age." The idea of a University for Spirit found a resonance within many hearts and minds. Perhaps we visit halls of learning during sleep, or in meditation, and long to see them materialize.

But big ideas have to find an anchor in practical form. Two Round Table discussions involving academics and educators from fifty organizations have met and are now forming a Forum for Spiritual Values in Education as a step towards an ultimate 'University for Spirit.' The Forum is bringing together in creative collaboration people from the many institutions, centres, and networks which are incorporating the spiritual dimension in their educational programmes and demonstrating spiritual values in their work. Some big visions are emerging with collaborative projects designed to implement these in practical action. The early seeds planted by Sir George at Attingham, and later under the umbrella of the Wrekin Trust, are beginning to take root and send out shoots. Sir George promised that if a chair were left for him at each planning meeting and exploratory gathering, he would attend. We have no doubt that he does.

(Contributed by Janice Dolley)

Sir George Trevelyan: a recollection

Caroline Myss, author of Anatomy of the Spirit *(Harmony Press, 1996), was a friend and colleague of Sir George Trevelyan.*

I first met Sir George at the Findhorn Community in 1985. I was captivated by his mythic nature and elegant persona. And then there was his spirit, so gregarious and magical that it could not be contained in his ageing body. He animated the world around him. People watched him with a quality of delight that was unearthly, as if they had finally encountered someone who truly lived half in this world and half with the angels. I believed that to be true about George, and that was why I loved him the instant I met him. I was honoured to teach with Sir George on several occasions. For several years we did workshops together in southern England. He began teaching in the morning, stirring the psyches and souls of the people in the room with his dramatic reading of spiritual poetry and an electric understanding of the coming New Age of love and humanity. When it was my turn to teach, I rather lowered the spiritual atmosphere in the room with my information about the relationship of our biography to our spiritual biology.

We adored each other's company. Never before or since my time with George have I taught with anyone who stopped in the middle of a poetry recitation to announce that the nature god, Pan, had entered the room! When it happened I bolted out of my chair and said, "Where is he?" The interesting part of this was that it never occurred to me that George might be imagining Pan — I simply accepted as fact the notion that the mythical god of the forest had joined us. On the other hand, what is imagination if not the ability to leave this rational plane constructed out of our five senses and slip into the realm of spiritual life? I should have imagined more back then, because perhaps I would have actually seen Pan. A few years ago, in memory of my friendship with George, I commissioned a painting of Mother Nature and Baby Pan in honour of my love and memory of George.

But our professional association is only a small part of my memory. It was the behind the scenes adventures that endeared him most to me,

like the time we were speeding down the M4. George suffered a substantial loss of hearing, and he also loved to drive very fast. I had taken
my mother on this particular workshop trip, and on our few days off,
George, my mother, a wonderful friend named Rhoda, and I, were pas-
sengers in this car that he turned into a speeding bullet. I watched as
my mom began to be curious about the speed we were travelling, her
curiosity stirred by the fact that we were approaching the point at
which objects on the side of the road were no longer recognizable. She
turned to look at me in the back seat and her gaze communicated that
she was about to disincarnate from fear — unless he saved her the
trouble by hitting a tree. I leaned forward and said, "George, you have
to slow down a bit. You're scaring my mother to death." Holding the
wheel tightly with his arthritically tormented hands, he bellowed back,
"Can't hear a thing! You'll have to wait until I slow down!"

On another adventure, George told me that he was going to take me
to where Camelot had been. I can't quite recall where this was, but as
soon as we were out of his car — that precious car of his — he was
bouncing through the forest. "It was here, can't you feel it?" I was positively enchanted in that moment. I can still see the colour of the green
leaves, penetrated by the light of the sun, and the sun-green shadow
that filled the silent forest. The ground was damp with moss and leaves
and the fragrance was rich with the quality of the humid earth. I loved
the feeling. I knew I was in the midst of a rare moment, with a rare
human being, the combination of which would never come into my life
again. I held on to that moment and committed everything I could to
memory. I remember what George was wearing, I recall that it was two
in the afternoon, and there was not a trace of wind. The silence was like
a barrier between dimensions — this one and the age of Arthur. So
extraordinary was that moment that if George had suddenly led me to
Excalibur and told me that he was King Arthur in disguise, I would
have believed him.

But whether it was really Camelot or not did not matter to me. I was
playing in the forest with the most extraordinary human being — a
man whose life was filled with rich contributions to humanity, and pri-
vately, with a great deal of pain. In his personal life, George knew what
it was to be lonely, to love and lose someone, and to collapse under the
strain of guilt, sorrow, and hurt. His sensitive body bore the scar tissue
of that experience, crippling him with arthritis and putting him in a
wheelchair. Then he faced the choice that he would spend the rest of
his life inspiring others to make — he would forgive himself, accept,

surrender in faith, move forward. Armed with this fire in his soul he fought back and regained the use of his legs, though his feet and hands remained forever bent. They were surely indicators that this man knew what it was to resurrect himself — the Self — and ascend to a new life.

I'm at the part in this small recollection of George in which I must say something of his spiritual contribution. But, how to summarize the measure of a spirit of his elegance and innocence? He truly had no sense of the negative side of humanity. He lacked a sense of the shadow. There wasn't a trace of the energy of greed, need for fame, recognition, or any hostile thought toward another in his energy field. He had no use for earthly belongings (not that there is anything wrong with enjoying every positive pleasure life can offer) — those concerns were simply no longer a part of his life. He was nearly eighty, and had long passed the stressful years of survival concerns. And that lightness of heart was delicious to be around. Doubtless he had these normal life concerns when he was a younger man, and had financial matters with his projects to contend with, but even then the grounded and practical level of life baffled him. He needed substantial "spiritual looking after," so it was given to him. He was provided for as needed, and that was a part of the magic that animated his energy field. George's spirit contained the experiences of a man who had to heal himself, as well as someone who had to trust that all would be taken care of in his life.

I am honoured to have known him. When I think of the enchanting chapter of my life, he's a leading figure. When I think of the New Age and the voices who lead its entry, I think of him. When I think of how I came to know about nature spirits, Pan, and other creatures who govern the domain of plants, animals, and the sky and seas, I think of him. I took my first tumble "down the rabbit hole" with George. He was the Knight who took me to Camelot — and I shall love this Knight for all the days of my life.

Caroline Myss

Index

Photographic acknowledgments

With many thanks to the following for supplying and helping with photographs:

Geseke Clarke
Alexandra Orgill and Roger Orgill, MBE
Paul Cook and Direction Journal
Catriona Tyson
Mari Hollander and The Findhorn Foundation
Alan J Wills, Archivist, Gordonstoun School
Eckart Schopf
Ruth and Bernard Nesfield-Cookson
Trustees of the Trevelyan Family Papers

All effort has been made to trace the copyright holders. The publishers apologize for any omissions.

Science and the Paranormal

Altered States of Reality

Arthur Ellison
with a foreword by David Fontana

Facts not Fiction: The Case for the Paranormal ...

Changing the way we look at the universe requires a true openness to exploration and experiment. Professor Ellison suggests that we are conditioned by our Western science-based education to think that the universe is much simpler and "material" than it really is. He argues that we should recognize the limits of the current scientific worldview which fails to account for genuine paranormal experiences, including phenomena such as out-of-body experiences, reliably reported by thousands of people. In exploring honestly these areas, rather than denying them, he felt we could look more deeply into the real nature of human existence.

Arthur Ellison was a distinguished voice in paranormal research and Emeritus Professor of Engineering at the City University in London. He joined the Society for Psychical Research in 1955 and was twice president of the Society. He died in 2000. This book is published in honour of his life's work.

  David Fontana is the author of more than 20 books on subjects such as meditation, dreams and personal development. Currently he is Distinguished Visiting Fellow at Cardiff University and Professor of Transpersonal Psychology at Liverpool John Moores University. His books have been translated into 26 languages.

Floris Books

Thinking Beyond the Brain

a wider science of consciousness

Edited by David Lorimer

... a very exciting book.   Breathe
... deserves both close and wide attention.   Universalist
... essential reading.   Christian Parapsychologist

Consciousness is the cutting-edge topic in scientific circles, its precise nature holding huge implications for the future of science itself.

With so many recent advances in brain studies, questions of mind and consciousness have become of critical importance for scientists and theorists alike. Are we 'nothing but a pack of neurons' that will reveal their secrets in the laboratory? Or do our conscious mind and self-awareness stem from some dimension beyond material investigation? How, too, are we to account for 'parapsychological' phenomena in which consciousness seems to defy space and time boundaries?

These recent contributions to the debate, selected from the annual 'Beyond the Brain' conferences, show that it is time for radical rethink of our theories and methods in investigating phenomena of the human mind.

Contributors include: Willis Harman, Peter Fenwick, Brian Josephson, Kenneth Ring, David Fontana, Erlendur Haraldsson, John Beloff, Michael Grosso, Charles Tart, Stanislav Grof, Andrew Powell, Marilyn Schlitz, Roger Woolger, Mark Woodhouse, Ravi Ravindra, Anne Baring.

David Lorimer is the former director of the Scientific and Medical Network, an international group of academics and professionals dedicated to an open-minded exploration of boundaries in science.

Floris Books

The Spirit of Science

from experiment to experience

Edited by David Lorimer

The huge technical successes of modern science have obscured a deeper understanding of its place in human knowledge and in our value systems. For many, science belongs in a separate 'compartment' from normal human experience, confined to the world of the laboratory. This can give rise to a dark, impersonal and inhuman image of science.

In this collection, distinguished scientists and thinkers from a wide range of disciplines examine the relationship of scientific knowledge and practice to the wider dimension of human life and awareness. For some this appears as a dialogue between science and spirituality, for others an investigation into consciousness and the intelligent heart of the cosmos. Whether in physics, cosmology or biology, these essays explore the very nature of knowledge itself and the continuing role of human creativity, emphasising the need for crossing disciplinary boundaries in our search for understanding.

The contributions are based on papers given over twenty years at the annual 'Mystics and Scientists' conferences in England, and this collection brings together some of the most remarkable and far-seeing thinkers of our time.

David Lorimer is the former director of the Scientific and Medical Network, an international group of academics and professionals dedicated to an open-minded exploration of boundaries in science.

Floris Books